Ethernet Networking
for the Small Office
and Professional
Home Office

Jan L. Harrington

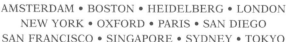
AMSTERDAM • BOSTON • HEIDELBERG • LONDON
NEW YORK • OXFORD • PARIS • SAN DIEGO
SAN FRANCISCO • SINGAPORE • SYDNEY • TOKYO

Morgan Kaufmann is an imprint of Elsevier

MORGAN KAUFMANN PUBLISHERS

Publisher	Denise Penrose
Acquistions Editor	Rick Adams
Publishing Services Manager	George Morrison
Project Manager	Marilyn E. Rash
Assistant Editor	Kimberly Honjo
Copyeditor	Joan Flaherty
Proofreader	Debbie Prato
Cover Design	Alisa Andreola
Interior Printer	Malpe-Vail
Cover Printer	Phoenix Color Corp.

Morgan Kaufmann Publishers is an imprint of Elsevier.
30 Corporate Drive, Suite 400
Burlington, MA 01803

This book is printed on acid-free paper.

Library of Congress Cataloging-in-Publication Data
Harrington, Jan L.
  Ethernet networking for the small office and professional home office / Jan L. Harrington.
    p. cm.
  Includes bibliographical references and index.
  ISBN-13: 978-0-12-373744-1 (alk. paper)
  ISBN-10: 0-12-373744-3 (alk. paper)
  1. Ethernet (Local area network system) 2. Home offices. 3. Business enterprises—Computer networks. I. Title.
TK5105.8.E83H273 2007
004.6'8--dc22   2007010951

For information on all Morgan Kaufmann publications, visit our Web site at
www.mkp.com or *www.books.elsevier.com*

Transferred to digital printing in 2009.

Contents

Part Two: Design and Connectivity

Part Three: Making the Network Work

Part Four: Ethernet Solution Examples

Preface

Computer networks—interconnected collections of computing hardware and software—are a fact of life today. You might use a network to connect to a printer located in another room, to interact with the Internet, or to share files with someone in your company who is working in another city. Each type of network has its own hardware and software requirements, all of which is surrounded by a bewildering array of terminology.

A network can be as small as two computers and a printer located in the corner of a family room or as large as the entire world. Although much of the theory of data transmission is the same, regardless of the network's size, the specifics of the hardware and software are somewhat different, and no single book could describe all of it (unless you wanted to move the book with a forklift, that is).

This book focuses on professional networks that are in either a small commercial space or a home. Today, such small networks use a single physical standard—Ethernet—that was designed primarily for networks that are contained within a single physical location. (Remote users can access the network through interconnections to other networks made, for example, by the Internet, but the permanent parts of the network are typically housed in one building or a group of buildings located in close physical proximity.)

If you need to design, install, and manage a network in such an environment, then this book will give you an understanding of the technology involved in an Ethernet network. It will teach you how Ethernets work and what you need to put one together.

Probably the toughest part of understanding networks is the jargon. If you're unfamiliar with networking terminology and acronyms, then a sentence like "To hook up to the legacy 10BASE2 segment, you connect the BNC connector to the NIC" is meaningless gibberish. One of the major goals of this book is therefore to demystify the secret language of networks for you so that you can speak in acronyms just like the rest of the network gurus.

One of my greatest frustrations with networking books is that they often focus on only one layer of the network. To be technically accurate, "Ethernet" refers to only one part of the hardware. However, if you are going to be responsible for an Ethernet network, then you need to know a lot more than just how to choose and configure your network hardware. You also need information about the devices you can attach to your network and the software you will need to make it all work. In addition, you will probably want to give some thought to managing the network. And most important, you will want to look at your network in terms of security; even if your network's only outside connection is to the Internet, you are vulnerable to a variety of system attacks! This book goes beyond the hardware aspects of Ethernet to look at the entire network from bottom to top.

Another major concern with writing a book of this type is the level of technical detail. How much do you really need or want to know about how network signals are transmitted? If you want to know which specific signals are carried on which wires within a network cable, then this is not the book for you. However, if you want enough technical detail to be able to make intelligent choices about what types of transmission media to use for your network and the way to interconnect the parts of that network, then you are holding the right volume.

What You Need to Know

To understand the material in this book, you need a thorough knowledge of basic PC hardware and at least one PC operating system—for example, Windows 2000 or newer, some flavor of UNIX, or Mac OS X. I have an unabashed preference for the latter, but we each go where our experience and hearts take us. You should also be comfortable with basic PC software such as word processors, e-mail, and World Wide Web browsers.

Acknowledgments

Writing a book for Morgan Kaufmann is an absolute delight. I'd like to thank both Rick Adams, my editor, and Rachel Roumeliotis, his assistant, for all their help. And, of course, much thanks to the project manager, Marilyn Rash; the copy editor, Joan Flaherty; and the proofreader, Debbie Prato.

In addition, a large number of vendors gave us permission to use illustrations and photos of their products. My thanks go out to all of them. (You can find contact information for those vendors in Appendix C.)

http://www.blackgryphon.info

Part One

Introduction

The first two chapters of this book present some introductory conceptual material about networking and Ethernet. By the time you finish reading them, you will understand exactly what Ethernet is and the part it plays in your network.

1

Introduction

One of the biggest problems when discussing networking is knowing where to start. The subject of computer networks is one of those areas for which you have to "know everything to do anything." Usually, the easiest way to ease into the topic is to begin with some basic networking terminology and then look at exactly what it means when we use the word *Ethernet*.

Anatomy of a Network

A computer *network* is a combination of hardware and software that allows computers and other devices (for example, printers and file servers) to communicate with one another through some form of telecommunications media (for example, telephone lines).

Note: As you read material about data communications, you may see references to POTS lines. POTS stands for "plain old telephone service."

Networks can be classified by the distances they cover and whether they include technology like that used on the Internet:

♦ *LAN* (local area network): A network confined to a small geographic area—such as a floor, single building, or group of buildings in close physical proximity (for example, a college campus or an office park)—that is almost always owned by a single organization. The organization owns the telecommunications lines as well as the hardware connected to the network.

♦ *Intranet*: A network (LAN or WAN) owned by a single company that uses technology similar to that used on the Internet.

♦ *MAN* (metropolitan area network): An outdated term describing a network that covers an entire city. Today, the concept of a MAN has been replaced largely by the WAN.

♦ *WAN* (wide area network): A network that covers a large geographic area, such as a city, state, or one or more countries. Although a WAN may be owned by a single organization, the network usually includes telecommunications media (for example, telephone lines or satellite transmissions) that are leased from commercial telecommunications providers.

♦ *Internet*: When in all lowercase letters (*internet*), a WAN that connects multiple networks into a larger network. When written with a leading uppercase letter (*Internet*), it is the global network that supports the World Wide Web. Because of the potential for confusion between internet and Internet, the term *internet* is rarely used today.

The technologies we will be discussing in this book are applicable to LANs and intranets. Although we will discuss connecting LANs to the Internet, the focus is on creating and maintaining networks that serve small to medium-size workgroups in small offices, regardless of whether they are located in commercial buildings or homes.

Network Components

A computer network is made up of three major components:

♦ *Hardware*: The equipment that connects to the network. Typically, this includes computers, printers, and modems. Each distinct piece of hardware on a network is known as a *node*. In addition to the hardware that actually uses the network to transfer data to perform work for an organization, a network may contain specialty hardware that helps manage the network and connects it to other networks. Such hardware includes routers, bridges, switches, hubs, repeaters, and gateways. You will read about network hardware of these types throughout this book.

Each device on a network is identified by two types of addresses. The first is a hardware address that physically identifies the piece of equipment. In many cases, this address is set by the hardware manufacturer and is not easily changed. These addresses, known as *MAC (media access control)* addresses, must be unique throughout the network segment. If a manufacturer happens to produce hardware with duplicated MAC addresses, then a network segment that uses that hardware cannot function.

The second type of address is a software address that is added by the software that handles data transmission. The software address can be changed as needed.

♦ *Software*: The programs that manage the transfer of data throughout the network, most commonly known as *network operating systems* (NOS). Current desktop operating systems—Windows, Mac OS X, and Linux—are capable of network operations right out of the box. However, they cannot provide the robust, centralized, shared services such as file sharing needed by commercial networks. Most organizations therefore end up investing in specialized network operating system software to provide services such as file sharing, user management, security, and directory management.

♦ *Transmission media*: The cables or wireless signals that carry data from one node to another.

In addition, there must be interfaces between the hardware and the network. These often take the form of expansion boards that are added to pieces of hardware (*network interface cards*, or NICs, such as that in Figure 1-1), although a significant number of today's computers and printers are shipped with network hardware already installed on their motherboards. Depending on the type of transmissions media in use, a network may also need hardware connections between the media coming from a piece of hardware and the network itself.

Figure 1-1:   A network interface card (Courtesy of Farallon Corp.)

In Figure 1-2 you can see a generalized diagram of how the hardware fits together. Each device you want to connect to a network must have either a network interface card or networking hardware installed on its motherboard. The NIC (or the motherboard) contains a port to which a cable can be attached. That cable runs to the network, connecting to the network transmission medium with some sort of attachment unit. Early networks had visible attachment units that physically tapped into the network cable. Today, however, most attachment units are part of the network interface hardware.

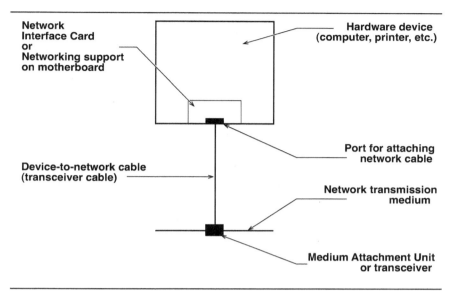

Figure 1-2:   Generalized network connections

A wide variety of hardware and transmission media are available for Ethernet LANs and intranets. We will therefore be spending a considerable amount of time in this book looking at hardware choices.

Clients, Servers, and Peers

When hardware devices exchange messages over a network, the software governing the exchange can view the hardware in one of two relationships: *client/server* or *peer-to-peer*. With a client/server relationship, the *client* device (usually a computer) makes a request for some type of network service—for example, printing or a file transfer—from a device (typically, but not always, another computer) dedicated to providing that service (the *server*). Servers may store files to be printed, manage files that are to be shared by multiple users, send and receive e-mail, or support a Web site. Because servers are designed to handle requests from multiple network users, they are typically the fastest and most powerful computers on the network. How many servers you have and the specific functions they perform depend on the needs of your network. We will discuss a number of types of servers throughout this book.

Servers are permanent parts of a network. They run software designed specifically for the functions they are intended to perform and allow network administrators to regulate who gains access to which network resources. However, at times you many need ad hoc simple networking functions, such as the transfer of files between two computers. When two devices agree to perform a network function between themselves without the help of a server, they are engaging in peer-to-peer networking. Although peer-to-peer networking is useful for ad hoc file or printer sharing in very small networks, it can present security and management problems because it isn't under the control of the network administrator who handles a computer's servers. You will therefore use it less and less for file transfer as your network grows. However, you may find that peer-to-peer activities such as instant messaging are useful to your business.

Note: Peer-to-peeer networking is used widely over the Internet for file sharing, some of it illegal (for example, using BitTorrent to transfer copyrighted movies). Aside from the large amount of network bandwidth consumed by such transfers, the dubious legality of much peer-to-peeer file transfers often make it prudent to prevent users from engaging in such activities.

Note: The idea of client/server data processing is subtly different from the roles taken by clients and servers over a network. Client/server data processing implies that the major part of the software is running on the server (for example, a database management system, DBMS). The client formulates a request to the server (perhaps a query for data from a database) which is then sent to the server over the network. The server processes the request and sends back unformatted, raw data to the client. The client's software then formats the data for display to the end user. In other words, the data manipulation chores are shared between the client and server computers, cutting down on the amount of traffic on the network. In contrast, a file server doesn't necessarily run software for the network client that is accessing it; it may simply deliver a file that is stored and processed completely on the client machine.

Data Communications Protocols

The procedures used to transfer messages over a network are known as network *protocols*, specifications of how a computer will format and transfer data. If a computer contains implementations of a set of protocols, theoretically it can communicate with any other computer that has implementations of the same protocols. The protocols provide a standardized way for computers to format and transmit data to one another. Protocols ensure, if you will, that computers communicating over data communications lines will be speaking the same language. Each group of protocols that work together is known as a *protocol stack*.

There are many standard sets of protocols in use. However, those that you may encouner with Ethernet include:

◆ *TCP/IP* (Transmission Control Protocol/Internet Protocol): The protocols used by the Internet. Because of the influence of the Internet, TCP/IP has been the most widely used group of protocols in the world. There are implementations of TCP/IP for virtually every computing platform today and it has for the most part eliminated the adoption of other protocol sets except for special uses.

Note: TCP/IP actually originated with the UNIX operating system. It was selected for use by ARPANET, the precursor of the Internet, and had a relatively minor role in networking until the Internet became widely used in the early 1990s.

◆ *NetBEUI* (network BIOS extended user interface): Protocols used by Windows 95, 98, and NT. NetBEUI was developed by IBM for OS/2 and was also used in Windows for Workgroups. Newer versions of Windows emphasize TCP/IP and NetBEUI is therefore largely outdated.

◆ *IPX/SPX*: The protocols developed for Novell NetWare, a network operating system, based on prior work by Xerox at its PARC (Palo Alto Research Center) facility. Novell added

TCP/IP support to its products to survive in the marketplace and today the only IPX/SPX installations you will find tend to be in legacy networks.

Note: Prior to the development of SPX/IPX, TCP/IP was the most widely used set of protocols. TCP/IP regained its dominance with the rise in popularity of the Internet.

◆ *AppleTalk*: A set of protocols designed primarily for use by Macintosh computers. However, AppleTalk protocols are also available for Windows and Linux. They are typically used in networks that are predominantly Macintosh and at this point are used largely just for printing. Otherwise, most heavily Macintosh network use TCP/IP, just as do Windows and Linux networks.

In addition to the protocol stacks just discussed, there is another, very important group of protocols known as the *OSI* (Open Systems Interconnect) Reference Model. Adopted by the *ISO* (International Standards Organization), it was anticipated that the protocols would be implemented and become an international standard. However, the rise of the Internet put an end to OSI's march to dominance; only a few of its protocols were ever implemented in software and used. Rather, as you will see shortly, TCP/IP and OSI now work together.

It is possible for one computer to use more than one protocol stack at the same time. For example, you might be using TCP/IP to pick up e-mail using a modem and telephone line. At the same time, your computer could be using AppleTalk to print a file and one of Novell NetWare's protocols to exchange files with another computer over a LAN.

Each data communications conversation in which your computer participates uses only one protocol stack. However, because all of today's desktop operating systems support some form of multitasking, a computer can handle multiple communications sessions at the same time, each of which may be using a different set of protocols.

Layered Protocols

The interaction of network hardware and software can be viewed as a layered stack. Each set of protocols mentioned in the previous section has its own distinct stack. However, for purposes of working with Ethernet and the Internet, only TCP/IP and OSI are significant.

The TCP/IP Protocol Stack

In Figure 1-3 you will find the TCP/IP stack. Such layering always has a hardware layer (the *physical layer* in Figure 1-3) at the bottom. The remaining layers are software and correspond to groups of data communications protocols.

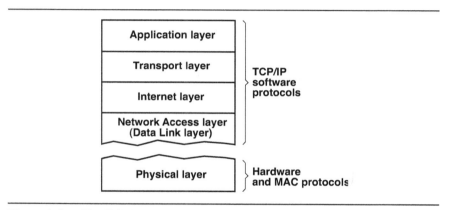

Figure 1-3:   The TCP/IP protocol stack

From the bottom up, the TCP/IP layers are

♦ *Network Access layer* (also known as the *Data Link layer*): The protocols in this layer cover the way in which hardware gains access to the transmission media.
♦ *Internet layer* (also known as the *Network layer*): The Internet layer contains protocols that are used when messages must travel between two interconnected LANs or intranets. This is where the protocols for the IP portion of TCP/IP can be found.
♦ *Transport layer*: The Transport layer ensure reliable transfer of data, independent of the application programs that are using the data. This layer contains the TCP portion of TCP/IP.

♦ *Application layer*: The protocols in this layer are those found in the programs that a node uses to access the network.

When you obtain networking software, you are getting implementations of protocols at one or more layers in a protocol stack.

The OSI Protocol Stack

The AppleTalk protocol stack and Novell NetWare's protocols are based on the OSI protocol stack. However, as mentioned in the preceding section, the OSI protocol stack is a theoretical model that provides a convenient framework for discussing groups of protocols. Most of today's protocol stacks can be mapped to the OSI layers.

As you can see in Figure 1-4, there is a Physical layer that includes the hardware and that is separate from the software layers above. The bottom three software layers are relatively equivalent to the bottom three layers of the TCP/IP protocol stack. However, the Session layer takes over some of the responsibility of managing communication sessions. The Presentation layer acts as an interface between the Application layer, which, as in TCP/IP, consists of the user's software and the Session layer.

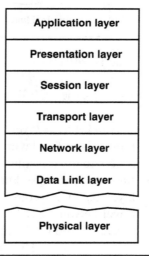

Figure 1-4:   The OSI Reference Model protocol stack

Combining TCP/IP and OSI

What happens in practice today, in particular on the Internet, is a combination of the layers from TCP/IP and OSI. We use the topmost three layers from TCP/IP (those layers that are hardware independent) and the bottom two layers from OSI (those layers that are hardware dependent), as in Figure 1-5. The OSI Data Link layer is split into two layers—Logical Link Control (LLC) and Media Access Control (MAC)—to provide further separation between software-only layers and hardware-dependent layers. Whenever this book talks about TCP/IP from now on, it will mean the combined protocol stack.

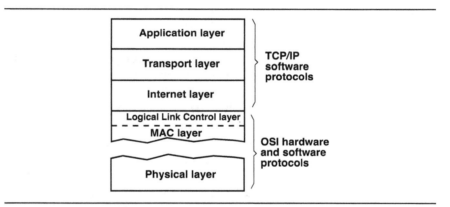

Figure 1-5   The combined TCP/IP and OSI protocol stacks

Another Word on Protocol Stacks

The beauty of the layered approach is that hardware and software can be relatively independent. The software portions of the protocol stacks you have seen (TCP/IP and OSI) are independent of the hardware on which they may be running. For example, TCP/IP can be used on all types of Ethernet transmission media, both copper wire and fiber optic.

Users rarely interact with the Application layer protocols directly. Instead, applications present a more user-friendly interface to the user and then formulate the communications command out of sight of the user.

Network Operating Systems

Although we will discuss network operating systems fucntions in some depth in Part Three, at this point you should at least be familiar with the names of the software that manages networking. Those that you are likely to encounter include:

◆ *Novell NetWare:* Novell NetWare was one of the first network operating systems. It made possible the networking of computers running MS-DOS. NetWare used DOS to boot the server and then installed itself as an alternative operating system. Although today Novell NetWare uses TCP/IP, its original file transfer protocol was IPX. Novell NetWare requires a server runing the server software and client software on all machines. Novell client software is included in recent Windows releases but must be purchased separately for other operating systems. Novell NetWare is the least commonly used of the major NOSs today and is the least likely to be installed in a new, small network.

◆ *Microsoft Windows:* Current desktop releases of Windows support peer-to-peer networking. In addition Windows server software provides a full range of network services, many of which are discussed throughout this book.

◆ *Mac OS X Server*: Like desktop versions of Windows, Mac OS X supports a variety of peer-to-peer networking services. However, if you want to use a Mac OS X server, you will need the separate server software.

◆ *UNIX*: The many variations of the UNIX operating system incorporate TCP/IP as their networking foundation. In this book, we will look at Linux, the open source version of UNIX that is the most commonly used UNIX in small offices.

Note: Linux networking is generally more complex to implement and manage than Windows and Mac OS X, in particular, because Linux has no single graphic user interface (GUI); the tools that you have to manage networking depend on the Linux distribution you purchase. Therefore, the only way to talk about networking that can be certain to apply to all distributions of Linux is look at the command line.

What Ethernet Really Means

Where does Ethernet fit into all of this? In the Physical layer. In a LAN or intranet, there are many pieces of hardware trying to gain access to the network transmission media at the same time. However, a network cable or wireless transmission frequency can physically allow only one node to use it at any given moment. There must therefore be some way to control which node has control of the medium (a *media access control*, or MAC, protocol).

Ethernet is a MAC protocol. It is one way to regulate physical access to network transmission media. You will learn how it works in Chapter 2.

> *Note: Until just a few years ago, there were viable alternatives to Ethernet (in partiuclar, IBM's Token Ring). However, Ethernet has become the only wired MAC protocol for which hardware is still being produced. You can have Ethernet, or you can have Ethernet, and if you don't like that, you can have Ethernet—unless you go wireless, which as you will see later in this book, has some major issues (primarily security, but also performance) that make it problematic for all but the smallest networks.*

Types of Ethernet

Ethernet is actually a collection of networking standards, some of which are outdated and not used any more. (See Appendix A for a discussion of the earlier versions of Ethernet.) Today there are three versions of Ethernet that you are likely to encounter in a small network, distinguished by their transmission speeds:

♦ *Standard Ethernet* (also known as *10BASE-T*): Transfers data at a maximum of 10 megabits per second (abbreviated 10 M bps). At today's prices, it is possible to set up a simple eight-device standard Ethernet LAN for less than $100. This assumes that all of the nodes require expansion boards. If all the nodes have built-in network adaptors, then you can get by for about $25. However, today standard Ethernet is largely gone because almost all computers are supplied with faster versions of the standard. Although we will discuss standard Ethernet in this book as a basis for Ethernet operation, it is highly unlikely that you would install it: The next faster version costs no more and, because it is more widely used, occasionally less.

◆ *Fast Ethernet*: transfers data at a maximum of 100 Mbps. At the time this book was written, it was the most common type of Ethernet in use for connecting client workstations.

◆ *Gigabit Ethernet*: transfers data at a maximum of 1 gigabit per second (abbreviated 1 Gbps). At the time this book was written, Gigabit Ethernet hardware was becoming common on client workstations, although its most typical use is to connect servers to the network. If your desktop computers come equipped with Gigabit Ethernet, it is certainly reasonable to use it throughout your network, as prices for network interconnection hardware have dropped to the point where they are affordable for even small networks.

◆ *10 Gigabit Ethernet*: Transfers data at a maxminum of 10 giga-bits per second (10 Gbps). Initially designed to run over fiber optic cabling for use in WANs, 10 Gb Ethernet has now migrat-ed to copper wire and can be used within a LAN. Keep in mind, however, that very few individual devices can transmit and re-ceive data at 10 Gbps. Therefore, LAN 10Gb Ethernet is best suited for large networks where many devices share the net-work medium. It is highly unlikely that you would run 10 Gb Ethernet to a single destkop device; such a setup would not be economically efficient.

Note: The next Ethernet speed jump will probably be to 40 Gbps, although there is no official standard for this speed yet. This WAN implementation is intended only for fiber optic cabling. Will there be an even faster version? Never say "never": Some writers are currently talking about 100 Gbps Ethernet, even though as of summer 2007, there wasn't even a committee working on a 40 Gb standard!

When considering Ethernet speeds, keep in mind that the transfer rates associated with each type of Ethernet are maximums. In practice, it is rare to achieve the highest transfer rate. Many factors limit network speed, including the nature of the transmission media, the amount of traffic on the network, and the speeds of the hardware manipulating the network. In addition, an Ethernet that supports between 30 and 60 percent utilization is considered saturated. You will therefore never realize total use of your network media. (However, the introduction of hardware known as switches as a replacement for hubs has significantly increased the utilization.)

Given that Ethernet and the data transmission protocols that run on top of it (TCP/IP, IPX/SPX, and AppleTalk) are independent, when you choose Ethernet over some other form of physical network, you are restricting your hardware choices rather than your software choices. As you will see, the type of Ethernet you choose dictates to some extent what hardware you use. However, your software choices are not limited.

The Speed and Bandwidth Connection

The types of Ethernet are defined in terms of their maximum transmission speeds. Nonetheless, they can in most cases use the same type of wiring. Assume, for example, that standard, Fast, and Gigabit Ethernet are all using the same wire medium. Electrical signals can travel at only one physical speed over the medium. How can this be true if there are multiple Ethernet speeds?

The answer lies in how we actually look at speed. The measures of Ethernet speed are actually what is known as *throughput*, the number of bits that arrive at a destination per unit time. There are two ways to affect throughput. The first is to speed up the rate at which the bits travel, but this is dictated by the physical properties of the wire. Since we cannot speed up the travel rate of a single bit, the only other choice is to increase the number of bits traveling together. For example, if you can send four bits per unit time, your throughput will be greater than if you can send only one. This is directly analogous to widening a road from two to four lanes but leaving the maximum speed limit the same. Widening the road does not allow an individual car to travel faster, but does allow more cars to cover the same distance in the same period of time.

The number of bits that can travel together at the same time represents the *bandwidth* of the transmission medium. If we can increase the bandwidth, we can increase the throughput without changing the maximum physical transfer speed of bits down the wire. Fiber optic cabling, for example, is very fast not only because each bit can travel at the speed of light, but because so many tiny glass fibers can be bound together into a single cable to provide a high bandwidth.

Ethernet Standards

The types of Ethernet about which you have just read are defined in a set of standards prepared by the Institute of Electrical and Electronic Engineers (IEEE). The committee in charge of the standards for LANs is known as IEEE LAN 802, and the group within it that handles media access controls standards as 802.3. Each 802.3 standard describes a method for media access control and the transmission media that should be supported.

> *Note: Although the name of the IEEE may not suggest that the organization has anything to do with computing, keep in mind that the IEEE predates computers. It has evolved to encompass a wide range of computing standards and applications.*

Although in most cases you won't be concerned directly with the specifications themselves and the rather strange numbering scheme that goes along with them, you may find that equipment and cable vendors use the standard numbers to identify the type of Ethernet for which a product is appropriate. You should therefore at least be familiar with the type of Ethernet each standard represents. This book identifies the standards that accompany each type of Ethernet cabling as we explore hardware details in the following chapters.

A Bit of Ethernet History

Originally, Ethernet was the brainchild of one person: Robert Metcalfe. In the early 1970s, while working at Xerox PARC on the "office of the future" project, Metcalfe was intrigued by a radio network in Hawaii known as AlohaNet. One problem faced by AlohaNet's media access control was that its maximum effeciency was 17 percent: That is, a maximum of 17 percent of the transmission units sent actually reached their destination. According to Metcalfe, the unreceived portions of the transmissions were "lost in the ether."

Metcalfe developed an alternative media access control method that allowed up to 90 percent of the transmission units to reach their destination. Originally known as "experimental Ethernet," it transferred up to 3 Mbps. As you can see in Metcalfe's original drawing in Figure 1-6, he refers to the cabling along with data travel as "the ether," hence the name *Ethernet*.

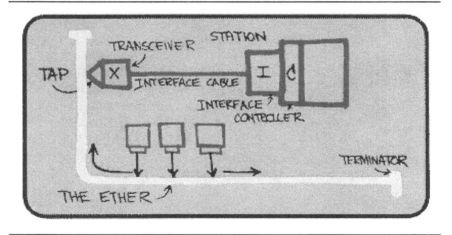

Figure 1-6:   Bob Metcalfe's original drawing for Ethernet (Courtesy of Bob Metcalfe)

> *Note: Bob Metcalfe went on to found the 3Com Corporation and currently is a networking pundit and guru. His columns appear in* InfoWorld *and elsewhere.*

The first Ethernet specifications were published in 1980 by a consortium of commercial hardware vendors—Digital Equipment Corporation (now a part of Compaq Corp.), Intel, and Xerox (DIX). By that time, the transmission speed had been increased to 10 Mbps.

The IEEE adopted Ethernet as a LAN standard and published its initial specifications as 10BASE5 in 1983. Later, Ethernet was also endorsed as a standard by the ISO. Ethernet is therefore an international standard for one way in which nodes on a LAN can gain access to transmission media.

Throughout its history, Ethernet has moved to faster and faster standards:

- *1986*: The standard for 10BASE2 was approved, still running at 10 Mpbs.
- *1991*: The standard for 10BASE-T was approved. Although still running at 10 Mpbs, it used copper wiring, making it much easier to handle than earlier standards.

Note: For more information on these earlier Ethernet standards, see Appendix A.

- *1995*: The standard for 100 Mpbs Ethernet was approved. This is the slowest speed in general use today.
- *1998*: The standard for 1000 Mbps (Gigabit) Ethernet using fiber optic cable was approved.
- *1999*: The standard for 1000 Mbps Ethernet using copper wire was approved.
- *2002*: The standard for 10,000 Mbps (10 Gigabit) Ethernet was approved. This type of Ethernet is for wide area rather than local area networks.

As of early 2007, standards committees were beginning to explore the possibilities for 40 Gigabit and 100 Gigabit Ethernet, although speeds beyond 1 Gigabit currently aren't designed for use in local area networks.

2

How TCP/IP and Ethernet Work

Regardless of the type of Ethernet you choose, the basic way in which data are packaged to travel over the network and the way in which devices gain access to the network media remain the same. In this chapter we will therefore look at both the packaging of the data and the way that Ethernet provides media access control.

However, before we can look at the physical layer in depth, you need to know how the upper layers of the TCP/IP protocol stack operate. This knowledge forms the basis for understanding how devices such as switches and routers determine where to send packets of information.

21

Network Data Transmission

The data that travel over a network can be *serial* or *parallel*. With serial data transmission, each bit (a 0 or 1 value) travels single file. Parallel data transmission sends rows of bits, 32, 64, 128, or more at a time. As you may remember from Chapter 1, the bandwidth of a data communications channel relates to the number of bits per unit time (usually a second) that arrive at their destination, thus the term *bits per second* for the speed of a data communications network.

It might seem at first that parallel transmission is faster than serial transmission—and it is—but we use serial transmission over data communications networks because there is a major drawback to parallel transmission—interference that gets worse over distance. Let's assume that you have a cable designed to carry 32 bits in parallel. Because each wire in the cable can carry only one bit at a time, you need to bundle 32 wires together to obtain the desired bandwidth. (If they aren't close together, it will be next to impossible to fit a connector to them.)

Unfortunately, the wires in the cable tend to leak signals to one another. The closer the wires are bound and the longer they get, the worse the interference. Therefore, parallel transmission of this type (using a flat *ribbon cable*) is only good for very short distances, such as a few feet. Today we use it most commonly for connecting peripherals such as disk drives inside a system box.

The speed of a serial transmission—the speed at which data reach their destination—is affected by many factors, including the following:

♦ The maximum physical speed that the wire can carry a signal.

   Note: When we speak of "wire" in this context, we mean copper wire and fiber optics.

♦ The speed at which a new signal can be placed on the wire. This is an effect of the equipment that places signals on the wire, as well as the method for giving hardware control of the wire.

♦ The ratio of overhead bits to data bits. (The more overhead bits you have, the lower the data throughput.)

Major TCP/IP Protocols

In a practical sense, you don't need to know anything about networking protocols to plug the right wires into the right interconnection hardware. However, if you really want to know how your equipment works, then you'll want to understand the material in this section. It looks at how protocols stacks work in general and how the major TCP/IP protocols work specifically.

The Operation of a Protocol Stack

The protocols in a protocol stack are organized so that protocols that provide similar functions are grouped into a single layer. As you saw in Chapter 1, the original TCP/IP provided four layers. (It has no physical layer.) However, the lower two layers of the original four have been replaced with protocols that were originally part of the OSI protocol stack.

The exchange of bits occurs only at the Physical layer. The remaining layers are software protocols. Conceptually, each layer communicates with the matching layer on the machine with which it is exchanging messages, as in Figure 2-1. However, because bits flow between machines only at the Physical layer, the actual communication is down one protocol stack, across the Physical layer, and up the receiving protocol stack (see Figure 2-2).

The top three layers in the TCP/IP protocol stack are independent of the hardware a network is using. The remaining layers, however, are hardware-dependent, often meaning that there will be multiple sets of protocol specifications corresponding to different types of hardware.

As a message moves down the protocol stack on the sending machine, it is *encapsulated*: Each software layer below the Application layer adds a header (and possibly a trailer) to the message before passing it down. On the receiving end, each layer strips off the header (and trailer, if present) before passing the message up to the next layer. By the time the message reaches the Application layer on the destination machine, it has been restored to is original state.

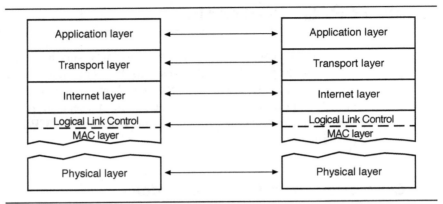

Figure 2-1: Logical protocol communication

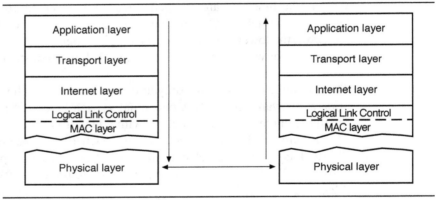

Figure 2-2: The actual path for protocol communication

The Application Layer

The Application layer handles the interaction with the end user. All messages originate there. Commonly, the Application layer sends a string of text down to the Transport layer, which begins the encapsulation process.

.Frequently used Application layer protocols are summarized in Table 2-1. In most cases, the specifications for a protocol include the syntax and commands to be used when formulating the message. For example, to retrieve

Table 2-1: Frequently Used TCP/IP Application Layer Protocols

Acronym	Name	Purpose
HTTP	Hypertext Transport Protocol	Manage the interaction between Web clients (browsers) and Web servers
SMTP	Simple Mail Transport Protocol	Transfer e-mail messages between client (e-mail client software) and e-mail server as well as between servers
MIME	Multipurpose Internet Mail Extensions	Provide format conversation for e-mail extensions so they can travel over a TCP/IP network
POP3	Post Office Protocol	Handle e-mail transfer
DNS	Domain Name Server	Manage the mapping of domain names to IP addresses
	telnet	Remote system login
FTP	File Transfer Protocol	Transfer files
NNTP	Network News Transfer Protocol	Exchange Internet news articles between servers and clients

a Web page, a Web browser formats a GET command, which includes the URL of the page to be retrieved

Users rarely interact with the application layer protocol directly. Instead, applications present a more user-friendly interface to the user and then formulate the communications command out of sight.

The Transport Layer

The Transport layer contains two protocols: TCP (Transmission Control Protocol) and UDP (User Datagram Protocol). They are fundamentally different in the way in which they operate. TCP provides a virtual connection between the communicating Transport layers and is suitable for long messages; UDP does not provide a virtual connection and is used mostly for short messages.

Transmission Control Protocol

TCP is known as a *connection-oriented* protocol because it establishes a logical circuit between sender and recipient that stays intact for the duration of a communications session. It is also known as a *reliable* protocol because it provides both error correction and detection.

The heart of TCP's operation is its *three-way handshake* for establishing a connection, which works in the following manner:

1. The sender transmits a segments with a SYN (Synchronization of Sequence Numbers) request (a request to open a virtual connection between the two machines). The sender chooses an ISN (Initial Sequence Number), either a 0 or some random number, that it sends in the initial SYN request.
2. The destination replies with a SYN containing the sender's original sequence number and an ACK (Acknowledge) containing the sender's original sequence number plus 1. (The segments may not arrive at the destination in the correct order, so the sequence numbers are essential to reassembling the message. They are also unique identifiers for each segment.)
3. The source responds with an ACK and the connection is established.

A similar process gives TCP its reliability and error correction ability. Each segment that TCP sends is acknowledged by the recipient with an ACK segment. This ensures reliability; if the sender doesn't receive the ACK message within a specified amount of time, it retransmits the segment. This also provides error correction for segments dropped when other layers and/or protocols detected errors in them. The beauty of having TCP handle the error correction is that lower level protocols need to worry only about error detection.

Because each segment received must be acknowledged, TCP is a *verbose protocol*, at least compared to UDP. It also is not a particularly fast protocol compared to UDP because it requires an extra exchange of messages.

When TCP receives a message from the Application layer, it attaches a header to the message, creating a *segment*. You can find the structure of a segment in Figure 2-3. The application layer message appears in the Data field; the rest of the segment is the header. The header fields are summarized in Table 2-2.

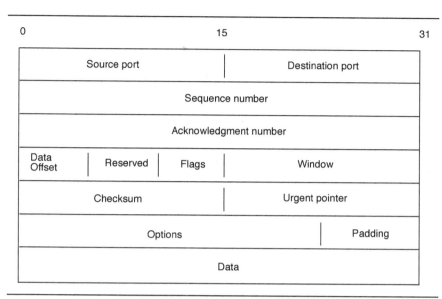

Figure 2-3: The structure of a TCP segment

Table 2-2: Fields in a TCP header

Field	Size	Contents
Source Port	16 bits	The TCP software port originating the message (for example, port 80 for the Web).
Destination Port	16 bits	The TCP software port to which the message is being sent.
Sequence Number	32 bits	A number indicating the segment's position in the set of segments that comprise the entire message. TCP counts the number of octets[a] in the data field of the entire message and assigns each segment a sequence number that represents the number of the first data octet in that sequence. The recipient uses the sequence numbers to reassemble a message into the correct order, even if the segments are received out of order.
Acknowledgment Number	32 bits	A number acknowledging the receipt of a segment. It is set to the number of the next octet the recipient expects to receive.

Table 2-2: Fields in a TCP header *(Continued)*

Field	Size	Contents
Data Offset	4 bits	The number of 32-bit units in the segment, indicating where the Data field begins.
Reserved	6 bits	Not used currently. Set to zero.
Flags (Control Bits)	6 bits	URG: Read Urgent Pointer field ACK: Read Acknowledgment field PSH: Push function RST: Connection reset SYN: Synchronize FIN: Last segment in the set
Window	16 bits	
Checksum	16 bits	A message digest (see Chapter 12 for details)
Urgent Pointer	16 points	An offset into the Data field indicating where urgent data begin. Read only if the URG flag is set.
Options	variable (multiple of 8 bits)	A collection of information about the segment, including the maximum segment size.
Padding	variable	Extra space added to ensure that the Data field begins on a 32-bit boundary

a. An *octet* is an 8-bit byte. In the early days of computing, a byte wasn't necessarily 8-bits. We therefore carry over the term octet in data communications for historical reasons.

TCP manages its error correction in the following way:

1. Establish a virtual connection using the three-way handshake. (See Chapter 6 for details.)

2. Send the first data-carrying segment. (This will actually be the fourth segement, since the first three were used to set up the connection.)

3. When the segment is received, the recipient counts the number of octets in the Data field and adds 1. This will be the value of the next sequence number.

4. Place the computed next sequence number in the Acknowledgment field of a segment and send it back to the sender.

5. If the source does not receive the acknowledgment segment in a preset amount of time, retransmit the segment.

User Datagram Protocol

UDP does not provide error correction and is therefore an *unreliable* protocol. In other words, delivery of packets is not guaranteed. UDP *datagrams* are transmitted without provision for an acknowledgment. Because there is no virtual connection between sender and receiver, UDP is also said to be *connectionless*.

Although it might seem that UDP's unreliability might make it unsuitable for much use, it is actually able to carry a number of Application layer protocol messages. (TCP carries about 80 percent of Internet traffic; UDP carries the rest.) The most common Application layer protocols carried by UDP datagrams can be found in Table 2-3.

Table 2-3: Application Layer Protocols Carried by UDP Datagrams

Acronym	Name	Comments
NFS	Network File System	Handles interactions with a remote server
Proprietary		Streaming audio and video
Proprietary		IP telephony
SNMP	Simple Network Management Protocol	Network management
RIP	Routing Information Protocol	Updates the routing tables in routers
DNS	Domain Name Server	Maps IP addresses to domain names

Because UDP doesn't require the error correction segments used by TCP, it is faster than TCP. It is therefore also well suited to streaming media, where retransmitting a corrupted segment won't provide any benefits.

The Internet Layer

Like the Transport layer, the Internet layer has only two protocols: IP (Internet Protocol) and ICMP (Internet Control Message Protocol). The latter is used to carry IP control messages. It is IP, however, that forms the backbone of the TCP/IP protocol stack because every data-carrying message passes through it.

IP is connectionless, and therefore unreliable. (Remember that it doesn't need to do error correction because TCP is taking care of that.) IP does error detection, however. It uses a checksum to verify that a message was received without alteration. If it determines that the message was altered, it discards the message. Because the Transport layer on the receiving machine will never receive the message, the Transport layer on the sending machine won't receive an acknowledgment for the packet, triggering a retransmission.

IP receives a segment from the Transport layer. It adds its own header and footer, creating a *packet*, which it then sends to the Data Link layer. IP also handles *fragmentation*, the splitting and reassembly of packets based on the largest packet size a network can handle. In addition, IP takes care of packet routing.

> *Note: Most routers don't have an entire TCP/IP protocol stack, but only the bottom layers, stopping with the Internet layer. They don't need the Transport and Application layers because they can route packets using IP.*

An IP packet encapsulates an entire Transport layer segment, placing the segment (including the Transport layer header) into its Data field, as in Figure 2-4. The uses of the fields in the header are summarized in Table 2-4.

Many of the fields in the IP header deal with fragmentation, which occurs because different types of networks have different limits on the size of packets they can carry. When a router receives a packet that is too large for the network over which it must send a packet, it extracts the data portion of the original packet and breaks it into chunks. Then it adds a complete IP header to each chunk, creating a message fragment. A packet may be fragmented many times before it reaches its destination. However, the fragments are not reassembled into the message until all fragments have been received by the destination machine. This is because all fragments may not travel by the same route to reach their destination. In addition, differences in the speed of network links may cause the fragments to arrive out of order.

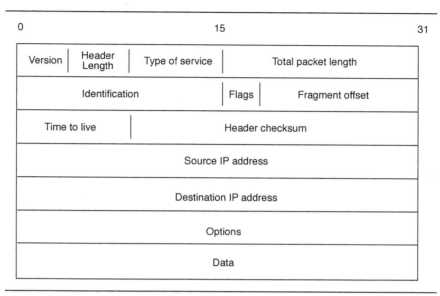

Figure 2-4: The structure of an IP packet

The Logical Link Control Layer

The Logical Link Control (LLC) layer provides the major interface between the hardware below and the software layers above. Because it sits between the protocols in the MAC layer that regulate access to transmission media and the rest of the protocol stack, the LLC layer lets the upper layers communicate with any form of transmission media in the same way.

The LLC layer receives an IP packet from the Internet layer and formats it into *frames*, the units that will be sent across the physical media. The organization of a frame, however, depends on the type of MAC protocol that will be used. This means that the LLC is hardware-dependent, unlike the upper layers in the protocol stack.

LLC layer protocols include specifications for the frames of many types of physical networks, including Ethernet, Token Ring (rarely used today because it has become nearly impossible to find parts to maintain the

Table 2-4: The Header Fields in an IP Packet

Field	Size	Contents
Version	4 bits	The IP version (4 or 6).
IP Header Length	4 bits	The number of 32-bit words in the header.
Type of Service	8 bits	The type of service requested. This field currently is very rarely used.
Total Packet Length	16 bits	Number of octets in the entire packet (header and data).
Identification	16 bits	If the packet is part of a set of fragments, a value that, when combined with the source IP address, uniquely identifies this fragment.
Flags	3 bits	Flags that provide fragmentation information. If the third bit is set, there are additional fragments for the packet. If the second bit is set, the packet is not to be fragmented.
Fragment Offset	13 bits	The position of this fragment in the original packet, indicated by the number of octets it begins from the start of the original packet.
Time to Live	8 bits	The maximum number of router hops allowed for the packet. The purpose of this value is to keep a packet from circulating forever around the network. Each router decrements this value by one.
Protocol	8 bits	The type of Transport layer protocol segment being carried by the packet.
Source IP Address	32 bits	The IP address of the originator of the message.
Destination IP Address	32 bits	The IP address of the message's intended recipient.
Options	Multiple of 32 bits	Used occasionally today but usually left empty because many routers drop datagrams with nonempty options.

hardware), and FDDI (Fiber Distributed Data Interface). LLC also includes WAN protocols such as ATM, Frame Relay, SONET, X.25, and PPP (Point-to-Point protocol, used for communication between dial-up modems).

The Ethernet MAC Protocol

Ethernet is really a MAC protocol and the media specifications that go with it. The MAC protocol includes details of how the data should be formatted when traveling over the wire and how devices should gain control of the wire to transmit.

Ethernet Frames

To transmit a message across an Ethernet, a device constructs an Ethernet *frame*, a package of data and control information that travels as a unit across the network. A small message may fit in a single frame, but large messages are split among multiple frames.

> *Note: Because software protocol stacks like TCP/IP refer to their units of transmission as "packets," Ethernet frames are also often called packets.*

There are two general types of frame. The first carries meaningful data (the content of messages two devices want to exchange). The second carries network management information. Nonetheless, the general structure of both types of frame is identical.

An Ethernet frame varies in size from 64 bytes to 1529 bytes. It is made up of the nine fields that you can see in Figure 2-5.

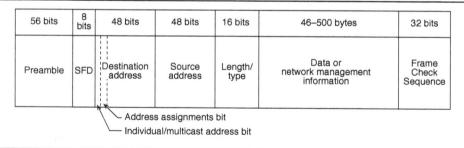

Figure 2-5:   An Ethernet frame (IEEE 802.3 standard)

♦ *Preamble*: The preamble contains a group of 64 bits that are used to help the hardware synchronize itself with the data on the network. If a few bits of the preamble are lost during transmission, no harm occurs to the message itself. The preamble therefore also acts as a buffer for the remainder of the frame.

The last 8 bits of the preamble are used as a *start frame delimiter*. This marks the end of the preamble and the start of the information-bearing parts of the frame.

♦ *Destination address*: The destination address (48 bits) contains the physical address of the device that is to receive the frame.

The first two bits of this field have special meaning. If the first bit is 0, then the address represents a hardware address of a single device on the network. However, if the first bit is 1, then the address is what is known as a *multicast address* and the frame is addressed to a group of devices. The second bit indicates where physical device addresses have been set. If the value is 0, then addresses have been set by the hardware manufacturer (global addressing). When addresses are set by those maintaining the network, the value is 1 (local addressing).

Note: A device's physical address is distinct from its software address, such as the addresses used by the Internet layer of the TCP/IP protocol stack. (For example, the author's printer has an Internet layer address of 192.168.1.105 and an Ethernet address of 00:C0:B0:02:15:75.) One job of data communications protocols is therefore to translate between hardware and software addresses. TCP/IP, for example, uses Address Resolution Protocol (ARP) to map TCP/IP addresses onto Ethernet addresses.

♦ *Source address*: The 48 bits of the source address field contain the hardware address of the device sending the frame.

♦ *Length field*: The contents of the length field depend on the type of frame. If the frame is carrying data, then the length field indicates how many bytes of meaningful data are present. However, if the frame is carrying management information, then the length field indicates the type of management information in the frame.

♦ *Data field*: The data field carries a minimum of 46 bytes and a maximum of 1500 bytes. If there are fewwer than 46 bytes of data, the field will be padded to the minimum length.

♦ *Frame check sequence* (FCS): The last field (also known as a *cyclical redundancy check*, or CRC, field) contains 32 bits used for error checking. The bits in this field are set by the transmitting device based on the pattern of bits in the data field. The receiving device then regenerates the FCS. If what the receiving device obtains does not match what is in the frame, then some bits were changed during transmission and some type of transmission error has occurred.

Note: FCS error checking will not catch all errors, but it is certainly more effective than having no error checking at all!

Ethernet Media Access

Whenever a device connected to an Ethernet network wants to send a message, it places that message in one or more frames. However, only one frame can be transmitted on any given network segment at a time because the network itself—at least conceptually—is a single electrical or light pathway that can carry only one signal at a time. A device must therefore take control of the network, making sure that it is not in use by another device, before it begins sending a frame. This is what media access control is all about.

To understand how Ethernet's MAC protocol works, you must first know something about how an Ethernet network is laid out (its *topology*). Originally, all Ethernet networks used a *bus topology*, a layout in which the devices all connect to a single network transmission line. As you can see in Figure 2-6, the ends of the bus are unconnected. Each device simply taps into the bus, which is conceptually—although not necessarily physically—a single unbroken transmission pathway.

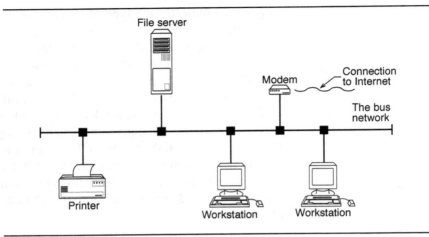

Figure 2-6:   A simple bus topology for an Ethernet network

> *Note: There doesn't seem to be any well-accepted story
> about why an electronic pathway into which devices plug
> is called a bus. However, think of the bus as a vehicle that
> bits ride from one place to the other. That is as good an
> explanation as any!*

To send a frame, a device makes sure that the bus is not in use and then
transmits its frame by placing its signal on the network media. This is
known as *broadcasting* the frame because it is placed on the bus for all
connected devices to read rather than being directed at a specific device.

All devices on the network read each frame as it passes. If the address is
for another device, the device reading the frame ignores the rest of the
frame. However, when a device recognizes its own address in the frame, it
then continues to handle the rest of the frame.

The trick in this scheme is to make sure the bus is not in use. Ethernet hardware is designed to detect the presence of a frame on the network. When
this condition occurs, a device detects a *carrier*. The device then waits a
short, randomly determined period of time and checks again.

> *Note: The use of the term* carrier *in this case is not the same
> as the carrier signal used by modems. A modem carrier is*

*a tone of a known frequency, which is raised or lowered
during data transmission to indicate patterns of 0s and 1s.
Ethernet uses the term merely to indicate the presence of a
signal on the network.*

If the network is idle (no carrier is detected), then the device begins transmitting its frame. But what if two devices checked the network at exactly
the same time, both determined that the network was idle, and then both
transmitted a frame at exactly the same time? This situation is known as a
collision, and it does occur with some regularity.

The Ethernet hardware can detect a collision. In that case, a device waits a
random amount of time and attempts the transmission again, first recheck-
ing to see if the network is idle. Assuming that the random wait interval is
different for the two colliding devices, it is unlikely the same collision will
occur again for the same frames. If, however, a second (or third or fourth
…) collision does occur, the random wait interval becomes longer each
time a collision occurs.

This scheme for regulating network traffic is known as *Carrier Sense Multiple Access with Collision Detection* (CSMA/CD). The "carrier sense"
portion, of course, refers to a device's ability to sense the presence of a
frame on the network. The "multiple access" portion represents the idea
that all devices on the network have equal access to the transmission media. Finally, "collision detection" describes a device's ability to detect a
collision and handle the situation.

Each bus to which nodes are attached constitutes a *collision domain* (or a
network segment, in more general terminology). All nodes within a single
collision domain are therefore contending for access to the same network
transmission medium. Large Ethernet networks are assembled by connecting individual collision domains using hardware such as switches and
routers.

The more devices there are in a collision domain and the more frames they
are sending (i.e., the heavier the traffic), the more likely collisions are. In
a very busy, heavily loaded collision domain, a collision may occur repeatedly for the same frame. Users will detect this as a general slowdown in
the network. It may mean that you need to reexamine the way in which the

network is laid out; breaking it into smaller collision domains or upgrading the type of Ethernet in use may be warranted.

Because only one signal can be on the transmission medium at one time, the original Ethernet networks were *half-duplex* (transmission in only one direction at a time). This is in contrast, for example, to *full-duplex* telephone transmissions, where signals travel in two directions at once. (You may have trouble hearing what is being said if you are talking at the same time as the person on the other end of the phone call, but the technology nonetheless supports full-duplex operations.) The newer forms of Ethernet that are installed today do provide full-duplex tramissions.

Alternative Protocol Stacks

You should be aware of two alternative protocol stacks that often run on Ethernet hardware: IPX/SPX and AppleTalk.

IPX/SPX was developed by the Novell Corporation for use by its Novell Netware network operating system. Although Netware now uses TCP/IP, you may encounter a legacy network that uses IPX/SPX. The IPX protocol is roughly analogous to TCP/IP's UDP protocol; SPX, which comes from the OSI protocol model, is roughly equivalent to TCP. For more information on IPX/SPX see *http://en.wikipedia.org/wiki/IPX/SPX*.

AppleTalk is a protocol stack developed by Apple Computer for Macintosh networks. Based on the OSI reference model, it originally used its own hardware (LocalTalk) but now runs on Ethernet. Most Macintoshes use TCP/IP today, but AppleTalk is also still widely used for printing. Implementations of the AppleTalk protocol stack are available for both Windows and Linux distributions. For more information on AppleTalk, see *http://en.wikipedia.org/wiki/AppleTalk*.

Part Two

Design and Connectivity

An Ethernet can be as small as connecting a couple of computers and a printer, or it can contain hundreds of devices in interconnected segments. This part of this book describes how network are designed and the hardware that connects small segments into larger networks.

3

Fast and Gigabit Ethernet Media and Standards

The Fast (100 Mbps) and Gigabit (1000 Mbps) Ethernet standards specify the use of either unshielded twisted-pair wire (UTP) or fiber optic media. UTP cabling is cheaper and easier to use than fiber optics, but it has some distance limitations. We therefore tend to use UTP to the desktop within a building, and fiber optics for heavy traffic network links either within a building or as a network backbone between buildings.

UTP Cabling

The most common cabling for Fast and Gigabit Ethernet today is twisted-pair wire. It is inexpensive and easy to set up and maintain.

41

Twisted-pair wire cables contain one or more pairs of copper wires that are twisted in a spiral manner. For example, the cable in Figure 3-1 has four pairs of wires. Because the cable itself includes no shielding, this type of cable is called *unshielded twisted pair* (UTP).

Figure 3-1:   Twisted-pair wire cabling (Courtesy of Belden Wire & Cable Co.)

The pairs of wires are numbered from from the top down in Figure 3-1 and referenced by the colors of the two twisted wires, as in Table 3-1.

Table 3-1:   Identifying the Wires in a UTP Cable

Pair	Colors
1	White (with blue stripe) and blue
2	White and orange
3	White and green
4	White and brown

UTP Standards

The Electronics Industries Association (EIA) has set standards for the quality of UTP cabling: Category 3, Category 4, Category 5, Category 5e, Category 6, and Category 7. The major difference among them is the number of twists in each pair of wires. For example, Category 4 cabling has three or four twists per *foot*, whereas Category 5 cabling has three or four twists per *inch*. (The illustration in Figure 3-1 is Category 5 cable.) Almost all new cabling installed today is Category 5e or better.

Why is this twisting important? Because when you bundle multiple pairs of wires in the same cable, the signals tend to bleed from one pair to another (*crosstalk*). The twisting of the pairs reduces the crosstalk and therefore the amount of *noise* (unwanted signal) affecting each transmission traveling down the cable, which in turn helps to reduce transmission errors.

Category 3 cabling is the standard voice-grade twisted-pair cable that carries telephone transmissions. (The typical telephone cable has two pairs of wires and can therefore carry two telephone lines.) Because it is already installed in most buildings, it can be attractive to consider employing unused telephone lines to carry network signals. However, Category 3 cable is designed to carry signals at a maximum speed of only 16 Mbps, restricting its use to 10 Mbps Ethernet.

Virtually all new Ethernet installations use Category 5e or better cabling, which can carry signals traveling up to 1 Gbps. Given that Category 5e cabling is relatively inexpensive, there is no reason to use cabling of lesser quality when installing new wiring for a network or during new construction.

> *Note: At the time this book was written, Cat 6 cabling was state of the art. The Cat 7 standard had not been developed, although a variety of commercial vendors were testing cabling in an effort to determine how such a cable should be manufactured, with an eye to eventually moving toward a standard.*

If you are installing cables inside walls, heating/air-conditioning ducts, or other spaces where the air is breathed by people, then you will need to use what is known as *plenum* wiring. Plenum cables have a plastic coating that is less toxic than standard cabling when burned. It costs a little more but is required by most building codes and is available in both Cat 5e and Cat 6 versions.

The UTP wire used in most networks connects to a devices network interface card (for an example, see Figure 3-2) and to the network itself with RJ-45 plugs. As you can see in Figure 3-3, it appears to be a larger cousin of the RJ-11 plugs used in modular telephone systems.

> *Note: The acronym RJ stands for "registered jack."*

> *Note: The "thingy" on the end of a cable is a "plug." The thing you plug the plug into is a "jack."*

An RJ-45 jack

Figure 3-2:   A port on an NIC into which an RJ-45 connector is plugged (Courtesy of Farallon Corp.)

Figure 3-3:   RJ-45 plugs (Courtesy of Belkin)

UTP Cabling Lengths

Each piece of UTP cable connecting a device to a hub must be no longer than 100 meters. The reasons behind this lie in the properties of the copper wire used in the cables.

♦ *Attenuation:* As signals travel over a piece of copper wire, they lose strength due to friction on the surface of the wire (*attenuation*). This effect, measured in decibels (dB), becomes progressively worse with distance. As the signal strength decreases, it falls toward the *noise floor*, the level of background noise on the cable. When the signal is not stronger than the noise, the receiving device can't separate data from noise, and the signal is unintelligible.

Note: Decibels (dB) is a measure of the loudness of sound. It is a logarithmic scale, such that 20 decibels is 10 times louder than 10 decibels, 30 decibels is 10 times louder than 20 dB, and so on.

As the quality of UTP cable goes up, the amount of attenution goes down. For example, Cat 5 and Cat 5e cabling must have no more than 24 dB attenuation over 100 meters; with Cat 6 cabling it drops to 21.7 dB and will theoretically drop to 20.8 with Cat 7 cabling.

♦ *Interference:* Interference from outside sources—for example, the crosstalk described earlier or other electrical sources in the environment—can change signal strength and type, introducing errors into transmissions. The effect of interference becomes worse the longer a signal is exposed to sources of interference. Therefore, longer cable runs are more susceptible to interference than are shorter lengths of cable.

♦ *Noise:* Noise (any unwanted signal) on the wire also introduces errors. In addition to the constant noise level on the wire (the noise floor mentioned earlier), noise can occur as spikes that destroy blocks of data. Networks can usually recover from errors that affect only a bit or two of data at a time. However, errors that wipe out a block of bits are much more difficult to handle. Noise therefore can be a significant issue with copper wiring and make it unsuitable for use in electrically noisy environments such as factory floors or kitchens where microwave ovens are in use. (The only solution in such situations is to use fiber optic cabling.)

Research has shown that these problems—with the exception of environmental noise—are kept to an acceptable level when the maximum length of a single piece of UTP cable is 100 meters.

UTP Jack Wiring

There are two standard ways in which RJ-45 jacks can be wired: T568A and T568B. As you can see in Table 3-2 and Table 3-3, the difference is in the handing of the second and third pairs of wire. Theoretically, it doesn't matter one bit which type you use in your network, but you need to settle on just one.

Table 3-2:   Wiring for T568A Jacks

Pair	Transmitting Wire Pin	Receiving Wire Pin
1	White: 5	Blue: 4
2	White: 3	Orange: 6
3	White: 1	Green: 2
4	White: 7	Brown: 8

Table 3-3:   Wiring for T568B Jacks

Pair	Transmitting Wire Pin	Receiving Wire Pin
1	White: 5	Blue: 4
2	White: 1	Orange: 2
3	White: 3	Green: 6
4	White: 7	Brown: 8

In practice, which should you choose? Before deciding, consider the following:

♦ Use T568A in a home. Although the standard states that new construction of all types should use the A version, most commercial installations use T568B, and that is a reasonable choice for a new commercial network.

♦ If one version or the other is already in use, continue with the same version.

♦ If network devices are wired for one version or the other, stick with that version.

♦ If you have network specifications that require one version or the other, use the specified version.

Note: The actual standard for UTP plugs and jacks (TIA/EIA-568A) is also known as WECO or AT&T 258A. The wiring methods — A and B — both exist within the same standard.

Fiber Optic Cabling

Fiber optic cable is made up of a collection of glass tubes spun as thin as hairs. Each tube can carry a single pulse of light that represents one bit in a data transmission. By bundling many of these fibers together, a single cable can transmit many bits at the same time. In a simple fiber optic cable, such as that in Figure 3-4, the optical fibers are surrounded by a semirigid material that gives the cable strength and protects the fibers within, which is in turn encased in a protective outer jacket (see Figure 3-5).

Figure 3-4:   Fiber optic cable (Courtesy of Belden Wire & Cable Co.)

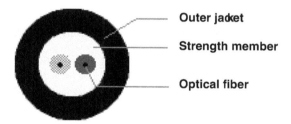

Figure 3-5:   The construction of a fiber optic cable (Courtesy of Belden Wire & Cable Co.)

The use of fiber optic cable has some very significant advantages.

♦ Because it uses light rather than electrical signals to transmit data, it is invulnerable to electrical interference, crosstalk, and attenuation. Fiber optic media can therefore be used in situations where wire media pose problems, such as on factory floors.

♦ It is much harder for someone to tap than wire media.

♦ It is much less susceptible to attenuation than wire media.

♦ It has much higher bandwidth than most wire media. The same fiber optic media can carry Ethernet signals at any standard speed.

On the other hand, fiber optic cabling is more difficult to work with than wire. It cannot be spliced and taped with electrical tape like wire, but instead requires special connectors that precisely line up the ends of two segments of cable with one another. In addition, fiber optic equipment is more expensive than equipment for wire media.

Nonetheless, in environments where many devices share network media (in particular, linking servers) or where severe electrical interference is a factor, fiber optic cabling is a viable choice. For example, in graphics and video design firms where large files move between workstations, fiber optic cabling can significantly speed up workflow by providing additional bandwidth.

Single versus Multimode Fiber Optics

There are two types of fiber optic cabling, *single mode* and *multimode*. Single mode, which can transmit a single wavelength of light long distances, is used primarily for WAN connections. Multimode can transmit multiple signals at one tim, but is more limited in length and typically used in LANs.

When light is introduced into an optical fiber, it can either go straight down the middle of the optical tube or it can travel at an angle, reflecting off the side of the tube as it travels. Each signal traveling down the tube at a time is known as a *mode*.

The diameter of the core of a single-mode fiber is very small (for example, 9 microns). A single ray of light is transmitted down the core, and it travels without reflection straight to its destination. In theory, one single-mode fiber link can be as long as 10 kilometers.

Multimode fiber has a larger core diameter and supports the transmission of multiple signals. Each ray of light has a different angle of reflection, making it possible for the receiving device to separate the individual signals. (See Figure 3-6.) However, the reflection angles disperse over distances (*modal dispersion*), spreading the signals and ultimately making it impossible to tell the signals apart. This limits the distance of multimode fiber. If the core is 62.5 microns in diameter, the maximum length is approximately 275 meters; 50 micron fiber can go as far as 550 meters.

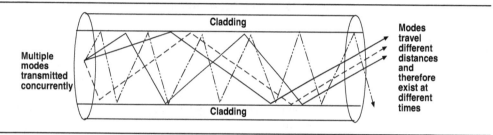

Figure 3-6:   Multiple signals traveling down multimode fiber

Multimode fiber is generally easier to work with than single mode. Because fiber optic cabling cannot be spliced, the ends of two pieces of single mode fiber must the aligned precisely when they are to be used as a single run of cable. Multimode fiber, because of its shorter runs, often doesn't need to be assembled out of multiple pieces of cabling; it can use a single unbroken piece of fiber.

Fiber Optic Cable Bundles

Just as UTP cable comes in several varieties, fiber optic cables come in seven basic types of bundle. As you can see in Table 3-4, they vary in where they are used and their strength. Each can use either single or multimode fiber. There are no standards for fiber optic cable assembly; therefore, these types of cable vary somewhat from one manufacturer to another.

Table 3-4:   Types of Fiber Optic Cable

Type	Use	Description
Tight-buffered	Inside	Each fiber is surrounded by 900 microns of aramid yarn. Then the yarn is surrounded by plastic. There is no reinforcement of each individual fiber. Used primarily for patch cords and from the wall to the desktop. A cable with just a single fiber is known as *simplex*; a two-wire cable is *duplex*.
Disribution	Inside	Made of many tight-buffered fibers. No reinforcement of individual fibers. Must terminate in a breakout box or patch panel.
Breakout	Inside	Many tight-buffered cables bundled together reinforcing fibers (e.g., aramid yarn). Because the fibers are reinforced, does not need to terminate in a breakout box or patch panel; may use quick-install connectors. Although more expensive per foot than distribution cabling, may be cheaper and easier to install and maintain.
Loose tube	Outside	A single fiber optic rod runs down the center to reinforce fibers wound around it. The outside coating can be filled with a gel to protect the fibers from water. Therefore, it can be buried.
Ribbon	Outside	Made from layers of fiber optic tubes.
Armored	Outside	Covered with metal for burying in areas where rodents are a problem.
Arial	Outside	Designed for running on utility poles. Usually hung from a "messenger" cable or from another utility wire.

Fast Ethernet Standards

There are four Fast Ethernet media specifications, three of which use UTP wire and one of which uses fiber optic cable.

Twisted-Pair Wire

The three Fast Ethernet options that are designed for UTP wire are summarized in Table 3-5. Current installations, however, are almost exclusively 100BASE-TX, using Category 5 or higher wire. Therefore, we will focus solely on 100BASE-TX.

Table 3-5:   Fast Ethernet Cabling Options

Standard	Cable type
100BASE-TX	Category 5 UTP (uses 2 pairs of wire)
100BASE-T4	Category 3 UTP (uses 4 pairs of wire)
100BASE-T2	Category 3 UTP (uses 2 pairs of wire)

As you can see from the preceding table, the predominant UTP standard for Fast Ethernet uses only two of the four pairs of wires in the cable. The specific wire usage for 100BASE-TX can be found in Table 3-6. The mirrored signals (-TD and -RD) are used to help identify and eliminate crosstalk (the *cancellation* technique). The receiving station can compare the positive and negative polarity signals. They should be the same except for the polarity. Any difference can be attributed to crosstalk and stripped out.

Another way to look at the same issue to to call it *differential signaling*. Any interference that affects one wire will almost certainly affect the other as well. The receiver can then calculate the difference between the two signals, which will always be constant, regardless of interference.

Fiber Optics

Fiber optic configurations for Fast Ethernet are covered by the 100BASE-FX standard. Like standard Ethernet wiring for fiber optic cables, Fast Ethernet fiber optics requires two cables, one for transmitting and one for receiving.

Table 3-6:   Fast Ethernet UTP Wire Usage

Wire color	Use	Comments
White (paired with green)	+TD	Transmit data
Green	-TD	Copy of transmit data signal but with the opposite polarity
White (paired with orange)	+RD	Receive data
Orange	-RD	Copy of receive data signal but with the oppostie polarity
White (paired with blue)	unused	
Blue	unused	
White (paired with brown)	unused	
Brown	unused	

Gigabit Ethernet Standards

Like Fast Ethernet, the Gigabit Ethernet standard has been written for two types of medium: fiber optics and copper wire. In this case, the fiber optic implementations came first and UTP implementations have become feasible to the desktop since about 2004. (The technology was available before that, but wasn't particularly affordable.)

Fiber Optics

Three standards deal with Gigabit Ethernet networks built from fiber optic cable.

   ♦ *1000BASE-CX*: Designed for the direct interconnection of clusters of equipment. This standard has been superceded by 1000BASE-T, the UTP implementation of Gigabit Ethernet.

♦ *1000BASE-SX*: Designed for horizontal cabling using multi-mode fiber. In other words, you can use this stanadard for inter-connecting network segments on a single floor or for creating a group of servers (a *server farm*).

♦ *1000BASE-LX*: Designed for interconnecting network segments, including vertical runs through buildings, using single-mode fiber. Most small offices do not need to use media based on this standard.

As you may have already concluded, the distance that you can run a fiber optic segment depends on the diameter of the fibers in the cable and the cable's bandwidth. As you can see in Table 3-7, segment lengths in the published standards vary from 230 to 5000 meters. There is, however, a large gap between the last two entries in the table (5000 meter maximum) and the remaining entries because the last two are single-mode fiber specifications.

Table 3-7: Sample Fiber Optic Cable Lengths

Standard	Diameter (in microns)	Bandwidth (MHz*km)	Cable length (in meters)
1000BASE-SX	62.5	160	2–230
	62.5	200	2–275
	50	400	2–500
	50	500	2–550
1000BASE-LX	62.5	500	2–550
	50	400	2–550
	50	500	2–550
	9	n/a	2–5000
	5	5000	2–5000

Twisted-Pair Wire

1000BASE-TX, which requires Cat 5 or better cabling, uses all eight wires in the UTP cable. In addition, each wire can handle a bidirectional signal (both send and receive). The signal is then sent in four parts, mirrored on each pair of wires, as in Table 3-8.

Table 3-8:   Fast Ethernet UTP Wire Usage

Wire color	Use	Comments
White (paired with green)	+BI_DA	Bidirectional data A
Green	-BI_DA	Mirror of +BI_DA
White (paired with orange)	+BI_DB	Bidirectional data B
Orange	-BI_DB	Mirror of +BI_DB
White (paired with blue)	-BI_DC	Mirror of +BI_DC
Blue	+BI_DC	Bidirectional data C
White (paired with brown)	+BI_DD	Bidirectional data D
Brown	-BI_DD	Mirror of -BI_DD

> *Note: To be completely accurate, Gigabit Ethernet over UTP cabling doesn't really run at 1 Gbps. It actually runs at the same speed as Fast Ethernet, but it uses all four pairs of wires at the same time and handles two signals per wire. That produces the 1 Gbps speed!*

4

Creating Network Segments

The basic building block of an Ethernet is a *network segment*, a group of devices whose message exchanges are controlled by a single *interconnection device*. *Hubs* (once also known as *repeaters*) and *switches* are interconnection devices that create individual network segments; switches and *routers* connect segments to make larger networks.

> *Note: Routing is such a complex topic that it is covered in a chapter of its own (Chapter 6).*

Although you can still purchase hubs today, and they are in use in many existing networks, the price of switches has dropped so significantly that there is rarely any reason to install a hub in a new or upgraded network. As you will see, switches provide better performance at about the price of a hub.

Hubs (Repeaters)

As you will remember from Chapters 1 and 2, Ethernet was created to allow multiple devices to share the same wire. The original *topology* (the layout of the devices and the wire) was a straight-through bus, as in Figure 4-1. All messages are *broadcast* to the network bus, where all devices can read them. Such topologies are based on coaxial cable. (See Appendix A for details on outdated Ethernet standards.) Such segments would often be equipped with *repeaters*, devices that read the broadcast signal and retransmitted it, thus extending the length of the bus.

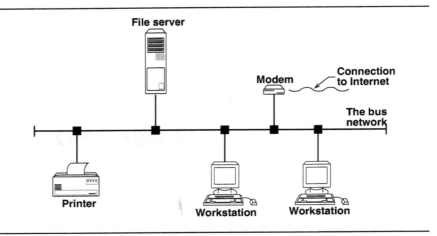

Figure 4-1:   A simple Ethernet bus topology

When Ethernet standards for UTP appeared, the bus was collapsed into a single small box called a *hub*. (See Figure 4-2.) Each device is connected to the hub with a single UTP cable. However, because the bus is a single wire, it can carry only one signal at a time. That means that a device can either transmit or receive, but not both, at the same time. Communication is therefore *half duplex* (bidirectional but only one direction at a time).

Transmission using a hub happens in the following sequence:

1.   A device checks the bus.
2.   If the bus is free, the device transmits using its transmit wire. If the bus is not free, the device waits, following the CDMA/CD protocol.

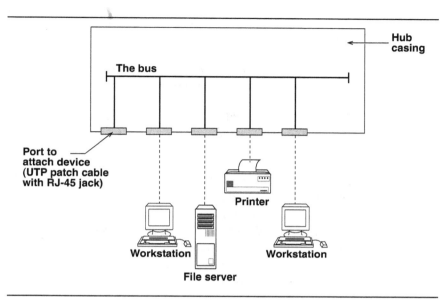

Figure 4-2:   The wiring inside a hub

3. The transmitting device handles a collision if one occurs.
4. When the hub receives a signal without a collision, it repeats the signal and broadcasts it out all its ports.
5. All attached devices recognize that there is a signal on their receive line. Each checks the MAC address of the frame to determine whether it is the receiptient of the frame.

Most hubs today can handle multiple transmission speeds. For example, a Fast Ethernet hub can handle 100 Mbps connections as well as the older 10 Mbps connections. The ports are said to be *autosensing* because they can automatically detect the maximum speed of the NIC at the other end of the UTP cable.

Unmanaged Hubs

A hub of the type we have been discussing is known as an *unmanaged* or *passive hub* and has no intelligence of its own. In particular, it has no idea what devices are connected to its ports. All it can do is broadcast a signal out all ports. A hub is a simple device with no moving parts that is reliable, easy to set up, requires virtually no maintenance, and has traditionally been quite inexpensive.

> Note: A hub operates at the Physical level of the joint TCP/IP and OSI protocol stacks.

All devices connected to one hub share the same bus. We say that they are in the same *collision domain* because they are all contending for access to the same wire.

The box containing a hub is a case with RJ-45 ports, as in Figure 4-3. Over time they have varied between 4 and 36 ports. If there were 36 devices attempting to communicate simultaneously (something that would rarely happen in a small network), performance remains very good. However, as the size of the network increases, performance suffers. In fact, when a single collision domain grows to around 200 devices, the network collapses during high traffic periods, unable to transmit acceptably clear signals.

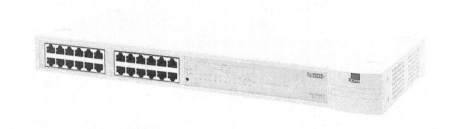

Figure 4-3:   A 24-port hub (Courtesy of 3Com Corporation)

Most unmanaged hubs are designed to be daisy-chained together to create larger networks. To make this possible, each hub has an extra port. For example, an eight-port hub designed for daisy chaining will actually have nine ports. The extra port is designed to be connected to another hub with a UTP cable joining the individual network segments into a single collision domain, as in Figure 4-4. When the ninth port is used to connect to another hub, the eighth port on the hub cannot be used to connect a network device because both the eighth and ninth ports are connected to the same wiring inside the hub.

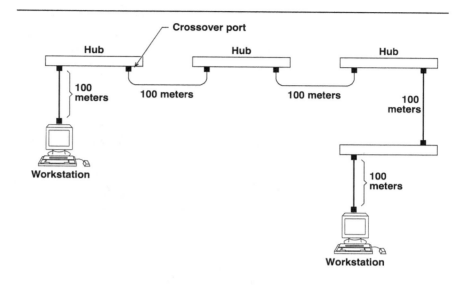

Figure 4-4:   A simple daisy chain of unmanaged hubs

The extra port in an unmanaged hub has a special electrical property: It is a *crossover port* in which the transmit and receive wires are reversed. This is essential so that the two hubs do not attempt to send and receive on the same wires. In fact, you can use any of the other ports in an unmanaged hub to connect to another hub *if* you use a *crossover cable*, a cable where the transmit and receive wires are reversed at one end.

The maximum length of a UTP cable is about 100 meters. The hub daisy-chaining technique can extend that reach. The major drawback is performance: The more devices contending for a bus, the slower the access.

Managed Hubs

Some hubs are equipped with the ability to capture statistics about network traffic and to accept control commands from a workstation on the network. Such *managed hubs* make it easier to troubleshoot and maintain a network.

The type of information and control a managed hub can provide usually includes the following:

◆ *View status of the hub*: As illustrated in Figure 4-5, the information provided to the user includes a measure of the utilization of the hub, the percentage of time taken up by collisions, the number of packets (frames) broadcast per second, and the percentage of errors detected in the Frame Check Sequence (FCS).

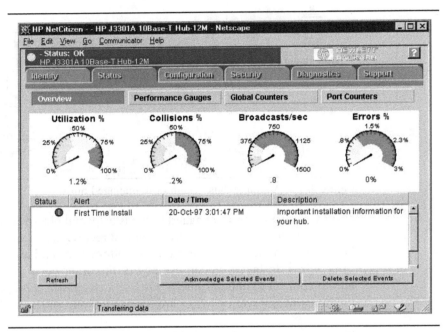

Figure 4-5:   Viewing the status of a managed hub

◆ *View the status of a single port*: As you can see in Figure 4-6, individual port statistics are the same as those for the entire hub.
◆ *Configure the hub*: In Figure 4-7, for example, you can see that the software shows a replica of the managed hub and allows the user to use a mouse to activate and deactivate individual ports. In addition, the user can set IP addresses and choose what information is gathered about the system.
◆ *Manage security.*
◆ *Collect hub and port usage statistics over time.*

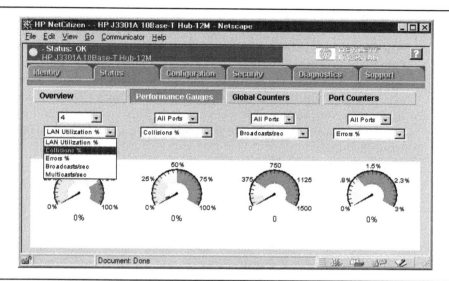

Figure 4-6:   Viewing the status of one port on a managed hub

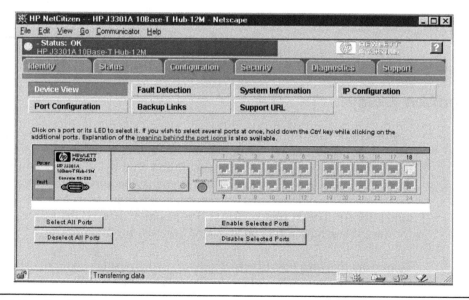

Figure 4-7:   Configuring ports on a managed hub

Stackable Hubs

Another way to extend a collision domain, getting around the 100 meter cable length limitation, is to use *stackable hubs* such as those in Figure 4-8. Stackable hubs are designed not only to sit one on top of another, but also connect with special stacking cables. The entire stack of hubs then looks to the network as if it were one hub. This is a simple and workable solution as long as no single network device is more than 100 meters from the hubs.

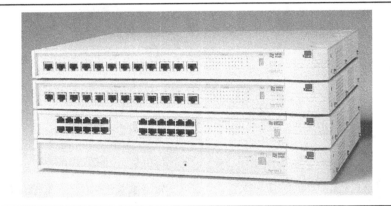

Figure 4-8:   Fast Ethernet stackable hubs (Courtesy of 3Com Corporation)

Propagation Delay

Cable length isn't the only problem that you can run into when you use hubs to build an Ethernet. Another major issue is *propagation delay*, the time it takes for a signal to be broadcast and read by all devices on a network. As a network grows, cable distances may become so long that a device may not be able to finish transmitting before it has a chance to detect collisions from other transmissions. Propagation delay is the major reason for the cable length limits on standard Ethernet installations.

To prevent this on a Fast Ethernet network, you must take overall cable distances into account when planning the network layout. You start with a table of the average round-trip delays, expressed in bit times, for the devices on your network (see Table 4-1). The maximum allowable bit times be-

Table 4-1:   Sample Fast Ethernet Round-trip Propagation Delays,
              Expressed in Bit Times

Type of Hardware	Delay per Meter	Maximum delay
Two 100BASE-TX or 100BASE-FX devices		100
Two 100BASE-T4 devices		138
One 100BASE-TX or 100BASE-FX device and one 100BASE-T4 device		127
Category 3 cable segment	1.14	114/100 meters
Category 4 cable segment	1.14	114/100 meters
Category 5 cable segment	1.112	111.2/100 meters
Fiber optic cable	1.00	412/412 meters
Fast Ethernet hub		92

tween any two devices is 512, Therefore, you add up the delays between the two devices on the network that are the farthest apart from one another. If the result is less than 512, then the network configuration is acceptable.

> Note: A "bit time" is the amount of time needed to send one data bit from one end of the network to the other.

As an example, consider the network in Figure 4-9. Assume that all devices are 100BASE-TX and that the network uses the lengths of Cat 5E UTP wire shown in the illustration.

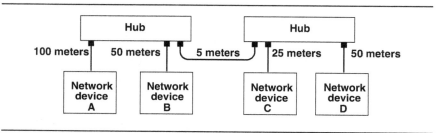

Figure 4-9:   A sample hub-based network

The longest path through the network is from device A to device D, through the two hubs. We can therefore calculate the propagation delay for a signal to travel that path as follows:

Network device A = 100 bit times
Network device D = 100 bit times
First hub = 92 bit times
Second hub = 92 bit times
Cable from device A to hub = 100 * 1.112 = 111.2 bit times
Cable from first to second hub = 5 * 1.112 = 5.56 bit times
Cable from device D to hub = 50 * 1.112 = 55.6 bit times

Total bit times = 556.36 bit times

Since the result is greater than the maximum of 512, this is not an acceptable network configuration. However, if we shorten the cable length between device A and its hub to 50 meters, then the network will work.

Network device A = 100 bit times
Network device D = 100 bit times
First hub = 92 bit times
Second hub = 92 bit times
Cable from device A to hub = 50 * 1.112 = 55.6 bit times
Cable from first to second hub = 5 * 1.112 = 5.56 bit times
Cable from device D to hub = 50 * 1.112 = 55.6 bit times

Total bit times = 500.76 bit times

Switches

OK. You've just spent nearly 10 pages reading about hubs, and now you're about to discover that they are pretty much outdated and that because switches cost only a tiny bit more, there is very little reason to use hubs. (Why discuss hubs at all? Because you can't appreciate switches and how they are and aren't exactly Ethernet unless you understand hubs!)

From the outside, a small switch doesn't look all that much different from a hub (for example, see the switches in Figure 4-10). They have RJ-45 ports and possibly fiber optic ports (the smaller, round ports in Figure 4-10). But what goes on inside a switch is fundamentally different from the operation of a hub.

Figure 4-10:   Cisco switches

Note: If you can't find a switch that has the right number and type of ports for your needs, you can purchase a chassis and add your own interface modules, like the switch in Figure 4-11.

First of all, a switch is an intelligent device. As you will see shortly, it can learn the configuration of its network so that it can send a packet out the correct port for a specific device. It also supports *full-duplex* operations (tranmissions in two directions at once) and can process tranmissions from more than one device at a time. All of these things work together to provide significantly better performance than what can be achieved using a hub.

When you use a switch, there is no longer any contention for a single bus. For this reason, some people believe that a network that is not built on hubs isn't really Ethernet. However, switches still use the Ethernet frame layout and adhere to all other Ethernet standards. Whichever way you view it, go for the switch; forget the hub unless someone gives you one and you can't afford a switch.

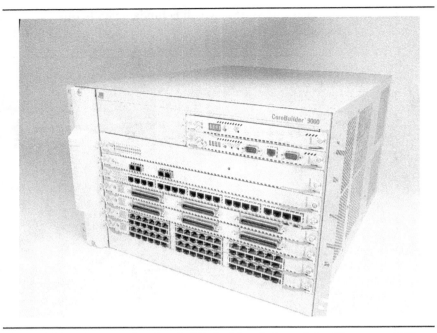

Figure 4-11:   A seven-slot chassis filled with switch modules (Courtesy of 3Com Corporation)

Note: Originally, switches had two ports that connected two networks, possibly of different types. They were then known as "bridges." The term bridge *has largely fallen out of use.*

Switch Learning

Power up a switch, and it knows little more than a hub: It doesn't know what is connected to any of its ports. Over time, however, the switch learns which device can be reached out of each of its ports. This process is known as *switch learning*.

Most switches operate at the Data Link layer in the joint TCP/IP and OSI protocol stack. They therefore have access to the MAC addresses of both the sending and receiving devices, which are part of the Ethernet frame that the Data Link layer handles. (A switch doesn't necessarily contain the entire TCP/IP–OSI protocol stack, but only the Physical and Data Link layers, which are all it needs to operate.)

When a switch first powers up, it has no idea what devices are connected to its powers. It must thereforefore broadcast the first packet it receives to all of its ports. However, before broadcasting that packet, the switch reads the packets to determine the MAC address of the packet's source. The switch knows the port through which the packet arrived and therefore knows that port through which the sending devices can be reached.

The switch puts that information in a two-column switch table. As each subsequent packet arrives, the switch first searches through the table to see if it knows the port out which the destination MAC address can be found. If the MAC address is in the table, then the packet can be sent to the specific port where the device is located. Otherwise, the switch can enter the new devices into the table and broadcast the packet. As the switch table fills up (for example, Table 4-2), the switch is doing very little broadcasting and instead is simpling switching packets to the correct destination port.

Table 4-2:   A Switching Table

MAC Address	Port
00:14:51:64:83:3f	1
00:18:ae:12:b6:3c	1
00:14:51:64:83:40	5
00:18:ae:12:b6:95	0
21:14:ab:12:14:16	0
10:cd:ef:81:13:04	2
88:15:46:64:36:46	2
88:15:51:64:83:45	2
01:33:51:64:83:40	1
00:2e:51:64:83:40	3
00:52:65:64:38:04	5
00:14:53:66:39:05	5

This method of learning works very well as long as the devices that are on the network do not change. However, over time, devices are powered up and down, making the table of locations that the switch has assembled obsolete.

The solution is actually simpler than you might think. Every few minutes, the switch erases its table and starts over; the switch also clears a table entry whenever it loses a link on a port. Because there are so many packets traveling between stations, the learning process is actually very fast and it does not take the switch long to recreate an accurate location table.

Creating a Simple Switched Segment

The simplest switch segment has devices connected directly to a switch, as in Figure 4-12. In this case, devices A and B could be computers, while C is a shared network-compatible printer. You can continue to expand this segment by filling the available ports with additional devices, simply by plugging them in. When the switch fills up, you might replace it with a larger switch.

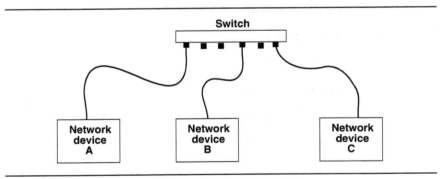

Figure 4-12:   A simple switched segment

Creating Hierarchical Switched Configurations

Continually replacing a small switch with one that has more ports may not be the most effecitve way—in terms of both cost and perfomance—to build a network. The single-switch design means that all network traffic must travel through that single switch. As traffic on the network increases, each packet will take longer to travel through the switch—the switching table becomes larger and takes longer to search—decreasing the response time of the network.

The solution is to break the network into more than one segment, creating a hierarchy of switches (and perhaps hubs). For example, if you have some hubs—don't buy any new ones—that you want to integrate into a single network, you might use a configuration like that in Figure 4-13. This network has three collision domains (one for each hub), connected by the switch. The switch receives all traffic broadcast by each hub. However, if a packet is destined for a device on the same segment from which the packet came, the switch ignores it, cutting down on the amount of traffic the switch needs to handle. The switch therefore only delivers packets that are destined for one of the other two collision domains.

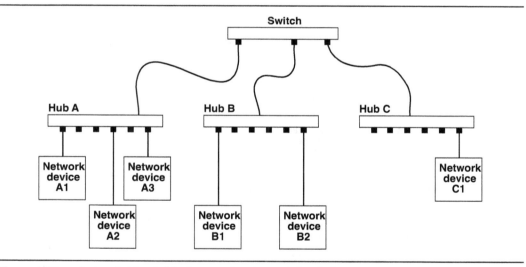

Figure 4-13: A simple hierarchical network using existing hubs

For example, a packet going from device A1 to device A3 will be broadcast out all of Hub A's ports, including the one going to the switch. However, if the switch has both A1 and A3 in its switching table, it will recognize that they are on the same segment and not bother to transmit the packet. In contrast, if A1 sends a packet to C1 and both devices are in the switching table, the switch will transmit the packet out the port to which Hub C is attached. Hub C will in turn broadcast the packet to all of its ports, at which point the packet is recognized by device C1.

If you are creating a hierarchical design from scratch, by all means use all switches, as in Figure 4-14. Each switch constitutes a distinct network segment. Unlike the design with hubs, however, not every packet reaches the switch at the top of the hierarchy. Instead, only those packets destined for other segments are sent to the top switch; each switch on the second level handles traffic for its own devices.

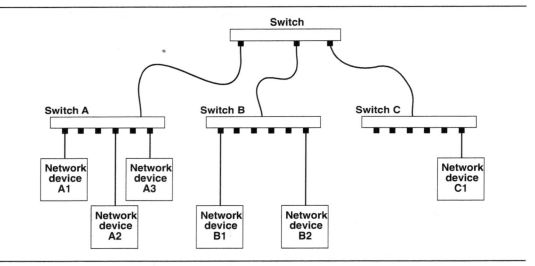

Figure 4-14:   A simple all-switched hierarchical network design

A hierarchical configuration is not limited to two levels. In theory, there is no limit to how deep you can nest switches. For example, a configuration such as Figure 4-15 is valid. We often call the switch at the top of the hierarchy the *core* switch. It is not necessarily the largest switch (i.e., the one with the most ports), but it should be the fastest.

When designing your switching hierarchy, you want to get the best performance possible, which means you need to consider the following:

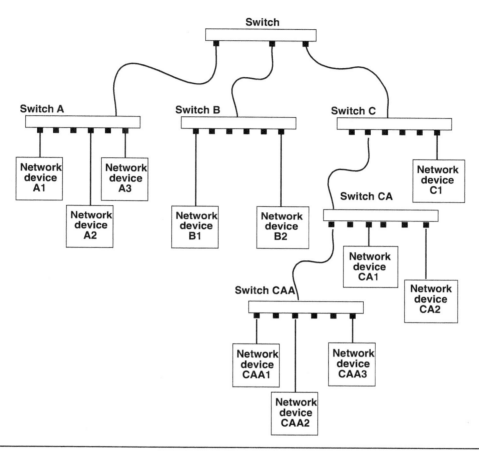

Figure 4-15:   A multilevel switched network

- ◆ The deeper the hierarchy (i.e., the more levels in the hierarchy), the slower traffic will be between devices on different segments because more switches will need to handle each packet.
- ◆ Devices that communicate frequently should be grouped on the same segment so that their packets don't need to travel up or down the hierarchy. (The fewer switches through which a packet needs to travel, the faster it will be delivered.)
- ◆ Some switches can handle both UTP and fiber optic cabling, making them suitable for linking faster and slower network segments.

♦ Fiber optic equipment is more expensive than UTP equipment. Use fiber optics only when you need the fastest performance, such as to shared devices such as servers. Printers are also generally shared, but a printer is a mechanical device that is relatively slow when it produces its output, and therefore putting it on a fast network link may be a waste of resources.

♦ You don't necessarily need to fill all ports on a switch. Having open ports also gives you flexibiity so that you can reconfigure the network to break up bottlenecks or to add new devices as the network grows.

What devices do you place on which segment? There's no straightforward formula, but the following guidelines can help:

♦ Many computers now come with Gigabit Ethernet on the motherboard. Given that eight-port UTP Gigabit switches cost less than $100, there is rarely an economic reason not to use switched Gigabit if your computers are equipped with it. Otherwise, Fast Ethernet over UTP to the desktop is more than adequate.

Note: Of course there will be exceptions to the preceding — there are always exceptions to just about everything! For example, if you are networking a graphics design firm and artists are exchanging large files over the network, then you may want Gigabit Ethernet throughout the network and feel that the expense of adding Gigabit expansion boards to those computers that aren't equipped with it out of the box to be justified.

♦ Fiber optics generally aren't necessary to connect end user devices or slower devices such as printers.

♦ When you have multiple file servers, you may want to group them on a fiber optic segment, creating what's known as a *server farm*. Because the servers receive the bulk of the network traffic, they need to be on the fastest segment on the network.

Note: In terms of security, a server farm can be both good and bad. It increases vulnerability because many servers, possibly containing sensitive information, are congregated together. If a hacker cracks that network segment, then all the servers may be accessible. By the same token, by grouping the servers you cut down the number of places that your network is vulnerable. You can concentrate your security efforts on that single point of vulnerability, rather than needing to secure servers at many locations. You can find more about security issues in Chapter 12.

♦ Devices that communicate with each other frequently should be on the same network segment. For example, if you have a workgroup printer used by the advertising department, place it on the same segment as the advertising department's end user machines.

Note: You can find examples of a variety of hierarchical switched configurations in the case studies at the end of this book (Chapters 14, 15, and 16).

Cabling Issues

Connecting two switches (or hubs, for that matter) is not quite as straightforward as simply plugging a patch cable in one and then into another. Why? Because the send line in the cable must become a receiving line at the other end. You need either a cable with the send and receive wires reversed on one end (a *crossover cable*) or a piece of equipment that accepts a *straight-through cable* (one with the send and receive wires in the same places at both ends) but has a *crossover port* (a port that switches the send and receive signals as they come in).

If one of your switches has a crossover port, then you can use a straight-through cable to connect two switches or hubs. In most cases, the crossover port is an "extra" port, doubled with the highest numbered port on the switch. (You can use either the crossover port or the standard port, but not both.) Run the cable from the crossover port on one switch to any regular port on the other.

If there is no crossover port or if the single crossover port is in use, then you must use a crossover cable. Run this cable between any two regular ports on the switches.

Note: A crossover cable has T568A wiring at one end and T568B wiring at the other.

Looping Issues

In theory, switches must be connected in such a way that they do not contain any loops. If a loop does occur, as in Figure 4-16, traffic may endlessly travel around the network, never reaching its destination.

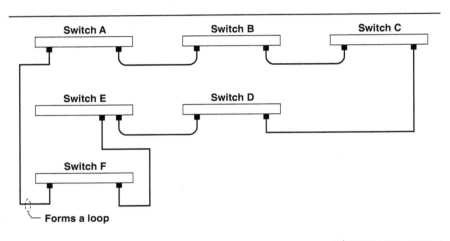

Figure 4-16:   A switched network containing a loop

The problem occurs because the loop introduces more than one path to a given network address. Assume, for example, that switch A in Figure 4-16 needs to send a packet to a device connected through switch D. Depending on how switch A learned to find switch D, the path may be A–B–C–D or A–E–D. Switch B must also learn the path to switch D, which could be either B–C–D or B–A–E–D.

For this example, assume that switch A is using an A–B–C–D path. When the packet reaches switch B, switch B uses the B–A–E–D path and sends the packet right back to switch A. The two switches will then endlessly exchange the same packet. As more packets get caught in this loop, the network will bog down with packets that are never delivered.

There are two solutions to this problem. The first is to ensure that a network never contains any loops. In a relatively small network, this is not terribly difficult. However, as networks grow, it can be hard to keep track of exactly how network segments are connected and therefore where a loop might occur. In that case, you need switches that implement a *spanning-tree algorithm*, a method for ensuring that there is only one path from one switch to another in a network.

A group of switches in the same "tree" select one switch as the "root" of the tree. (This is usually the switch with the lowest Ethernet address.) Then, the root collects configuration information from all the switches in the tree and sends that information to every switch involved. Each switch then computes a single path from its location to the root, therefore ensuring that there is no more than one path between any two switches.

> *Note: To make it easy to communicate with all the switches in the tree, the root switch uses a multicast address, an address that is recognized by a group of devices on a network. In fact, a broadcast (a packet sent to all ports) is simply a multicast address that is recognized by all devices connected to the switch.*

Where Do You Put It? Wiring Closets, Walls, Floors, and Ceilings—Oh, My!

Designing the network hierarchy is only part of the job of configuring a network. You also need to decide where you are going to physically place each component, including wiring, switches, and the network devices. You certainly don't want employees and clients/customers to be walking over network cabling, nor do you want your switches accessible to anyone who might be in the office. This is where *wiring closets* come in.

When Ethernets were new, a wiring closet was exactly that—a place where all the network wiring came together. The closet would be locked so that only a network engineer could gain access to make physical changes to the connections. Today's wiring closets may not always require manipulating the individual wires in a cable, but they often contain switches, hubs and other equipment that you need to keep away from unauthorized hands.

A hub-based Ethernet wiring closet would contain one or more *patch panels*, devices like those in Figure 4-17 into which RJ-45 plugs could be inserted. The patch panels are *rack-mountable*, which means that they can be housed in a vertcal storage rack like that in Figure 4-18. This means that the interconnectivity wiring can be in one secure place.

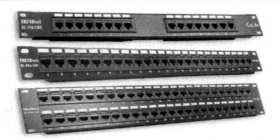

Figure 4-17:   Rack-mountable patch panels (Courtesy of TRENDnet)

Today we still use wiring closets for security purposes. However, the rack-mountable equipment tends to be switches rather than hubs or simple patch panels. A wiring "closet" may also be large enough to house one or more servers. The servers need to be secured, as does the wiring, and the locked wiring closet is a good first step in providing that security.

> *Note: We're not so much concerned here about a disgruntled employee with an axe, but with a knowledgeable person who can either tap the wiring or hack into a server.*

So what does this mean for the overall architecture of your network. If your network is in a commercial space—any office space you rent that isn't in your home—then you will want some type of secure facility for your wiring termination and servers, regardless of the size of your network. In most home settings, the layout is much more informal: You can set the switches on a table or in a closet or in a drawer or wherever makes sense to you. Your physical security needs depend on your living situation rather than on a general wariness of strangers.

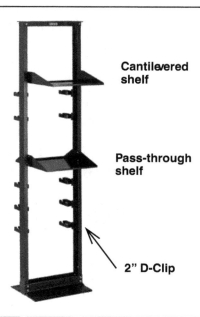

Figure 4-18:   An empty equipment rack

Note: I have two very active cats who constantly knock my switch and router off the desk where they normally reside. You'd think I could find a better place for the equipment, eh? Perhaps I should just give up and leave the devices on the floor.

Note: As far as household use goes, the best of all worlds is to be able to wire while a house is being constructed. Then your Cat 5 or better UTP can run through the studs, just as your telephone wires do. In fact, you can find wire bundles that include coaxial cables for TV signals and Cat 5 or better cables for data and telelphone. (Although telephones can use Cat 3, there is no reason it can't also use higher-rated UTP cabling.)

As a very simple example of what you might do in a small office, take a look at Figure 4-19, which contains a floor plan and wiring diagram of an office. There are wall outlets near each desk or table that is to be connected to the network. A UTP patch cable (a short length of cable with an RJ-45 plug on the end) runs from each computer to the wall jack. In most cases, you want to run the patch cables under carpeting or from a desktop directly to a wall so that people are less likely to trip. (One hopes that common sense prevails in all such things. ...)

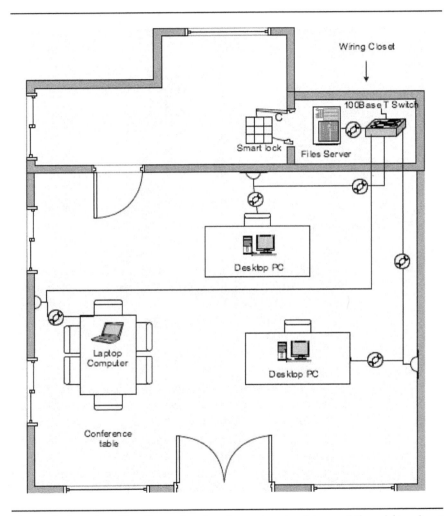

Figure 4-19:   An office floor plan showing network wiring and the wiring closet

Note: The ✪ symbol that appears on some lines in the diagram indicates that the line represents UTP wiring.

A file server and a Fast Ethernet switch are housed in a wiring closet. UTP cabling runs from each wall outlet, above a dropped ceiling, and into the wiring closet, which is secured with some type of *smart lock*. (A smart lock, at the very least, supports giving each person who should have access to the room a different entry code and records when each code is used to enter and exit.)

The UTP cabling that runs from the wall jacks to the switch has RJ-45 plugs at the ends that plug into the switch. The cables are wired into connectors that are then inserted into the wall plates. The cables are run in the ceiling space above the ceiling tiles and dropped down the wall spaces to where the wall plates will be attached. Is this a do-it-yourself job? That depends on how comfortable you are with climbing up and down ladders to run the cabling in the ceiling and how comfortable you are with wiring the connectors. (For details on the wiring process, see the appendix to this chapter. If you won't be involved with the hands-on wiring process, you can just skip that material.)

What can you do if you don't have a dropped ceiling? You will need to run the cables along the floor or through the attic. You can hide cables under carpets, or use cable protectors that you can purchase; the latter allows the cable to lie on top of the floor, regardless of its type. As an example, look at the small piece of cable protector in Figure 4-20(a). The cables run down the middle, in channels hidden under the hinged door. The size and number of channels vary, depending on the type of protector you purchase. (The diagram in Figure 4-21 shows three cable channels.) Given that the type of cable protector you purchase depends on the specific wiring you are trying to hide, you should definitely plan your wiring before running out to purchase the cable protectors. Alternatively, if you are in a lower traffic area, you can use cable protectors that simply drop down on top of your cables (Figure 4-21b).

If you have a crawl space under the floor and can drill holes in the floor, you can run the wiring underneath the floor; alternatively, you can go through an attic above the ceiling. The worst-case scenario is that you have a leased office that can't be modified structurally in any way. Then you'll

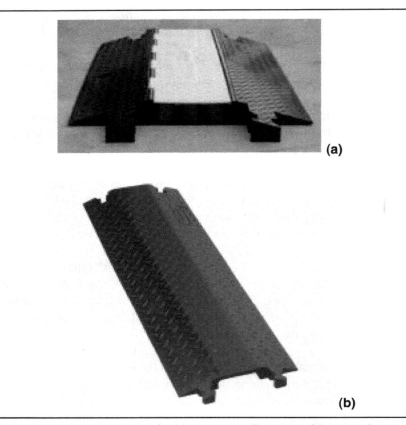

(a)

(b)

Figure 4-20:   A small section of cable protector (Courtesy of Peterson Systems International)

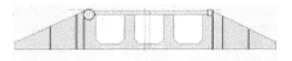

Figure 4-21:   A cross section of a cable protector, showing three channels for running the cables (Courtesy of Peterson Systems International)

need to lay your cables on the floor and protect them with cable protectors. Long cable runs in the junction between the wall and the floor work well—until you come to a door—in which case you can go over and around the door. Not elegant, but it works and keeps the cables out of the way of feet!

Note: The diagram in Figure 4-19 was created with a program called ConceptDraw NetDesigner. It is one of several products that provide tools and images for drawing network layouts and floor plans. (Others include Microsoft Visio and SmartDraw.) I like this one because it's easy to use and inexpensive, and it comes in a Macintosh version.

Appendix: Wiring RJ-45 Plugs and Connectors

For short cable runs (up to, say, 15 or 25 feet), we typically purchase patch cables with the RJ-45 plugs already attached. However, when you need longer distances or when you need a custom length that will run from a switch to a wall plate, you will probably take cable from a bulk roll and add your own plug and/or connector.

Note: You don't need to use connectors; you can wire jacks directly. However, it is a lot easier to use a connector, with its color coding for the wire layout.

The wiring process is very similar for plugs and connectors. The first thing you need is a *punchdown* tool like that in Figure 4-22. Once you've placed a wire in the correct place in a connector, you use this tool to insert and cut the wire. Although wiring does take a bit of practice, it's not too difficult with the aid of one of these handy, dandy devices.

The connectors that are plugged into wall plates, like those in Figure 4-23, come in a wide variety of shapes and sizes, depending on the exact type of cabling you are using and the manufacturer from whom they are purchased. However, most work on the same principles. You pop off a small cap—the entire connector isn't much more than an inch long—to expose the area for connecting the wires. In Figure 4-24, for example, the white portion will be inserted through the wall plate from the back so that the jack is accessible to a patch cable. The wiring is on the black portion, which is hidden behind the wall plate by the white cap at the top of the connector.

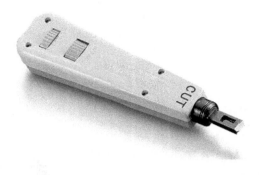

Figure 4-22:   A punchdown tool (Courtesy of Leviton Voice & Data)

Figure 4-23:   Wall plates that accept connectors with RJ-45 jacks (Courtesy of Leviton Voice & Data)

To wire a connector:

1. Assuming that you are working with a cable that will be attached to a wall plate, run the cable into the wiring box in the wall. Pull out enough wire so that you can work comfortably.

    Note: You can wire one end of a cable before you put it through the walls, ceiling, and/or floor, but at some point, the other end will probably need to be wired in place.

Figure 4-24:   A connector containing and RJ-45 jack (Courtesy of Leviton Voice
& Data)

2. Strip the plastic coating from no more than 1/2" of the wires at the end
    of the cable. (Most crosstalk occurs at the ends of the cables, where the
    ends are untwisted. Therefore, you want to strip and untwist as little of
    the cable as possible.)

3. Take the cap off the connector, if necessary.

4. Look at the color codes on the connector—they're usually on the side
    or top—to determine how the colored wires should be laid out (see
    Figure 4-25). Most connectors have diagrams for both T568A and
    T568B connections. In this example, we'll be wiring a T568A jack.

5. Lay the stripped bundle of wires in the connector (Figure 4-26).

6. Bend all but the blue and blue-striped white wires out of the way. Lay
    the blue-striped white wire through the opening for pin 5; lay the blue
    wire through the opening for pin 4 (Figure 4-27). As you can see in
    Figure 4-28, you want to place the wires so that the plastic coating on
    the cable is as close to the edge of the connector as possible.

7. Push down on the blue wire using the punchdown tool (Figure 4-29).
    This will make the connection with the connector and cut off any ex-
    cess wire.

8. Do the same for the blue-striped white wire (Figure 4-30).

9. Bend the orange and orange-striped white wires down into the connec-
    tor (Figure 4-31).

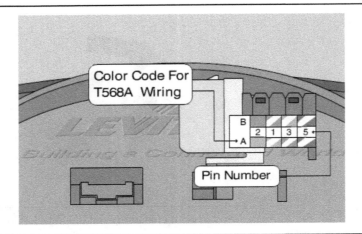

Figure 4-25:   Finding the correct wiring diagram (Courtesy of Leviton Voice & Data)

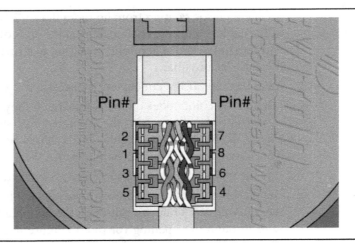

Figure 4-26:   Placing the wires in the connector (Courtesy of Leviton Voice & Data)

10. Repeat steps 5 through 7 for the orange and orange-striped white wires.

11. Place the green and green-striped white wires through pins 1 and 2 (Figure 4-32). Notice that unlike the blue and orange pairs, both green pairs of wire go on the same side of the connector.

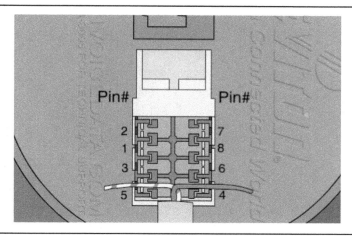

Figure 4-27: Laying the blue and blue-striped white wires (Courtesy of Leviton Voice & Data)

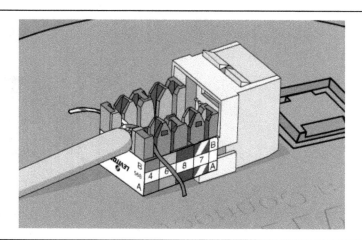

Figure 4-28 Another view of the blue and blue-striped white wires in the connector (Courtesy of Leviton Voice & Data)

12. Repeat step 10 for the brown and brown-and-white striped wires, placing them in pins 7 and 8, as in Figure 4-32.
13. Replace the cap on the top of the connector.
14. Insert the connector into a wall plate with the jack facing out.

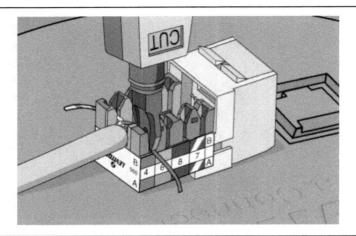

Figure 4-29:   Connecting the wire using a punchdown tool (Courtesy of Leviton Voice & Data)

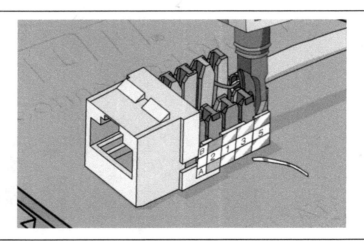

Figure 4-30:   Securing the blue-striped white wire (Courtesy of Leviton Voice & Data)

15. Attach the wall plate to the wall.

If you happen to need a T568B jack, then switch the green pair and the orange pair. (See Figure 4-33.) That's all there is to it.

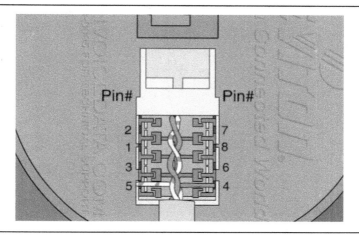

Figure 4-31:   Preparing to connect the orange and orange-striped white wires (Courtesy of Leviton Voice & Data)

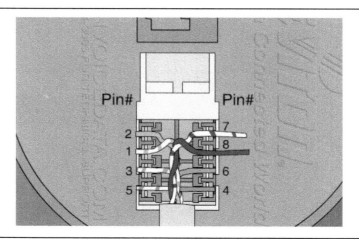

Figure 4-32:   Placing the remaining wires in the T568A connector (Courtesy of Leviton Voice & Data)

To wire the plugs, take the top off the RJ-45 plug and follow the wiring layouts in Table 3-2 or Table 3-3, whichever is appropriate for the type of plug. Use the punchdown tool to secure and clip the wires and then replace the top of the plug. Remember to get the plastic coating on the cable as

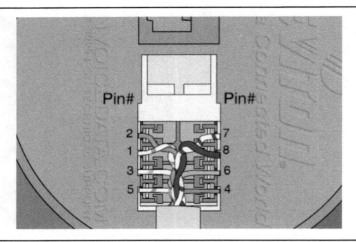

Figure 4-33:   The wiring of a T568B connector (Courtesy of Leviton Voice & Data)

close to the edge of the plug as possible so that the smallest amount of wire is untwisted.

Keep in mind that if you are wiring both ends of a patch cable, you will need to ensure that the wiring at both ends is identical for a straight-through cable. However, if you are wiring a crossover cable, you will use the T568A wiring at one end and T568B at the other.

5

Connecting to the Internet

Although there are undoubtedly a few small business and home networks that are not connected to the Internet, most networks have some sort of access to the global network. Such access is a mixed blessing for most network administrators, because it opens up the network to a huge range of security problems. (We'll cover many of those problems in Chapter 12.) In this chapter, however, you'll read about the various options for connecting your network to the Internet; Chapter 6 will delve into how to share that connection over your network. But first, we'll look at what happens when a connection is made to the Internet.

ISPs and IP Addresses

Today we don't connect directly to the Internet. Instead, we use an intermediary known as an *Internet Service Provider* (ISP). The ISP provides the

Internet connections for thousands, if not hundreds of thousands, of computers and networks at one time.

> *Note: ISPs also provide Web hosting, e-mail accounts, security, and often additional services. Theoretically, you should choose your ISP based on the services you need. In truth, however, the type of Internet access you choose will limit your choice of ISP. In some cases, there may be only one in your area that provides a particular type of access. You'll find more about this throughout this chapter.*

Each network that is connected to the Internet must have a unique address, known as an *IP address*. This allows a message from anywhere on the Internet to reach your network. In most cases today, a device known as a *router* then takes a message and sends it to its specific destination on your network. (Routing is a fairly complex topic that is covered in Chapter 6.)

IP addresses come from ISPs. When an ISP goes into business, it is given a range of IP addresses for its customers to use. In most cases, you are given an IP address whenever your network connects to the ISP. This *dynamic IP address* may change each time you connect. However, if you are going to be hosting your own Web site, you will need what's known as a *static IP address*, one that remains the same regardless of how many times you connect to your ISP.

> *Note: It costs a lot more to have a static IP address than a dynamic IP address. Therefore, it may be more cost effective to let your ISP host your Web site — in other words, put your Web files on one of the ISP's computers — than to do it in house. A static IP address also makes a computer far more vulnerable to security breaches than does a dynamic IP address. My Web site, for example, resides on a virtual Linux server on one of the mainframes at the college where I teach. I could have a static IP address for my home network and run the Web site from here if I chose, but why pay extra when it's not necessary?*

The need for an IP address is the same regardless of how you connect to the Internet. The choice comes down to whether you need a dynamic or static IP address and what is available in your area. Then you can evaluate the types of access against speed, reliability, cost, and services provided by each ISP.

Internet Connection Protocols

In Chapter 1 you were introduced to the combined TCP/IP and OSI protocol stack along with many of the protocols specified for each layer. There are, however, a number of protocols with special uses that we have not discussed. At this point we need to look at two of those protocols that are used to make connections to the Internet: PPP and PPPoE.

Point-to-Point Protocol

Most dial-up connections use the LLC layer *Point-to-Point Protocol* (PPP) to make and maintain their connection. PPP itself uses Link Control Protocol (LCP) and a collection of network-specific Network Control Protocols (NCPs) for negotiating connection characteristics. Once PPP has established a connection, higher-layer protocols, such as IP, can use the connection to exchange packets.

PPP's work is done primarily by the four phases of LCP:

1. Establish the link, and determine the link configuration.
2. Test the link quality and decide whether the quality is sufficient to run higher-layer protocols such as IP and TCP.

    Note: Phase 2 is optional.

3. Decide which Network layer protocols will be used. Once this is complete, LCP steps out of the communications exchange until the end of the conversation.
4. Terminate the link. Most of the time, this occurs when the user gives a command to sign off. However, LCP can also clean up after a link that was terminated abnormally, such as in a loss of carrier signal.

Point-to-Point Protocol Over Ethernet for Cable and DSL

If you are connecting the Internet through DSL or cable, you will typically use *Point-to-Point Protocol Over Ethernet* (PPPoE) to make the connection. This is an extension of the same PPP used by dial-up connections. Its purpose is to handle sending the signal over an Ethernet so that it can reach internal network devices. It works by encapsulating a PPP frame in an Ethernet frame. Like PPP, PPPoE is an LLC layer protocol.

> *Note: If you are connecting a single computer to the Internet using DSL or cable, then you configure your computer to use PPPoE. However, if you have a shared connection, then the connection is made by a router, and it is the router that uses PPPoE. Network devices simply connect to the Ethernet in their normal way.*

Dial-up Connections

People have been using telephone lines to access other computers long before there was public access to the Internet. Such connections require that the computer dial a telephone number and therefore are generally known as *dial-up connections*. There are two types available today, one that uses standard telephone lines and another that uses specially conditioned digital lines. Both are part-time connections; they are connected from the time the dial-up process begins to when the call is disconnected. Although you could theoretically leave a dial-up connection open for an indefinite amount of time, most dial-up connections are connected and disconnected as needed. Because of their intermittent nature, dial-up connections support only dynamic IP addresses.

Modems and POTS

The simplest, and oldest, type of connection to the Internet uses standard landline telephone lines (*plain old telephone service*, or POTS) and a device called a *modem*. The word "modem" is a concatenation of two terms—*modulate* and *demodulate*—that refer to what the device actually does.

The Analog-to-Digital Conundrum

When the telephone was developed over 100 years ago, no one had any thought of using the lines for anything other than voice communications. The signals carried by landlines are *analog*. In other words, they carry a wave-shaped, continuous signal like that at the top of Figure 5-1. Computers, on the other hand, use *digital* signals, discrete signals that we interpret as varying between two values, 0 and 1, as at the bottom of Figure 5-1.

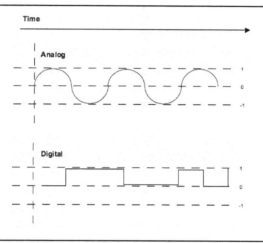

Figure 5-1:   Analog and digital signals

The problem is that there is no straightforward way to send that digital signal over an analog telephone line. That's where modems come to the rescue. There must be one modem at each end of a connection, typically one for the end user and one at the ISP. (ISPs who handle dial-up connectivity typically have hundreds, if not thousands, of modems.)

Early dial-up data communications sessions were analog from the end user's telephone line to either the destination or an ISP's modem. However, the North American telephone system is now almost exclusively digital beyond the lines that connect each user premises to the first telephone switch. (This is known as a *local loop*.) This means that the analog to digital conversion happens much earlier in the telephone call and that the signal may be converted from digital back to analog when traveling over the ISP's local loop.

A data communications session might go something like this:

1. The end-user modem (or whoever/whatever is initiating the session) dials the telephone number of the destination's modem.

2. The call reaches the first telephone switch and is translated from analog to digital until it reaches the destination's local loop. It is then translated back to analog to travel over the local loop and reach the destination.

3. The destination's modem answers the call and begins a process called *handshaking*, during which the two modems negotiate the configuration of the communications session. In most cases, this includes determining the maximum speed at which data transfer can occur. (More on speed in a bit.)

4. Once the handshaking is complete, each modem sends out a distinct *carrier tone*, a steady tone that will be used to transmit the digital signal.

5. To send a digital signal, a modem changes (or *modulates*) the carrier tone by changing either its frequency (speed), amplitude (loudness), or phase. (Most of today's modems use some sort of phase modulation.) This will be converted to digital at the sender's first switch and back to analog before entering the destination's local loop.

6. To recreate the digital signal, the receiving modem strips off the carrier tone, or *demodulates*, the incoming signal.

7. The two modems continue sending and receiving messages, each acting as both modulator to send and demodulator to receive, until the conversation is terminated.

You can find this process illustrated in Figure 5-2. There is one major exception to the illustration. Most ISPs can transmit digital signals directly into the telephone network, without converting them to analog for travel over the local loop. In other words, the ISP can bypass the local loop by using a digital line when sending data; receiving data must still go through two modems. (Typically ISPs use leased lines, which will be discussed later in this chapter.) The impact of this bypassing of the local loop becomes important when looking at the speed of dial-up connections.

> *Note: All-digital telephone systems exist on a number of business campuses and in some commercial buildings such as hotels. Don't try to attach an analog modem to a digital phone*

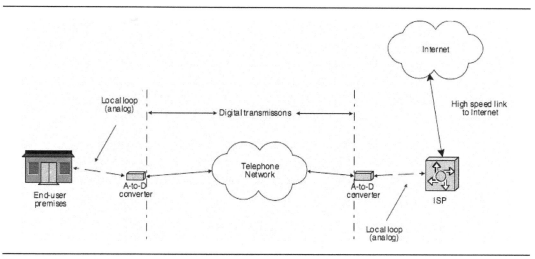

Figure 5-2:   A dial-up connection

system: There is power coming down the digital phone line and
it will literally fry your analog modem. If you aren't sure about
the type of phone system in a building, ask!

Modem Speeds

The speed of a modem is measured in bits per second, just like any other data communications medium. However, there is a second type of speed measure related to modems that can be important in the accuracy of a conversation: *baud*. The term *baud* refers to the number of times a signal's value switches each second. Because each signal value can carry one or more bits of information, the baud rate will be equal to or less than the actual throughput (the bps) of the connection.

To make this a bit clearer, let's assume that a modem works by changing the frequency of its carrier tone. (As mentioned earlier, most of today's modems use a type of phase shifting, but this is much more difficult to visualize than a frequency change. Fortunately, the principle is the same.) If we shift the frequency up to transmit a 1 and down to transmit a 0, then each frequency shift sends one bit. If the modem were to change frequencies 1000 times a second, the throughput would be 1000 bps; it would also be 1000 baud because baud measures the number of times the frequency changes each minute.

But what if we decided to use four frequencies instead? Each one could then represent a sequence of two bits: 00, 01, 10, and 11. If the modem continues to change frequencies at 1000 times per second, we are still transmitting a 1000 baud. However, the throughput has doubled to 2000 bps because each frequency change carries twice the information. By the same token, if we used 16 frequencies, each change would send a pattern of four bits, and we would end up with a throughput of 4000 bps at 1000 baud.

There is a big advantage to keeping the baud rate low: The receiver has more time to decipher the incoming signal if it comes more slowly. Therefore, current modems use many phase shifts and keep the baud rate as low as possible.

The fastest modem is rated at 56 Kbps (approximately 56,000 bps). This does not mean that you will actually connect at or transmit/receive at anywhere close to that speed. In North America, power restrictions on the telephone lines keep speeds down to 52 Kbps. In addition, when you transmit to an ISP (or another computer), there are two analog-to-digital conversions, one at the sending end and one at the receiving end. The technology of the A-D converters limit the speed to 33 Kbps. However, if your ISP can bypass the A-D converter when transmitting back to you, you will have only one A-D conversion when receiving data. Your downloads will therefore be closer to 50 Kbps, all things being equal.

In addition to all of the speed limitations placed by the hardware, the speed of a dial-up over POTS connection is also affected by the amount of noise (unwanted sound) on the telephone line. During the handshaking phase of the connection, the modems test the connection to determine the fastest speed at which a signal can be interpreted. The modems will step down the speed on a noisy connection, sometimes down to as slow as 28 Kbps.

> *Note: Other types of Internet connectivity also have devices called "modems," but they really aren't modems. They do act as an interface between your internal network and the outgoing communications line, but they don't modulate and demodulate a carrier signal the way a true modem does. Rather than fight the incorrect terminology, it's easier to just shrug your shoulders, know that you know better, and call the other devices modems so that everyone else knows what you're talking about.*

Modem Pluses and Minuses

There are a few good reasons to use a dial-up modem to connect to the Internet and a lot of reasons to avoid it. On the positive side, you can connect anywhere you can find an analog phone line. This is great when you happen to be traveling in areas not otherwise equipped for Internet access. Dial-up accounts are also inexpensive (as low as $10 a month for unlimited access).

But for a permanent, business network connection, there are many reasons to look elsewhere:

◆ Dial-up is slow.
◆ Dial-up is unreliable. Signals are dropped frequently.
◆ Being realistic, dial-up requires a dedicated phone line for all but casual, short communications sessions.
◆ Dial-up is difficult to share over a network.
◆ Dial-up provides only a dynamic IP address; it can't be used if your network is hosting a Web server, for example.

Note: The question of whether you should host your own Web site or pay someone else to host it can be a difficult one and is discussed in depth in Chapter 9.

Integrated Services Digital Network

Integrated Services Digital Network (ISDN) is a technology that uses existing telephone wires to transmit digital signals over the local loop. Like a connection using a modem, it is a dial-up connection. However, it is much faster than a modem connection due to higher bandwidth. At one time, ISDN was predicted to become the dominant high-speed data communications technology. It has, however, largely been superseded by cable Internet and DSL service.

ISDN Services

ISDN breaks its transmissions into *channels*, which are summarized in Table 5-1. The basic type of ISDN, Basic Rate Service (BRI), provides two

B channels and one 16 Kbps D channel, for a total bandwidth of 144 kpbs. The intent was that this level of service would be sufficient for individual and small business users.

Table 5-1:   ISDN Channels

Channel Name	Speed	Comments
B (Bearer)	64 Kbps	Carries voice and data
D	16 Kbps or 64 Kpbs	Speed depends on the type of service; carries signaling information and other conversation control information
H0	384 Kbps	Aggregate of 6 B channels
H10	1472 Kbps	Aggregate of 23 B channels
H11	1536 Kbps	Aggregate of 24 B channels
H12	1920 Kpbs	Aggregate of 30 B channels; available in Europe only

Those businesses with needs for greater bandwidth could subscribe to Primary Rate Service (PRI), which provides an H0 channel and one 64 Kbps D channel.

Note: In Europe, PRI uses an H12 channel rather than an H0 channel.

BRI service must use some of its bandwidth for signalling (instructions to control the connection). Therefore, the throughput for data is about 128 Kbps. Considering that dial-up service provides, at best, less than half that speed, ISDN appeared as a viable high-speed alternative when it was first developed.

To use BRI service, the switch at the end of an end user's local loop must be equipped for ISDN service. In addition, the end user pre rmises must be no farther than 18,000 feet (3.4 miles) from the ISDN-equipped switch. You would then subscribe to an ISDN telephone line, which connects to an *ISDN Network termination device* or perhaps to an *ISDN router* (to distribute the connection over your local network).

BRI service uses two types of network termination adapters: NT-1 and NT-2. The first connects to the two wires of the Cat 3 cable coming into the premises and converts the signal into a four-wire interface (S/T). A simplified ISDN connection can be found in Figure 5-3.

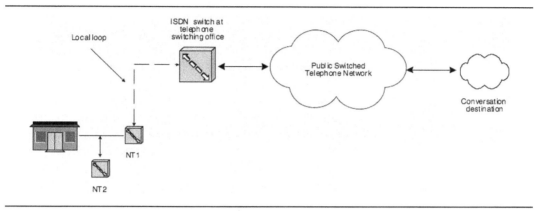

Figure 5-3:   An ISDN connection

An S/T interface supports up to seven devices connected in a bus configuration. Devices that can connect directly to the ISDN bus through the S/T interface include ISDN telephony equipment, computers, routers, and *terminal adapters* (TA). TAs include the NT-2 interface, which allows nondigital devices to connect to ISDN. TAs can also provide the connection between an Ethernet and ISDN.

ISDN Pluses and Minuses

As with POTS dial-up service, there are a few advantages to ISDN, and at this time, many diadvantages. Among the advantages are the following:

- ♦ With a dial-up service, you pay for the bandwidth you use. In other words, costs are assessed on how long you are connected. You can also purchase flat-rate usage plans, just as you can with dial-up telephone service today.
- ♦ Because ISDN uses existing Cat 3 wiring, no rewiring is required to connect to the service.
- ♦ ISDN may be available in areas where no other high-speed Internet connectivity is available.

Despite the advantages, ISDN is rarely chosen for Internet connectivity because

- ◆ An ISDN connection does not automatically connect you to the Internet. You must contract with an ISP who has ISDN capabilities.
- ◆ ISDN is not widely avaiable in North America. Its developers envisioned it as a widespread service, but implementations are present in only small pockets. It is more widespread in South America and Europe.
- ◆ You pay based on the time you are actually connected to an ISDN line, this type of data communications is more expensive than other Internet connectivity options. Unlimited Internet connectivity via ISDN costs about the same as cable or DSL access. However, this cost is on top of all other ISDN costs. In other words, the Internet connectivity pays for the serivces of an ISP and not the ISDN itself.
- ◆ Like dial-up with POTS, ISDN cannot support a static IP address.
- ◆ ISDN is not as reliable as a full-time Internet connection.
- ◆ ISDN is slower than alternatives such as cable Internet and DSL. For example, in some areas, $29.95 unlimited Internet connectivity per month provides a maximum speed of 128 Kbps for both uploads and downloads.

Direct Connections

Most of us need full-time, direct connections to the Internet. Which you choose depends on what is available in your area, cost, speed, and whether you need static IP addresses.

Satellite

If you're the IT specialist at somewhere like Yellowstone National Park, then you have a major problem: There is no wired direct connection to the Internet at all! You don't even have ISDN. One solution is to use a satellite connection. Most satellite Internet implementations use satellite dishes that are similar to those used by direct view satellite television. However, the shape and configuration of the dishes are somewhat different, and FCC regulations do not allow self-installation because the equipment has uplink capabilities.

Satellite Connections

With satellite Internet access, your Internet signals are bounced off a satellite in *geosynchronous* orbit (fixed over one place on the planet) as they travel between you and your ISP. At your end of the link, you will have a small earth station (AKA satellite dish) and equipment that translates between your signal and the signal the satellite expects. At the other end, your ISP will be sending and receiving satellite signals in a similar manner, although the ISP will be dealing with signals from many customers at the same time. (See Figure 5-4.)

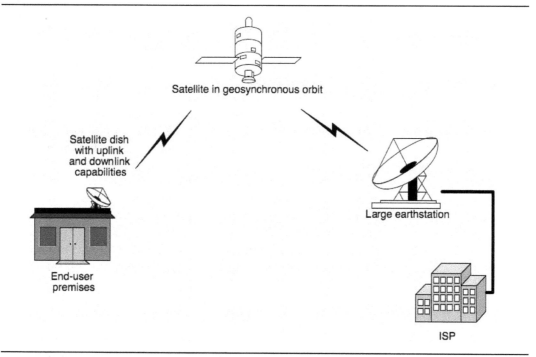

Figure 5-4: The structure of a satellite Internet connection

When you transmit a signal, there is an approximately half-second delay between the time you initiate your transmission and the time it reaches the satellite. The same is true for downloads. This means that downloads take a bit longer to start than they do with other types of always-on connections. Once a download has started, you can get speeds of up to 2 Mbps. (Notice that this is considerably slower than the Ethernet that you are using for your internal network.)

Satellite Pluses and Minuses

A satellite connection is not a good selection for all businesses. It is a "better than nothing" solution if you have no other type of full-time Internet access available—at least you can get an always-on connection and static IP addresses—but its drawbacks are fairly serious:

- The primary problem is the uplink and downlink delay, which makes satellite service unsuitable for a number of uses, including Web sites with heavy download traffic, Internet telephone service, videoconferencing, and online day trading.
- The service is disrupted during heavy rain storms, just as is satellite television service.
- Satellite Internet is relatively expensive. Not only is the equipment expensive, but it must be professionally installed. In addition, the monthly charges are more than cable or DSL access.
- A satellite link, being wireless, is more vulnerable to security breaches than a wired link. (More about this in Chapter 12.)
- Satellite transmissions are a shared medium: The more users there are, the slower the transmission rate for each user. It would be unusual to obtain the maximum download speed during business hours.
- Although a satellite link can be used with a VPN (virtual private network), an active VPN session can slow the transmission speed by 50 to 75 percent.

Note: You'll read about VPNs in Chapter 12.

In short, you should look to a satellite Internet solution when you have no other alternative for always-on service. It can be a business saver for a company in a remote (or underserved) location, but probably isn't a good choice in most cases.

Cable

Cable Internet access brings Internet service into a home or business using the same cabling as television service. Cable TV providers have upgraded many of their lines to fiber optics to carry both digital Internet signals and digital television. The lines from the end-user premises to the street are still generally coaxial cable (the same stuff that you use to connect your TV to the cable). In most cases, the cable TV provider also functions as the ISP.

The general architecture for cable delivery of Internet service is diagrammed in Figure 5-5. The network uses fiber optic cable from the regional cable headquarters, through the distributions hubs, to the fiber optic nodes. In most cases, the cabling from the nodes to end-user premises (either homes or businesses) is coaxial cable.

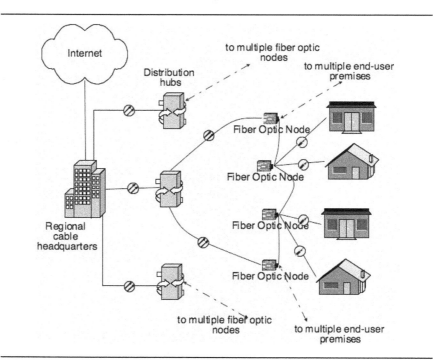

Figure 5-5:   The high-level architecture of the delivery of cable Internet service

Note: Many people refer to cable Internet service as "cable modem." Yes, there is a device that sits between the network entry point (a router, switch, or computer) and the cable network. It's a box, just like a modem. But it doesn't modulate and demodulate like a dial-up modem. It's really a network interface device. So humor me: I just can't stand to call it a modem when it isn't.

The cable Internet signal travels from the cable provider's distribution hub to a fiber optic node that serves 500 to 1000 premises. Each node has an approximate speed of 2 Mpbs upstream (going from the cutomer premises to the provider) and 27 Mbps downstream (going from the provider to the customer). The important thing to recognize here is that the bandwidth is shared by all customers connected to that node. This means that as the amount of traffic increases, the speed for each end-user goes down.

Note: The different speeds for uploads and downloads are not unusual. It's the same for satellite access and for the most common type of DSL. The theory is that end users spend most of their time downloading rather than uploading. If you're hosting your own Web site, it's a whole different situation!

What kind of performance can you expect? The typical download speed to a home is in the range of 5 Mpbs. A home premium service can provide downloads of 8 Mpbs and uploads in the range of 512 Kbps. High-end services support downloads of up to 30 Mbps and uploads of a maximum of 2 Mbps. Of course, you pay more for the higher speed services.

Business services offer a range of speeds: downloads from 256 Kbps to 5 Mpbs and uploads from 192 Kbps to 2 Mbps, although the latter is not widey available. Static IP addresses are available for an extra charge.

Cable Pluses and Minuses

For a small or home business, cable Internet access is a viable choice, regardless of whether you are hosting a Web site. The positives include:

♦ *Wide availability*: Cable Internet service is generally available anywhere cable television service is available. (There are exceptions as the cable providers continue to update their coaxial feeder cables to fiber optics. However, if you can get digital television via cable, then you almost certainly can get cable Internet access as well.)

♦ *Reasonable cost*: Competition among cable providers and telephone companies that provide DSL has kept the cost of cable Internet service at a reasonable level. You will pay more for faster service and for static IP addresses, however.

♦ *High reliability*: Cable Internet service is not affected by weather. It has a record of being very reliable with very little downtime.

♦ *High speed*: Home and small business cable Internet services are about the fastest you can get for under $200 a month.

On the downside,

♦ If you are in a high-density area where many people are using cable Internet services, then you may notice a degradation in performance during high-use periods, such as the late afternoon.

♦ Business services for small business are intended for very small networks. One provider, for example, allows only four users for its first-tier business service. Larger networks require more expensive programs.

Digital Subscriber Line

Digital Subscriber Line (DSL) is the major competitor to cable Internet access. Commonly offered by telephone companies, home service can share a telephone line with a voice line; business service requires a dedicated telephone line. Because DSL uses existing telephone lines, it would seem logical that DSL would be even more available than cable Internet access. Actually, the opposite is true. There are some significant distance limitations to DSL; as a result, many areas in North America do not have DSL access.

DSL provides digital tansmission of data between the end-user premises and the first telephone company switch (known as the *central office*, or CO, although it may not be much of an office, but just a box of electronics). Because it uses telephone lines, the connection to the CO is dedicated to a single user's premises.

DSL piggybacks onto the copper wire that runs from the CO to the end-user premises by using frequencies higher than those used by voice communications. The separation between the two is not perfect, however, and DSL installations therefore require that filters be installed between each telephone and its wall jack.

> *Note: The definition of a "telephone" can be very broad today. If you have an alarm system that uses the telephone to notify a monitoring company, for example, you need to get the alarm company to install a special DSL filter. Also, don't forget filters for devices such as cable and satellite TV boxes that call their services providers occasionally with billing information.*

DSL designed for home use is *asynchronous* (ADSL): It has faster download speed than upload speed. Typical speeds include 768 Kbps downstream and 128 Kbps upstream; a more costly, faster service is 3 Mbps downstream and 768 Kbps upstream. This provides only dynamic IP addressing. If you want to add a static IP address to the faster service, the price more than triples. Even faster service (7.1 Mbps downstream) with 768 Kpbs upstream) with static IP addressing more than quadruples the price.

> *Note: ADSL and cable Internet access cost about the same to the home. Therefore, price usually is not a major factor when choosing between the two.*

The type of DSL designed originally for business has the same upstream and downstream speed (*synchronous* or SDSL). However, given the current high upload speeds of ADSL and the availability of static IP addressing, there does not seem to be much demand for SDSL at this time.

Like cable Internet access, DSL uses a device at the end-user premises that is commonly called a *DSL modem*, and as with cable access, it isn't a modem. It's a network interface device that provides translation services between equipment at the end-user premises and the telephone line. Exactly which services are provided by the DSL modem depends on the model. For example, some act as routers, switches, and wireless access points, eliminating the need for some other pieces of network equipment for a very small network.

DSL Pluses and Minuses

Like cable access, DSL is a viable choice for Internet access for a small or home business. The positive aspects of DSL service include:

♦ *Good performance*: DSL is a dedicated line over the local loop to the CO. It therefore is not subject to the slowdowns that can occur with cable service when traffic to and from the fiber optic node is very heavy. (To be fair, most users won't see cable service slowdowns from heavy traffic; this only occurs in very high-density, heavy-usage areas.)

♦ *Reasonable cost*: Depending on the speed and type of service you purchase, DSL will cost anywhere from $15 to $150 a month.

♦ *High reliability*: DSL has very high uptime, with relatively few service outages.

♦ *High speed*: DSL is very fast compared to dial-up access.

Note: The DSL-versus-cable access choice can be a tough one. Both cost about the same, provide good performance, don't require a dedicated phone line, and are very reliable. Often the choice is based simply on which service is available in a given area. If you have both available, then you can look at package content and prices.

DSL does have several disadvantages:

♦ DSL is generally limited to a distance of 15,000 feet from the CO. This measurement relates to cable length rather than physical distance.

♦ Even within the 15,000 foot limit, the farther you get from the CO, the slower the transmission speed.

♦ DSL requires a telephone landline. If you are a "cell phone only" user, then this could be a major stumbling block.

♦ DSL's availability is more limited than that of cable access.

Note: Which do I use? DSL. Why? Because when bundled with my telephone service, DSL is $15 a month cheaper than the cable service. (I have satellite TV rather than cable.) In addition, my premises are only 1,250 feet from a CO. The service might be rated at up to 3 Mbps, but I've had much faster downloads.

Leased Lines

If you need high bandwidth that is dedicated to your use between your premises and your ISP, you can consider leasing the use of a line from a telecommunications provider. A leased line is a specially conditioned digital line that can support data and voice traffic.

Leased lines come in varous speeds and capacities, some of which are summarized in Table 5-2. As you can see, once you move beyond a fractional or full T1, you're looking at much more bandwidth than a small or home business is likely to need. The cost is also significant.

Table 5-2:   Leased Line Options

Designation	Speed	Sample Cost	Comments
Fractional T1	256 Kpbs to 768 Kbps	Under $300 per month (for example, $260 per month for 512 Kbps)	Supports 5 to 30 users.
T1 (also known as DS1)	1.5 Mbps	$300 to $1200 per month	A full T1 supports 20 to 50 data users, up to 24 voice channels, or a mixture of both voice and data.
Fractional T3	10 Mbps to 40 Mpbs	Depends on bandwidth	May be cheaper than multiple T1s.
T3 (also called DS3)	45 Mpbs	~$2600 and up per month	Supports more than 100 users or upt to 672 voice channels.
OC3	155 Mbps	~$5000 per month	Used by large Internet backbone providers.
OC12	620 Mpbs	~$15,000 per month	Used primarily for point-to-point WAN connections.
OC48	2.5 Gbps	~$80,000[a] per month	Used only by the largest Internet providers.
OC192	9.6 Gbps	(Prices not publicly available)	Used only by the largest Internet providers.

a. No, this is not a typographic error!

Note: Specific costs for leased lines are very difficult to obtain because they depend on location, line availability, and the specific services ordered. The only prices you are likely to find published are T1 and fractional T1; the rest require specific quotes from service providers.

Leased lines provide better privacy and security than cable access or DSL, high reliability, low error rates, support for static IP addresses, and, of course, high bandwidth. They are generally also available in places where DSL and cable may not be. In addition, the bandwidth of a leased line can be shared by voice and data signals. Should you have a leased line, you can probably do away with regular telephone lines.

The biggest drawback to a leased line is cost. Leased lines may also require a professional to install and configure the line on your premises.

Wireless

It is possible to use a wireless connection to access the Internet, bypassing telephone and cable wires completely. To obtain such a connection, you contract with a wireless ISP for service, just as you would a wired ISP. A number of cable and cell phone providers also have wireless Internet service available.

Note: This is different from connecting wireless devices to your internal network. What we're talking about here is a wireless connection to an ISP. Although some of the issues surrounding wireless Internet are the same, connecting wireless devices to your wired Ethernet is covered in Chapter 7.

Wireless Internet uses radio waves to transmit data signals from terrestrial towers to a wireless *access point* on your premises. You can then share that bandwidth across your network. However, the signals do not travel well through natural or manmade objects. In other words, you must have a good line-of-sight to a tower to receive the signal. Most wireless providers therefore are limited to a small geographic area. Generally, service is available in densely populated metropolitan areas, but is fairly sparse in small towns and rural areas.

Wireless Pluses and Minuses

There are several benefits to having wireless connectivity to your business or home network:

- ◆ You avoid relying on a wired solution. Your employees can connect from anywhere in your ISP's service area, as well as from your internal network.
- ◆ Cost is reasonable (comparable to DSL and cable).
- ◆ Installation and maintenance are simple.

However, there are some significant drawbacks to wireless Internet service as well:

- ◆ Wireless data rates are significantly slower than wired data rates. Although current wireless services are based on standards that support speeds up to 54 Mbps, actual speeds are significantly slower, as slow as 2 Mbps. The chances of obtaining anywhere near the maximum speed are very slim. (More on this in Chapter 7.)
- ◆ Service is not available in many areas, and when service is available, it is limited to a relatively small geographic area. The idea that you could have one wireless Internet provider that you could use anywhere in the country is very appealing, but not realistic. For example, Verizon, one of the largest wireless Internet providers in this country, has wireless Internet connectivity in 181 metropolitan areas. They continue to expand their offerings, but they are many years away from nationwide coverage.
- ◆ Even if you are within a wireless ISP's service area, you may not be able to pick up a wireless Internet signal if there are physical obstacles blocking your line-of-sight to a tower that relays the wireless signal.
- ◆ Wireless networking has serious security vulnerabilities. (In fact, many people consider these vulnerabilities so serious that this issue should be the first drawback listed, rather than the last.)

Note: We will look at the security issues surrounding wireless networking in some depth in Chapters 7 and 10.

6

Routing

As we've been discussing, you use a switch (or a hub, if you must) to create a single network segment. You use a hierarchy of switches to create multiple segments, generally to improve performance by spreading the traffic over the multiple segments. If such a network has no outside connectivity (in other words, if it doesn't connect to any type of WAN), then you can give each device a unique static IP address of your choice and all will work well. However, if you need WAN connectivity, then the situation becomes more complicated:

 ◆ The IP addresses must be unique across the entire WAN, which, in most cases, means the Internet. How are you going to ensure that you don't duplicate an IP address in use somewhere else in the world?
 ◆ Switches work with MAC addresses, unique identifiers that are part of network hardware. How can you send a message over the Internet to a device whose MAC address is unknown and

unknowable? (Remember that switches learn the location of MAC addresses as messages pass through them. They can't possibly gain access to MAC addresses of devices that aren't on the same network; the Internet is in the way!)

♦ Opening up your network to a WAN makes it significantly more vulnerable to security problems. Without Internet connectivity, you generally only need to worry about what your end users are doing. But when the Internet enters the picture, the entire world of security problems becomes your concern. (End users are responsible for at least half the security breaches that occur, so adding Internet connectivity can double your security headaches.)

The solution is a device known as a *router*. In most cases, a small network will need only one (an *edge router*), which acts as an interface between Internet traffic coming from an ISP and your internal network. It will then be the router that actually makes the connection to the ISP through a single WAN port. It provides a single point of connectivity to a WAN.

The router, which directs messages based on the software-assigned IP addresses rather than hardware-encoded MAC addresses, also provides a first-line security buffer for your internal network, handles assigning internal dynamic IP addresses, and directs traffic to the correct devices on the internal network.

Routers (once known as *gateways*) are part of the system of IP addresses and associated *domain names* that drive the Internet. Most function at layer 3 of the joint TCP/IP and OSI protocol stack (the Network layer). To understand how a router works and how its function differs from that of a switch, we have to begin by talking about IP addresses in some depth and about domain names.

IP Addressing

IP addresses are software addresses. Although we've said that each device connected to the Internet must have a unique IP address, that doesn't mean that the IP address must be hard-wired to the device or that it must always be the same. IP addresses can be changed as needed, and because they are assigned either through a device's operating system or by a router, having them in software provides the necessary flexibility. Flexibility is particularly important because devices enter and leave a network frequently, as they start up, shut down, sleep, and wake up.

There are two schemes for IP addressing: IPv4 and IPv6. IPv4 addresses are 32 bits long and are the primary type of address used today. However, the people who developed the IP addressing scheme underestimated the growth of the Internet, and we are running out of unique IPv4 addresses. IPv4 provides only 4.3 billion ($4.3 * 10^9$) unique addresses, fewer addresses than the number of people on this planet!

IPv6 addresses are 128 bits long and are slowly being phased in. The 128 bits can provide 50 octillion ($5 * 10^{28}$) addresses. However, initial predications were that we would run out of IPv4 adresses by 1980; at the time this book was written, the prediction had been moved ahead to 2013. Meanwhile, both forms of IP addresses are coexisting on the Internet, although there are very few IPv6 addresses in use.

IPv4 Addressing

To makes IPv4 addresses easier to read, we typically group the bits in the address into four sections and write it in the format X.X.X.X (*dot-decimal notation*), where each X is a value between 0 and 255 (a byte). The first one, two, or three Xs represent the *network part* of the address because they identify an entire network. The number of bytes used as the network part of an IPv4 address indicates the class of the network and limits both the number of unique networks allowed in that class and the number of nodes supported per network. In Table 6-1, you can see the three classes of networks currently in use.

> *Note: Class D addresses (224.0.0.0 to 239.255.255.255) are reserved for multicasting (broadcasts within prespecified groups of addresses). Class E addresses (240.0.0.0 to 247.255.255.255) are reserved for future use.*

Table 6-1:   IP Address Classes

Address class	Address range	Bytes in network part	Number of networks in the class	Number of nodes per network
A	0.0.0.0[a] to 127.255.255.255	1	126[b]	>16 million
B	128.0.0.0 to 191.255.255.255	2	16,384	65,534
C	192.0.0.0 to 223.255.255.255	3	2,097,152	254

a. 0.0.0.0 cannot be assigned to a network; it is used as a broadcast address to refer to all nodes on the current network.
b. There are only 126 (rather 128) addresses in class A because 0.0.0.0 is reserved as the broadcast address and 127.0.0.1 is reserved as a loopback address to enable nodes to communicate with themselves.

Not all IPv4 addresses are designed for external Internet use. In Table 6-2 you will find ranges of IPv4 addresses that cannot be used for Internet routing; these are reserved for internal network addresses. In most cases, these are used for dynamic IP addressing and are assigned by a router to a device as it joins a network. The use of these internal addresses (and dynamic IP addressing in general) has slowed the use of unique static IP addresses, helping to extend the life of IPv4.

Table 6-2:   IPv4 Address Spaces for Internal Networks

Network class	Address range	Bytes in network portion
A	10.0.0.0 to 10.255.255.255	1
B	172.16.0.0 to 172.31.255.255	2
C	192.168.0.0 to 192.168.255.255	3

For example, the machine on which I wrote this book typically has the IP address of 192.168.1.101. The first byte of the address tells you that it is a class C network; the actual value of the first byte indicates that it is an internal IP address that can't be used on the Internet.

The network portion of an IPv4 address may also identify a *subnet*, a switched network segment attached to a router. As an example, take a look at Figure 6-1. This network has a single router providing a shared connection to the Internet. The router actually has four network interfaces, one for whatever device is providing the interface to the Internet service and three to connect to switches. Each switch connects to its own network, a subnet. Notice the IP addresses: The first two bytes (also known as *octets*) are the same throughout the entire entwork, the 192.168 used for internal networks. However, the third octet is unique to each subnet and therefore identifies the subnet to which a device is connected.

The remaining numbers uniquely identify a network device (the *host part*). In Figure 6-1, each host part is unique within its own subnet. Notice that the host parts can duplicate, as long as the entire IP address is unique.

To extend the life of IPv4 addressing, some networks allocate the bits in the IP address in a different way (*classless addressing*). You can recognize such an address because it ends with a / (slash) and a number. For example, 192.168.124.18/22 tells you that the first 22 bits of the IP address are being used as the network portion and that the last 10 represent the host.

IPv6 Addressing

It makes economic sense to extend the life of IPv4 as much as possible: The majority of existing routing equipment hasn't been programmed to deal with IPv6 addressing and the cost of replacing the equipment would be substantial. Nonetheless, if the increase in devices that connect to the Internet continues at anywhere near the current rate—and don't forget things such as cell phones and PDAs!—it is inevitable that we'll need the longer addressing scheme.

Rather than decimal numbers to represent IPv6 addresses for human consumption, we use eight groups of four hexadecimal digits. For example, fe80:0000:0000:0000:0214:51ff:fe64:833 is the full IPv6 address of my main publishing workstation; to shorten it, the address can be abbreviated as fe80::0214:51ff:fe64:833f by removing contiguous groups that are all 0s and replacing them with a single extra colon.

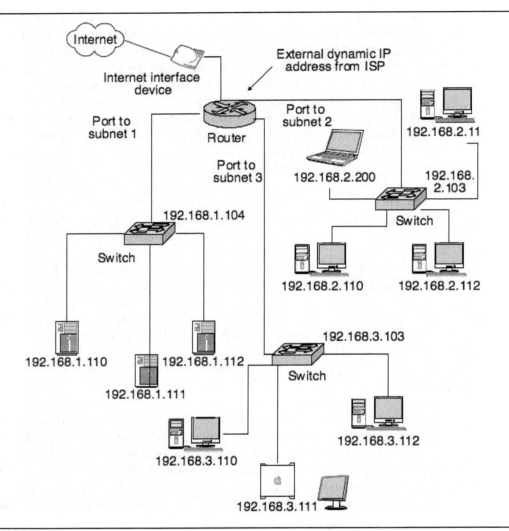

Figure 6-1:   A network with one router and multiple switched segments

*Note: There can be only one :: in an IPv6 address. It re-
places a string of contiguous 0s that is expanded to make
the address a full 128 bits. If there were more than one ::,
it would be impossible to determine the number of 0s to insert when expanding the address.*

Originally, the first 64 bits in an IPv6 address were allocated to identifying the network; the remaining 64 identified the host. However, other allocations are used with the /## notation, where ## indicates the number of bits used to identify the network, just as it does with IPv4 addresses. The network portion is also known as the address's *prefix*. A network (or subnet) is therefore a group of IPv6 addresses with the same prefix.

IPv6 networks have no classes. However, some addresses have special purposes. (See Table 6-3.)

Table 6-3:   Special Purpose IPv6 Addresses

Address	Use/comments
::/128	All 0s means an unspecified address; for use only by software.
::1/128	The IPv6 loopback address; expands to all 0s except for a 1 in the rightmost bit.
::/96	The prefix is 32 bits of 0s, used for IPv4 compatibility.
::fff:0:0/96	A 32-bit prefix used for mapping IPv4 addresses.
fc00::/7	Nonroutable addresses for use on an internal network, similar to the IPv4 addresses in Table 6-2.
fe80::/10	A 10-bit prefix that restricts the use of the address to the current physical link (i.e., the current subnet, if applicable).
ff00::/8	An 8-bit prefix indicating a multicast packet.[a]

a. IPv6 does not have a separate broadcast address. Instead, you would send a multicast message addressed to "all hosts."

Important note: From this point on, unless we state otherwise, all references to an IP address mean an IPv4 address.

Getting an IP Address

Throughout this chapter we've mentioned that IP addresses come from ISPs. That is true in the sense that your IP address, whether static or dynamic, does come from your ISP. But where does your ISP get IP addresses? And how does your computer actually get one? That's what this section is all about.

ISPs and IP Addresses

Ultimate responsibility for assigning IP numbers rests with the Internet Assigned Numbers Authority (IANA). However, numbers are actually assigned by regional registries. In the United States, for example, registration is handled by the American Registry for Internet Numbers (ARIN). IP numbers are assigned in large blocks to ISPs.

ARIN will also assign blocks of IP addresses to end users, but at this time, it seems reluctant to do so:

> Assignments of IPv4 address space are made to end-user organizations or individuals for use in running internal networks, and not for sub-delegation of those addresses outside their organization. End-users not currently connected to an ISP and/or who do not plan to be connected to the Internet are encouraged to use private IP numbers reserved for non-connected networks.
> *Source: http://www.arin.net*

The private IP numbers to which the quote refers are the ranges of non-routable addresses in Table 6-2. This is part of the global strategy to extend the life of IPv4 addresses.

> *Note: Blocks of IP addresses are not free. Depending on the size of the block allocated, an ISP pays from $1,250 to $18,000 per year. An end user pays an initial fee of $1,250 to $18,000 (again dependent on the size of the block of addresses) plus a $100 annual maintenance fee. Add in the cost of T3 lines, and setting yourself up as an ISP begins to look like a very expensive business!*

Static IP Addresses

If you want to host your own Web site, you will need a static IP address. You will be given this address by your ISP. You must then manually configure the server to use this address. How you do so depends on your operating system.

Windows

You can set a static IP address for a Windows machine through the GUI, although finding the right place to enter the address takes a bit of digging. As it so happens, the path for both XP and 2000 is exactly the same:

1. Follow the path My Computer->Control Panel->Network and Dial-up Connections or Network Connections.
2. Open the icon for the interface for which you want to set the IP address.
3. Choose Internet Protocol (TCP/IP) to display the correct dialog box.
4. Click on the *Use the following IP address* radio button. (See Figure 6-2.)
5. Enter the IP address in the appropriate text box and save the changes.

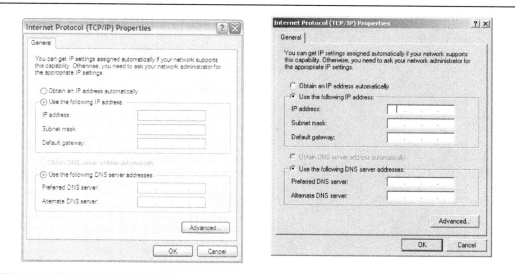

Figure 6-2:   Setting a static IP address for Windows XP (*left*) and 2000 (*right*)

Note: You will also need to enter a subnet mask, which we'll discuss in a later section in this chapter.

Macintosh OS X

Entering a static IP address for a Mac OS X machine is not significantly different from doing so for a Windows machine; it's just not buried as deep:

1. Launch System Preferences and open the Network preferences panel.
2. Highlight the interface for which you want to enter a static IP address and click the Configure button.
3. Choose *Manually* from the *Configure IPv4* popup menu. (See Figure 6-3.)
4. Enter the IP address in the appropriate text box and save the changes.

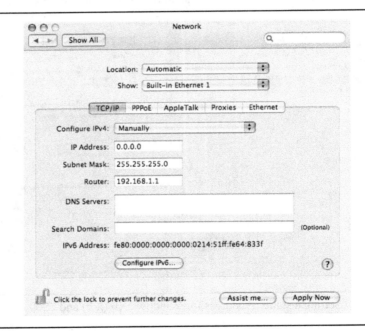

Figure 6-3:   Entering a Mac OS X static IP address

Linux

Many Linux distributions ease the assigning of a static IP address through the GUI used to install the operating system. However, if you need to set the IP address from the command line, you'll need to use the *ifconfig* command to set up at least two network interfaces (loopback and one other) for your machine. It has the general syntax

ifconfig type_of_interface IP_address

The type of interface is the name of the device driver for the interface. The ones you are likely to need can be found in Table 6-4.

Table 6-4:   Linux Network Interface Driver Names

Interface	Meaning
lo	Loopback[a]
ppp	PPP (Point-to-Point protocol, used for dial-up connections)
ethX	Ethernet, where X is the number of the Ethernet interface. If you have only one network adapter, it will be *eth0*. A second adapter will be *eth1*, and so on.

a. Loopback addresses take the form 127.X.X.X. Once a loopback address has been configured, a line for *localhost* (usually with the IP address of 127.0.01) can be found in the */etc/hosts* file.

For example, if I want my Ethernet adapter to have the IP address of 10.148.6.118, the command would be

ifconfig eth0 10.148.6.118

The *ifconfig* commands makes the interface active. The next step is to add the interface to the Linux kernel's routing table so that your machine can find other computers:

route add IP_address

To add the preceding Ethernet interface, you would use

route add 10.148.6.188

Note: To remove an IP address from the kernel's routing table, issue the route command again, substituting "del" for "add."

Dynamic IP Addresses

Dynamic IP addresses are assigned to a device whenever the device connects to the network. You router, for example, will be given an IP address by your ISP when the router connects to the ISP; workstations and printers will be given IP addresses by the router when they join the network. The router's dynamic IP address will be taken from the ISP's block of IP addresses; internal devices will usually be given addresses from the non-routable block of internal addresses.

DHCP and BootP

There are two protocols in wide use for assigning dynamic IP addresses, DHCP (*Dynamic Host Configuration Protocol*) and BootP (*Bootstrap Protocol*). These Network layer protocols typically give a device a new IP address when it connects to a network. Both require "servers" running the protocols to issue IP addresses. However, for a small network, the servers are built in to most small routers; you don't need a standalone machine acting as a DCHP or BootP server.

Dynamic Host Configuration Protocol

DHCP allocates IP addresses in one of three ways:

♦ *Manual allocation*: The device running DHCP (a server or router) has a table that pairs MAC addresses with IP addresses. Whenever a device powers up and enters the network, it requests an IP address from DHCP. DHCP looks up the MAC address in its table and issues the associated IP address. If the MAC address isn't in the table, the device doesn't get an IP address and therefore isn't allowed on the network. The setup of manual allocation is time consuming for a network administrator, but does provide a measure of security because only authorized devices can connect.

An alternative point of view is that it is less time consuming to configure a set of manual IP addresses in one central location (the DHCP server) than to go around and configure all of the clients with static IP addresses. By doing it with manual allocation, all the clients have to do is plug in and they will start working. Additionally, if a device is used in multiple environments (home/office/and so on), it is more difficult to use static settings on the client since they have to be changed each time the device moves to a new network.

♦ *Automatic allocation*: A network administrator supplies a range of IP addresses to DHCP. DHCP then issues an unused IP address from this range the first time a device requests an address. The address is permanently assigned to the device and will not be reused on the network, even when the device powers down.

♦ *Dynamic allocation*: A network administrator supplies a range of IP addresses to DHCP. DHCP then issues an unused IP address from this range to a device each time the device connects to the network. When the device disconnects—usually when it powers down—the IP address is returned to the pool of unused addresses to be assigned to another device.

Bootstrap Protocol

BootP is a simpler protocol for dynamically assigning IP addresses. A network administrator gives BootP a range of IP addresses. It then assigns an IP address to a device as it boots up. Like DHCP dynamic allocation, IP addresses are released when a device powers down and reused for other devices.

One advantage of BootP is that is can be used to assign an IP address to a diskless workstation so that it can connect to a server to obtain its operating system. DHCP is the more capable protocol, but it relies on a request from a network device's NIC to initiate assigning an address. BootP, however, works as part of the computer's boot process, before most of the operating system is loaded and can therefore assign an IP address that can be used to load the OS before the drivers to operator a NIC have been loaded.

Configuring Windows and OS X for Dynamic IP Addresses

Configuring the GUI-based operating systems to use dynamic IP addressing is straightforward:

1. Open the Control Panel/Preferences Pane used to set a static IP address (see Figure 6-2 and Figure 6-3).
2. For Windows, click the *Obtain an IP address automatically* radio button. For OS X, choose BootP or DHCP from the *Configure IPv4* popup menu.

Configuring Linux for Dynamic IP Addressing

Most Linux distributions include two pieces of client software for connecting the computer to a DHCP server: *pump* and *dhcpd*.

> *Note: Some Linux distributions have GUI support for configuring dynamic IP addressing. For example, with Red Hat Linux you can find it in the Network Configuration control panel.*

The *pump* client is the default for distributions such as Red Hat. However, it does not seem to work reliably for all users; if it isn't working for you, try adding a *-h hostname* switch. To make this work, edit the file */etc/sysconfig/network-scripts/ifcfg-eth0*—replace the *0* with the appropriate number for your Ethernet adapter—and add the following three lines:

DEVICE="eth0"
MACADDR=MAC_address_of_your_machine
DHCP_HOSTNAME="any_hostname_neednt_be_real"

Notice that you need to include the MAC address of your machine along with a name for a DHCP host, which can be anything you want. Because this is a change to a configuration file, you'll need to either reboot the machine or type

/sbin/ifup eth0

to get the change to take effect.

The *dhcpd* is a daemon that is the default for distributions such as Denebian and Slackware. It is shipped as a separate package that you will need to install. For distribution-specific details of how to install, test, and use *dhcpd*, see *http://www.tldp.org/HOWTO/DHCP/index.html*.

Many Linux distributions also include *bootpcd*, a BootP daemon that is installed with the operating system. (It doesn't require installation from a standalone package file.) You can configure BootP with the *bootpc* command. For example, to connect a network interface to the server, you could use

bootpc -dev eth0

For complete documentation of the command, see *http://www.penguin-soft.com/penguin/man/8/bootpc.html*.

Domain Names and DNS

A *domain name* is a human-understandable name associated with a static IP address. The mapping between a domain name and an IP address is what makes it possible to use *www.aol.com* to reach AOL's Web site, for example. Something, somewhere, must translate the URL to an IP address, however, before a packet can be routed to the correct location. This is where DNS (the *Domain Name System*) comes into play.

When you send a message that is addressed using a domain name—whether it be a URL or an e-mail address—the domain name must be resolved into an IP address before the router can make any routing decisions. Your computer must therefore consult a *domain name server* in an attempt find the correct static IP address before a packet can be assembled and routed.

> *Note: There are 13 root domain name servers on the Internet, backbone sites that know which top-level DNS servers hold complete databases for each top-level domain (e.g., .com or .org). The Internet can function with only four of those sites in operation, but you can bet that performance is significantly degraded at that point! Seven of the servers are wholly located in the United States; the reamining are distributed throughout the world rather than physically being in one place.*

Unless you have specified otherwise, your computer first consults the closest DNS server it can find, usually located at your ISP. Your ISP's DNS servers will usually contain that portion of the DNS database that is used most frequently through that ISP. If a domain name cannot be resolved at the ISP, then the ISP's DNS server will contact another DNS server with a larger portion of the DNS database and repeat the search. The search will progress up the hierarchy until it reaches a root DNS server that knows where the top-level domain database can be found. If the search fails at a top-level DNS server, you receive a message that the location can't be found, typically from your browser or from the ISP's e-mail server.

> *Note: Because the results of DNS lookups are cached, building "local" DNS databases, it is rare for a search for an IP address to end up at one of the root servers.*

When you use dynamic IP addressing, your DHCP or BootP server will supply the IP addresses of the closest DNS servers to your network (i.e., those at your ISP). The ISP supplies the IP addresses of the DNS servers to the DHCP or BootP server, which in turn passes them on to your computer when it supplies an IP address.

However, if you are using static IP addressing, you will need to enter the IP addresses of the DNS servers manually. First, get those IP addresses from your ISP. For Windows or OS X, enter those addresses into the TCP/IP configuration control panels, using the DNS server text boxes. (Once again, look back at Figure 6-2 and Figure 6-3.)

If you are using Linux, you'll need to edit */etc/resolv.conf.* Add the following lines:

search name_of_isp.com
nameserver IP_address1
nameserver IP_address2
nameserver IP_address3

You can specify a maximum of three DNS servers.

Making Routing Decisions

Routers are used to move packets between networks. Most make decisions where to send packets based on the IP address; they work at layer 3, the Network layer, of the TCP/IP protocol stack. Routers can exchange information with other routers, especially the *next hop* router, the next router down the road. This information can help a router optimize routing for packets and to route packets around network segments that may be down.

> *Note: We say that a packet makes a "hop" when it travels through a router. One way to figure out how long a packet bounced around an internet before it reached its destination is to look at the packet's "hop count," the number of routers it visited along the way.*

Routers and the TCP/IP Protocol Stack

Because a router makes its decisions based on IP addresses, it must contain enough of the TCP/IP protocol stack to strip off Physical- and Data Link-layer headers and trailers to expose the Internet layer packet. After making the routing decision, it must send the packet back down the protocol stack so that it can be reencapsulated for travel over the network wire. As you can see in Figure 6-4, a packet coming into Router 1 travels up the protocol stack for handling and then back down the stack to go out onto the wire to the next hop router. The process continues until the packet reaches the router to which the packet's destination subnet or device is connected.

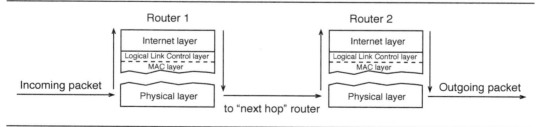

Figure 6-4:   Router packet handling

Routing Tables

How does a router know where to send a packet? Like a switch, it keeps an internal table that indicates the port out which it should send a packet with a given address. And like a switch, a router learns destinations, although unlike a switch, a router can exchange information with other routers; switches generally don't talk to one another.

> *Note: Switches running the spanning tree protocol (STP) do exchange messages, looking for downed links between the switches. A downed link signals the need to enable a redundant link that has been disabled to avoid a loop in the wiring.*

A router's routing table contains IP addresses (or parts of IP addresses) and the ports out which the addresses should be sent. For an example, see Table 6-5. The last row in the table, 0.0.0.0, is the default IP address that matches any address that isn't matched by an earlier row. The port associated with the default address will be the "next hop" router, the router that gets the packet one step closer to the Internet.

Table 6-5:   Sample Routing Table

IP address prefix	Port
10.148.0.0	3
10.148.10.0	4
10.16.0.0	0
10.16.10.0	1
10.16.10.2	1
0.0.0.0	1

The remaining entries in the table contain IP addresses (or just the network prefixes) and ports that the router has learned. When a packet reaches the router, the router matches as much of the IP address as it can. For example, if a packet with a destination of 10.148.10.0 enters the router, if will match the first two rows. The router then chooses the longest match, the match of the most bits in the IP address. In this example, it will choose the second row and send the packet out port 4.

Like a switch, the router builds the table by looking at the source addresses of packets and noting the port through which the packet entered.

Subnet Masking

An IP address contains both network and host portions in a single value. How does a router look just at the portion it needs? The trick is something known as *subnet masking*, a method for stripping off the host portion of an IP address, leaving just the network portion.

Masking is a binary operation that combines two binary values one bit at a time using either the AND or OR logical operation. Take a look at the examples in Figure 6-5. Each consists of the same two eight-bit quantities being combined using logical bit-wise operations. When two bits are combined with AND, the result is 0 unless both input bits are 1. If you want to preserve the value of a bit, you use the AND operation and a value of 1. A value of 0 always produces the result of 0.

```
1 0 1 1   0 0 1 1
0 0 1 1   1 1 0 0     Logical AND
0 0 1 1   0 0 0 0
```

```
1 0 1 1   0 0 1 1
0 0 1 1   1 1 0 0     Logical OR
1 0 1 1   1 1 1 1
```

Figure 6-5:   Logical operations used in masking

With the OR operation, it takes only a single 1 to produce a result of 1. The only way to get a 0 result is to have two input 0s. Therefore, the OR operation can be used to force bits to take the value 1: OR a bit with a 0 and you'll get the original value (1 or 0); OR a bit with 1 and you'll get a 1.

Each IP address assigned to a network device is accompanied by a *subnet mask*, a pattern of bits that is the same length as the IP address but contains 1s in all positions occupied by the network portion of the address and 0s in positions occupied by the host portion. The mask is combined with an IP address using the logical AND operation to set the host portion of the address to all 0s. What remains is the network portion.

A class A IPv4 address will have a subnet mask of 255.0.0.0. For a class B address, it will be 255.255.0.0, and a class C address, 255.255.255.0.

If you are using dynamic IP addresses, then the appropriate subnet mask will be supplied by DHCP or BootP along with the IP address. However, if you are using static IP addresses, then you must enter the subnet mask manually. For Windows and Mac OS X computers, look once again at Figure 6-2 and Figure 6-3. You'll see that each Control Panel/Preferences Pane has a text box for a subnet mask. The mask you enter, of course, depends on the class of the network you are using; in most cases, your ISP will be able to tell you the correct subnet mask.

If your Linux system doesn't have a GUI method for setting a subnet mask, you can do it with the *ifconfig* command:

ifconfig eth0 10.148.6.118 netmask 255.255.0.0

Router Capabilities

If you walk into an office supplies store and ask a salesperson for a router, that's exactly what you'll get—and then some. Today's small routers are a combination of several devices, including a router, a switch, a wireless access point, and a firewall. You have to read the box carefully to find out exactly what you're buying! This is not necessarily a bad thing. If your network is relatively small—no more than four subnets or devices connected directly to the router—a "router" may be all that you need for the complete setup.

> *Note: Ironically, if you're using DSL or cable to connect to the Internet, you may not need a router at all: Router*

capabilities may be built into the "modem" supplied by your ISP. In other words, the DSL or cable interconnection device may include a four-port Ethernet switch, wireless access point, and a firewall. The drawback to this setup, however, is that the "modem"may not be configurable like a true router. It may not provide VPN (virtual private network) support, not allow you to open and close TCP ports, not have a firewall, and so on. Check with your cable or or DSL provider about the hardware it providies to determine exactly what you will be getting!

Making Connections and Network Address Translation

When you add a router to your network, network devices are no longer attached direrctly to an Internet interface device. Instead, the connection to the ISP through the "modem" is made by the router. The router obtains a single dynamic IP address from the ISP. It then distributes packets to the internal network, using *network address translation* (NAT).

In most cases, the devices on your internal network will have dynamic IP addresses issued by DHCP on the router. These addresses typically come from the pool of nonroutable IP addresses. It's then the job of the router to translate information in incoming packets to determine the correct internal address for a packet. The router must also modify outgoing packets so that they contain the router's external IP address as the packet's source address.

Incoming packets are all directed to the router's external IP address. The router must therefore have some way to determine the internal destination of a packet. It uses *ports* for this purpose. A TCP port is a software concept and totally distinct from the hardware ports into which we plug cables. A software port represents an application running on a nework device. For example, normally a Web server uses port 80, but if an organization is running more than one Web server, it needs to assign a different port number to the second Web servier (often 8080). A router can then distinguish between incoming packets for the two Web servers by checking the port numbers.

A packet header contains not only the source IP address, but also the source port. The router will make an entry for the packet in a table, showing its internal source port as well as its IP address. When a packet comes back in reply, the router can match information in the incoming packet to determine where the packet should go on the internal network.

> *Note: There are several types of NAT. The one we have been discussing, which is most commonly used by small routers, is known as "overloaded NAT."*

One of the major advantages of NAT is that it hides the internal network from the Internet. This makes it much more difficult for someone to probe the network from the outside to determine its configuration. Having a dynamic IP address on the router also helps prevent the network from becoming the target of attacks that flood the network with spurious packets (*denial of service* attacks).

Firewalls and Port Management

Most routers today contain *firewalls*, software that can prevent many unwanted packets from getting onto your network. Although we will talk about firewalls in more depth in Chapter 10, we should note here that although firewalls work in several ways, the firewalls that are supplied with most small routers work by blocking packets destined for specific ports. (Here, again, we're talking about the TCP software ports that represent applications running on network devices.)

A router's software allows you to open and close ports through the firewall. If you have a Web server on your internal network, for example, you'll want to open up port 80 but close most other common ports. By blocking all ports and then opening only those you specifically want to let through, you can cut down on traffic that, for example, is looking for peer-to-peer file sharing services (e.g., Kazaa).

In most cases, a router comes with all incoming ports closed through its firewall; outgoing traffic is allowed by having all outgoing ports open. However, you will need to check your own specific model to determine its default configuration. Applications and network protocols receive fixed port numbers. Those used most commonly are called *well-known ports*. You can find a table of them in Appendix B.

Adding Routers to an Ethernet

When you are ready to connect your internal network to the Internet, you will need to add a router to your network. As mentioned earlier, a small router can also provide you with a core switch for your network (usually one to four ports). You can build your network hierarchy from that core switch.

Be careful when you shop for a router. The small routers that sell for less than $100 have only 10/100 ports, meaning that they are limited to Fast Ethernet speeds. Those with 10/100/1000 ports (up to Gigabit Ethernet) currently sell for between $100 and $200. Nonetheless, you can expect any of these routers to have a wireless access point, firewall, and switch with between one and eight ports.

Physical Connections

The architecture of a small network that includes a router is usually quite straightforward: The edge router makes the connection to the Internet and also acts as the core switch. For a *very* small network, you may be able to connect all devices to the router, as in Figure 6-6. This network will need a 10/100 switch in its router and can be cabled with all UTP wiring.

However, if your network is likely to grow beyond eight wired devices, or you need to include fiber optic links, then you will need switches and a hierarchical structure. There are no hard and fast rules about how you should configure the network; the specific devices you have and the amount of traffic each handles will to a large extent determine what you do. In general, you want to spread the traffic load as evenly as you can across network links, keeping in mind any of the following that apply:

- ♦ Traffic loads don't necessarily stay constant; at some point, you may want to reconfigure your network to improve performance. Using plug-and-play cabling, switches, and routers makes doing so much, much easier, especially if all the interconnection hardware is in the same wiring closet.

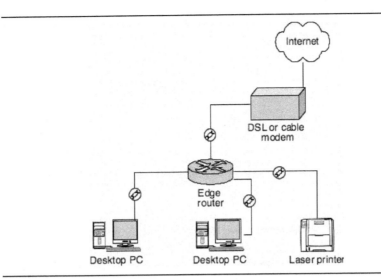

Figure 6-6:   A simple network with a router

♦ Fiber optic hardware is considerably more expensive than UTP
hardware. At the time this book was written, switches with fiber optic ports were selling—at the low end—between $1,000
and $2,000. (Like all things networking, these prices are likely
to decrease over time, but fiber optics will be more expensive
than UTP for the foreseeable future.)

♦ Fiber optics cables are very difficult to splice. You can actually
fuse the ends of two fibers together with heat. *Mating sleeves*
can also be used to line up the ends of two fibers precisely. Because either process is hard to accomplish well, you may want
to avoid fiber optic runs that are longer than the longest preter-
minated cable you can purchase.

♦ When it comes to expansion of your network, never say "never."
It makes sense to leave empty ports on each interconnecton device to allow for the future. Many IT professionals will suggest
that you install switches with twice as many ports as you need
for the initial network installation. (An eight-port UTP switch
doesn't cost much more than a four-port; go for the eight-port!)

*Note: For more examples of actual network architectures,
see Chapters 12 through 14, which contain case studies of
networks of different sizes.*

Configuring the Router

Even small "home" routers are intelligent devices and provide a variety of configuration options that typically can be accessed from a Web browser. The router itself has an IP address, which takes you directly to the configuration screen. To reach it, enter the router's IP address (given to you in the instruction manual) in your browser's address field and press Enter.

Note: The examples in this section are from a Linksys router. Other manufacturers' products have similar capabilities, but the screens will look somewhat different.

Making Connections

As mentioned earlier, when you put a router into your network, the router makes the connection to your ISP through whatever interface device you happen to have. To make the connection, however, the router needs to know your account number and password and the protocol to be used.

Each router will typically have a setup screen for entering basic connection information, such as that in Figure 6-7. The top section lets you choose the connection protocol (PPPoE in this case), enter the user name and password, and indicate whether the router should always stay connected or connect only when it has an outgoing packet.

Note: There is one advantage to "connect on demand": Each time you connect you may get a different IP address from your ISP. This provides an extra layer of security because your IP address changes frequently. On the other hand, incoming traffic will be delayed until an outgoing packet triggers a connection.

The setup screen also makes it possible to enter the router's internal IP address, which in this example is a class C, unroutable address. You can also enable DHCP for internal network and enter static IP addresses for DNS servers, if necessary. (If you are getting a dynamic IP address from your ISP, you'll normally leave these blank.)

In most cases, a router automatically attempts to make a connection as soon as it detects a signal from the Internet "modem." You can check the status of the connection, find the router's external IP address, and control the connection manually from the status screen (for example, Figure 6-8). The IP address, subnet mask, default gateway (next hop router) and DNS servers are all supplied by the ISP.

Figure 6-7:   A router setup screen

> *Note: Yes, you've read correctly. The router has two IP addresses, one to identify it as a destination to the internal network and another for its WAN port, which identifies it to the Internet.*

Routers and Security

Most of the information about network security can be found in Chapter 10 of this book. However, at this point it makes sense to show you the types of security that a router can provide. First and foremost, most routers supply a firewall. (See Figure 6-9.) You may choose to use or not use it.

Figure 6-8:   Router status screen

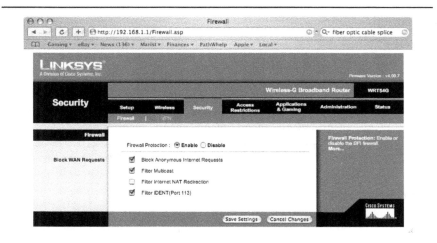

Figure 6-9:   A router's security screen

Note: If you supply a firewall as a standalone appliance, you may want to turn the router's firewall off. More in Chapter 10.

By default, most of today's small routers block packets from well-known ports. If you want to let them through, or want to let through traffic from specific Web applications such as games, then you will need to open the ports manually, as in Figure 6-10. You enter the ports you want to open in the Start and End boxes. (These make it easier to enter a range of ports.) If you have a Web server or FTP server with static IP addresss, you will need to open their ports, for example.

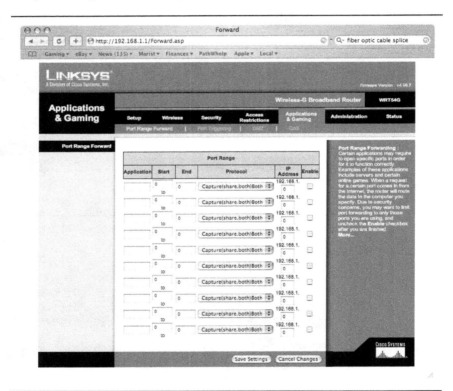

Figure 6-10:   Configuring a router to open specific ports

Finally, you can usually configure Internet access policies (Figure 6-11), providing access controls for specific machines on your internal network.

First, you create a list of workstations to be affected by the policy, as in Figure 6-12. Then you indicate when you want to deny or allow access. Notice also at the bottom of the access policy screen that you can block Web sites by URL or keyword. (It may not be as flexible as many stand-alone parental control applications, but it's a start!)

Figure 6-11:   Configuring Internet access policies

Note: You may have noticed that this router also has a screen for configuring wireless connections. We'll look at that in Chapter 7.

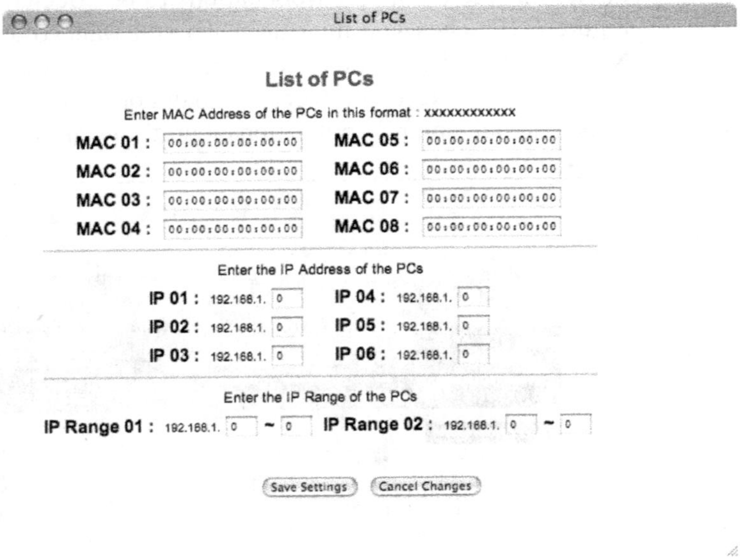

Figure 6-12:   Setting up a list of PCs for an Internet access policy

7

Integrating Wireless Transmissions

If you read the popular press, you would think that small networks were wireless, and nothing but wireless. The ostensible ease of setting up and using a wireless network seems to be endlessly appealing. And there is no question that a wireless connection is convenient for connecting a computer such as a laptop that needs only occasional access to your network or that changes its location frequently. However, there are major drawbacks to wireless networks—especially in terms of security—that should make even the smallest of small business users think twice.

In this chapter we'll look at why the most common wireless networks aren't truly Ethernet (and why they can't be). We'll also talk about wireless standards and speeds, along with how wireless connections work. Along the way we'll explore the security issues that still plague today's wireless connections.

Wireless MAC Protocol versus Ethernet MAC Protocol

As you will remember, the Ether MAC protocol (CSMA/CD) relies on the ability of connected devices to detect the presence of a signal on the network wire. When a device detects a signal, it knows that the wire is in use and that it must wait to transmit. Wireless connections, however, can't use CDMA/CD. Why? Because wireless devices can't detect collisions. And why not? Because wireless transmissions are half duplex.

With CSMA/CD, the transmitting device must send a frame and then immediately listen for a collision. But a wireless device can't send and listen at the same time. Therefore, if it transmits and a collision occurs, it has no way to detect that collision. CSMA/CA (Carrier Sense Multiple Access/Collision Avoidance) tries to minimize collisions. It works in the following way:

1. A device waiting to transmit checks to see if there is a carrier signal (access point is busy).
2. If the access point is not busy, it sends a jamming signal to alert other devices that it will be transmitting.
3. If there is a signal, the device waits a random amount of time and then checks the transmission channel again.
4. If the access point is still busy, the device doubles its wait time, and continues to do so until it can gain control of the tramission frequency.

The randomness of the wait intervals and the increasing wait time minimize the collisions. Packets that are mangled by collisions won't generate TCP acknowledgment packets and will therefore be resent.

Wireless Speeds and Standards

One reason that wireless networks aren't as widely used in business networks as they are in home networks is speed: Although some current standards are rated to perform as well as wired networks, in practice wireless networks almost never achieve anywhere near their rated throughput. The standards are constantly pushing speeds upward, and we can only hope that eventually wireless technologies actually will be able to achieve rated speeds.

At this point, the standards for wireless tranmissions are subsets of the IEEE's 802.11 and 802.16 specifications. (See Table 7-1.) Notice first that with the exception of the as yet unreleased 802.11n, the Wi-Fi standards are all slower than wired networks. In addition, they operate in the same bands as most coredless telephones!

Table 7-1:   Wireless Networking Standards

Standard	AKA	Maximum Speed	Security	Comments
802.11a	Wi-Fi	54 Mbps (5 GHz band)	WEP; WPA, WPA2	Good for multimedia, voice, and large images. Nonetheless, not widely used.
802.11b	Wi-Fi	11 Mbps (2.4 GHz band)	WEP; WPA	Greater range than 802.11a. First widely implemented wireless standard.
802.11g	Wi-Fi	54 Mbps (2.4 GHz band)	WEP;WPA	Compatible with 802.11b. Widely used.
802.11i			AES	Specifies additional security for 802.11x networks.
802.11n[a]	Wi-Fi	540 Mbps (2.4 GHz or 5 GHz bands)		Has a range of up to 250 meters. Interferes with 802.11b and 802.11g networks.
802.16	WiMax	75 Mbps[b]	DES3; AES	Intended for wireless MANs.
Bluetooth		2 Mbps (2.45 GHz band)	SAFER+; E22; E0	Intended for connecting small peripherals, such as keyboards, PDAs, and cell phones, to computers.

a. This standard is not as yet approved. It is scheduled for final approval in July 2007 and release in April 2008. Currently, you can purchase products labeled "pre-n," but there is no guarantee that those products will be compatible with the standard that is ultimately released.

b. WiMax speeds depend heavily on distance. The 75 Mpbs speed is achievable for up to four miles, but drops to 50 Mbps between 4 and 6 miles, and to 17 Mbps over 6 miles.

Most of wireless access points handle both 802.11b and 802.11g transmissions. Most laptops come equipped with 802.11g wireless adapters. Nonetheless, the compatibility doesn't work in the same way as autosensing ports on an Ethernet switch. The switch can operate with one port at 10 Mbps, several ports at 100 Mbps, and yet even more ports at 1000 Mbps; the speed of the transmissions between each device and the switch is a matter for the switch and device, independent of the speed of other devices connected to the switch. However, if both 802.11b and 802.11g devices are communicating with the same access point, the access point slows down to 802.11b speeds for all of its transmissions, removing the advantage of having the faster devices.

At the time this book was written, it made sense to purchase 802.11g equipment, especially for new installations where no 802.11b devices would be in use. It was somewhat risky to purchase pre-n equipment, given that there was no guarantee that it would be compatible with 8012.11n equipment that was produced in response to the final accepted standard.

Wireless Access Points

Wireless network adapters communicate with wireless *access point*s (APs). As you read in Chapter 6, an access point may be built into a small router, along with an Ethernet switch (for example, Figure 7-1). Alternatively, you can purchase stand-alone access points, which don't look much different from the all-in-one router. (The little antennas sticking up are a dead giveaway that you're dealing with a wireless device.).

> *Note: The irony of the preceding is that a stand-alone access point costs the same as, if not more, than a small router with a switch and access point built in.*

Service Set Identifiers

Wireless access points are limited in range. It therefore is not unusual to have more than one access point with overlapping ranges in the same network. To distinguish themselves, APs have names known as Service Set Identifiers (*SSIDs*). When a remote device wants to connect to an AP, it

Figure 7-1:   A router with a built-in wireless access point (Courtesy of Belkin Corportation)

supplies the SSID of the access point it wants to use. In public hot spots, however, many APs may share an SSID to make it easier for clients to move from one AP to another without signal interruption.

By default, APs broadcast their SSIDs for any wireless adapter in range to pick up. This is why it is so easy to connect to the wireless service in an airport, for example. The driver for a laptop's wireless adapter searches for SSID broadcasts and identifies the strongest signal it can find. That is the network to which it will attempt to connect first.

APs broadcasting their SSIDs are therefore wide open to any device in range, a major security problem. There are two very simple things you can do to prevent just anyone from connecting to your wireless access points: Turn off the broadcast of the SSID and change the default name of the AP.

The default names are usually something like the name of the manufacturer of the AP or the word "wireless" or something else equally insecure. For example, there are probably tens of thousands of unsecured wireless routers in the United States broadcasting the SSID "linksys." For more well-known SSIDs, see Table 7-2.

Table 7-2: Well-Known SSIDs

Vendor	SSID
Addtron	WLAN
Cisco	tsunami
Compaq	Compaq
Intel	intel
Linksys	linksys
Lucent	RoamAbout Default Network Name
3Com	101
Others	Default SSID
many	Wireless

If your access point is part of a router, you'll use the router's Setup utility to take care of this (for example, Figure 7-2). Otherwise, you'll use the Setup utility that is part of the AP.

Figure 7-2:   Configuring SSID broadcast

Note: How big a problem is the SSID broadcast, really? You decide: From the second floor of my house, which is set 150 feeet back from the road, a guest in my guest room can pick up the SSID broadcast of my neighbors across the street. The signal is going through two stick-built houses and traveling at least 250 feet. Although brick, stone, and metal can restrict the range of wireless signals, don't count on your walls keeping in your wireless transmissions.

Turning off the broadcast of the SSID and changing the default SSID will go a long way toward deterring *war drivers*, individuals who use specialized equipment and antennas to find open wireless networks. However, it isn't enough to deter the sophisticated service and data thief. For that you need encryption, which is discussed in the last section of this chapter.

Adding Access Points to a Wired Network

It's relatively simple to add a wireless access point (or two, or three, ...) to a wired network:

♦ If you purchase a router with a built-in access point, just add the router to your network. The access point automatically becomes part of the network.

♦ If you purchase a stand-alone access point, be sure that it has an Ethernet port. Then, use a short Cat 5 or better patch cable to connect the AP to a port on an Ethernet switch. Each AP you add to the network will consume one port on a switch.

You do, however, need to pay some attention to where you place your access points. Wi-Fi signals do travel through wood quite well, but not as well through metal and concrete. Floors tend to present more of a barrier than walls. Therefore, you want to place APs fairly high where they are least likely to encounter barriers in the transmission path. (Line-of-sight is optimal but does defeat the purpose of allowing equipment to move from place to place in the office!)

If you have office space that is broken up with cubicle partitions, try to place the APs above the level of the cubicle walls. Although Wi-Fi signals will certainly go through cubicle walls, with too many walls the signal strength will attenuate to such a point that it is unusable.

Wireless Security Issues

We've talked a bit about the problems with a wide-open wireless network: If an AP broadcasts its SSID, then anyone with a wireless-equipped device can piggyback off your network, stealing your Internet service and perhaps intercepting packets traveling on your network. The simplest protection is to turn off the broadcast of the SSID and to change the SSID from the AP's default value. Neither of these actions, however, will prevent a knowledgeable hacker from picking up network packets as they travel through the air.

It's unfortunate, but we have to operate our wireless networks under the assumption that someone is intercepting network traffic and looking inside our packets to steal confidential information. The first line of defense against such actions is *encryption*, changing the payload of the packets so that the payloads are unintelligible to unauthorized users.

Encryption schemes today are key based. Using one or two keys (depending on the type of encryption), an encryption scheme uses secret values to change the data field of a message; the recipient of the message must also have a key to change the data field back to its original, unencrypted form. Some keys can be cracked with an appliction of high-end desktop computing power. The strength of a key generally depends on how long it is and the complexity of the method used to transform the data based on the key. The longer the key, the better; the more complex the method, the better.

WEP

The 802.11b standard includes a type of encryption known as *Wired Equivalency Privacy* (WEP), and most access points do support it. Sound good? Uh uh.

WEP uses an encryption method called RC4. By encrypting the message payload, it ensures message privacy; by adding what is known as a *checksum*, it ensures message integrity. There is nothing intrinsically wrong with the RC4 algorithm, but WEP uses it poorly. As a result, WEP has some significant weaknesses:

♦ The RC4 algorithm relies on a secret cryptographic key. However, in many cases all wireless access points and clients use the same key.

♦ The default cryptographic key used by WEP is only 40 bits long and rarely changes. WEP also uses a 24-bit *initialization vector (IV)*, which changes every transmission. Even if a network changes the IV for each conversation, a moderately busy network will end up recycling and reusing IVs about every five hours. Whenever keys are reused (or not changed, in the case of the encryption key), a system cracker has the opportunity to collect multiple packets using the same key, making extracting the message content from the packet much easier.

♦ WEP encrypts only data. It doesn't encrypt the initialization of a connection, including client authorization information. The IV is also sent in the clear with every packet. (Many encryption sessions must start with an IV in the clear, but not all send it with every packet!)

♦ Access points ship with WEP turned off. Network administrators need to turn it on to get any benefit at all. (You can argue whether this is the manufacturer's fault or WEP's fault, but nonetheless, you have to turn it on.)

♦ WEP can be difficult to configure because the key must be entered identically into every system. Therefore, many users don't bother to turn it on.

Note: As mentioned earlier, WEP uses an encryption key that may be used by multiple clients and that doesn't change frequently. Here is how it works: The key and the IV are used as input to the RC4 algorithm to generate a pseudorandom stream, which is used as the key stream for the stream (Vernam) cypher for the data. The problem is that the same input to the RC4 algorithm produces the same Vernam cypher key stream. Therefore, as the IVs are reused and combined with the unchanging encryption key, all a cracker needs to do is obtain an unencrypted message and its encrypted version. It isn't too hard to deduce the key stream and then use it to decrypt all messages using the same IV. Even without an unencrypted message, a cracker can perform a logical XOR operation on two messages encrypted with the same IV to produce a weakly encrypted message that is easier to crack.

All this being said, WEP is better than nothing! If your access point provides no other security measures, at least turn on WEP, using your router or AP's management facilities. For example, you can see the setup of WEP using a 128-bit key in Figure 7-3. You enter a passphrase—something longer and more difficult to guess than "test"—and tell the router/AP to generate the keys. Each device that joins the network will need to supply the passphrase, as well as knowing the SSID of the AP (assuming that you have turned off the broadcast).

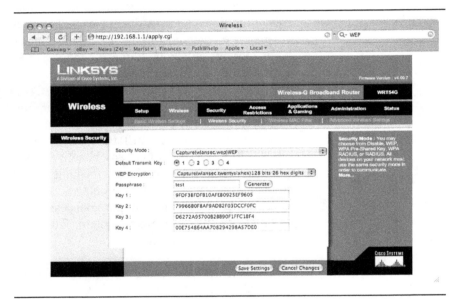

Figure 7-3:   Setting up WEP

WiFi Protected Access

The 802.11i standard is not a physical layer standard, such as a, b, and g, but instead was designed to provide security for existing wireless technologies. However, because it took so long to develop 802.11i, an alternative security solution, which is compatible with 802.11i—*WiFi Protected Access* (WPA)—also emerged.

WPA replaces WEP with stronger encryption, including a 48-bit IV. It also can operate in two modes. The first requires preshared keys—such as passwords—between an access point and a client. The second mode allows the use of external authentication services, such as RADIUS.

WPA's encryption uses the *Temporal Key Integrity Protocol* (TKIP) and is support by most current APs. (See Figure 7-4.) Its major provisions include a method for changing the encryption key with each packet sent during a communications session, making it much more difficult for a system cracker to decipher a message, even if he or she should intercept all packets from a single session.

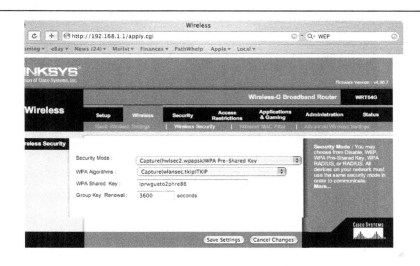

Figure 7-4:   Setting up WPA

WPA includes secure user authentication, something missing from WEP. As noted earlier, the WPA provisions allow access points to use a authentication server (for example, RADIUS) and also allow clients to authenticate access points. This can significantly reduce the chances that clients will connect to an unauthorized access point that has been inserted into a wireless network. If a network is too small to support an external authorization server, then WPA operates in its preshared key mode.

802.11i on Top of WPA

802.11i includes the WPA encryption methods, but in addition provides *Robust Security Network* (RSN), a procedure that allows access points and clients to determine which type of encryption will be used during a communications session. The beauty of this approach is that encryption methods can be updated as new algorithms are developed.

802.11i also mandates the use of *Advanced Encryption Standard* (AES) to provide even stronger encryption. Unfortunately, AES can't be added to existing access points with simply a software upgrade, as can WPA; it requires changes to the hardware, although most wireless equipment manufactured after 2002 is compatible with 802.11i, as in Figure 7-5.

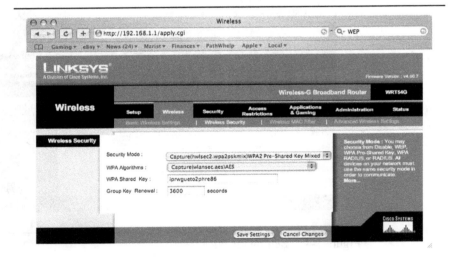

Figure 7-5:   Configuring WPA2 (802.11i) security using AES

Note: The U.S. government has endorsed AES as its primary encryption method, replacing the original Data Encryption Standard (DES).

Note: 802.11i is known familiarly as WPA2.

Part Three

Making the Network Work

As you read in the preface, it's not enough to simply put hardware in place. You need software on top of it. In particular, you need to be concerned with what you are going to share over the network, how you are going to secure the content of the network, and how you are going to manage both the hardware and software. This part of the book looks at a variety of tools for doing just that.

8

Network Servers: Files, the Web, and Printers

One of the most basic uses of computer networks is the sharing of printers and files. You can place applications used by multiple users in a central location. When the applications change, you need to update them only once. Not storing the applications on end-user machines saves hard drive space. You can also store document files that are needed by multiple users in a single repository. This repository for files—applications and documents—is commonly known as a *file server*.

Many printers today are designed to be shared over a network, either with small stand-alone devices known as *print servers* or by attaching them to netework server computers, which then act as the print servers.

In this chapter we will look at network servers—what they can do for you and how their operating systems differ from desktop operating systems—and at print serving. We'll also look at alternatives for Web hosting (should you or shouldn't you?).

Client-Server versus Peer-to-Peer File Sharing

For sharing files over most small networks, there are two architectures: client-server and peer-to-peer. A client-server architecture tends to be a permanent setup, while peer-to-peer sharing tends to be generally ad hoc.

In a true client-server environment, the processing is split between a client machine and a server machine. The client sends a data processing request to the server, which handles most of the data manipulation. The server then sends the unformatted results back to the client, which handles the formatting and display for the end user. The benefit of such an arrangement is that the server, which tends to be a more powerful computer, handles the more demanding data manipulation tasks. However, the server doesn't need to waste time formatting the results for output. In addition, the raw results typically require less network bandwidth than data that have been formatted for display using a GUI. Therefore, a client-server arrangement minimizes network usage and also makes efficient use of high-end server resources.

Most of the database access we perform today uses the client-server model. An application or query language utility runs on the client machine. The user issues a data manipulation request (retrieval or modification) that usually is translated into SQL (Structured Query Language, the most widely used query language for a database). The SQL then travels to the database server across a network. The server is running the database management system (DBMS) software and typically also stores the database files. The DBMS accepts the SQL, processes the query, and prepares an unformatted result (the result of a query, a message indicating that a modification has been performed, or an error message), and sends it back over the network to the client. The client software then formats the result for the end user to see. Except in cases where the data include images or other multimedia content, the network traffic involves only plain text.

The client-server architecture can also be extended to simple file sharing. The file server holds files and applications that need to be shared by various users on the network. Users are given accounts on the server and can then mount server volumes to which they have access as if the server volumes were local disks.

In contrast to client-server configurations, peer-to-peer file sharing does not use a permanent file respository. It is designed to allow individual end users to share files on an ad hoc basis. A desktop user gives permission to one or more users on the network to access something on his or her computer. The second user can then access the files to which he or she has been given access.

Uncontrolled peer-to-peer file sharing can be a significant security problem. First, many end users don't have the knowledge necessary to restrict access to just the files they intend to share; they inadvertently open up too much of their computer to the network (and perhaps to the Internet). Second, peer-to-peer file sharing can be used illegally, especially to copy copyrighted music and movies. Not only does such file sharing consume massive amounts of network bandwidth, but it can open up the owner of the network to legal prosecution for allowing such activity to occur. Depending on your network and users, prohibiting peer-to-peer file sharing may be a valid choice. As an alternative, you can provide a "drop box" folder on a file server where users can place files without an account for other internal network users to pick up.

Server Operating Systems

Regardless of whether it is going to act simply as a repository for shared files or host an application such as a DBSM, a file server is generally the fastest, most powerful computer on the network. Because it handles a higher volume of network traffic than most other computers, it also should be on the fastest network segment. Today that means that servers should be connected by gigabit Ethernet (over either UTP wire or fiber optic cabling).

File Server Services

A file server is more than just a piece of hardware. It includes software that supports file sharing and, in particular, handles access restrictions to the contents of the machine's hard drives. The services you should expect from your file server include the following:

♦ Maintaining user accounts and passwords to provide some level of security for the network

- ◆ File management on the server
- ◆ Scheduling of programs and services to be run at regular intervals
- ◆ Printing
- ◆ File locking and synchronization
- ◆ Accounting

Widely Used Server Operating Systems

To provide the features mentioned in the preceding section, a file server needs an operating system that is somewhat different from from a desktop operating system. Such software is sold separately from desktop OSs and is usually priced based on the number of concurrent users it will allow.

> *Note: What we're calling a "server operating system" was once known as a "network operating system." That term is a bit oudated because even OSs that are designed for a single-user machine, such as Windows Vista, have a significant network support component.*

You can choose an SOS based on Windows, Linux, or Mac OS X. You might also want to consider Novell Netware, a third-party server operating system. Each can support users from the other OSs, so your choice will probably be based on price, features, and comfort level with a given platform.

Novell NetWare

Novell NetWare was the first widely used network operating system. Early releases made it possible to network computers that ran MS-DOS, a single-user operating system that had absolutely no native networking capabilities.

Versions 3.x and 4.x, which are still widely used, rely on the proprietary Novell NetWare protocol stack. However, NetWare 5—the version released about the time this book was written—has taken a different approach. Novell recognized the overwhelming acceptance of TCP/IP and has switched its primary protocol support to the Internet protocols. However, NetWare 5 still provides support for the Novell protocol stack to ensure backward compatibility with existing installations.

As with any NOS, NetWare requires two types of software: server software installed on all servers on the network, and client software installed on all workstations.

Network Management and Server Software

Like all server operating systems, NetWare provides software to manage servers and to manage the overall network. The network as a whole appears to a network administrator as a single directory tree. This is the visual component of NetWare Directory Services (NDS), which makes it possible for network administrators to keep track of all resources on the network. The window in the center of Figure 8-1, for example, shows the directories available on a server named NW5_SYS.

In addition to directory services, NetWare's administrative capabilities include creating and maintaining user accounts (including user security), creating and maintaining print servers, and collecting and preparing network-user accounting information. In Figure 8-2, for example, you can see the way in which NetWare 5.0 handles establishing domain name services for groups of users.

NetWare is available from Novell Corporation for Intel-based servers. A Linux version has been ported by Caldera Corporation. In addition, the MARS project is working on a version of all of the free UNIX implementations.

NetWare is known for being particularly strong in its directory services. This portion of the operating system—NDS (Novell Directory Services)—can be purchased separately and used in conjunction with other server operating systems (particularly Windows).

Client Software

Client software is available for Windows, Max OS, and a variety of UNIX computers. All are supported by both the Novell product and the Caldera product. Therefore, NetWare is a good choice for a multiplatform environment.

> *Note: The NetWare client software is shipped as a part of the Windows family of operating systems. Nonetheless, you must purchase the server software if you are going to use Novell NetWare as your network operating system. In addition, many network experts believe that the Windows client implementation is weak; Novell recommends that you use its client software instead.*

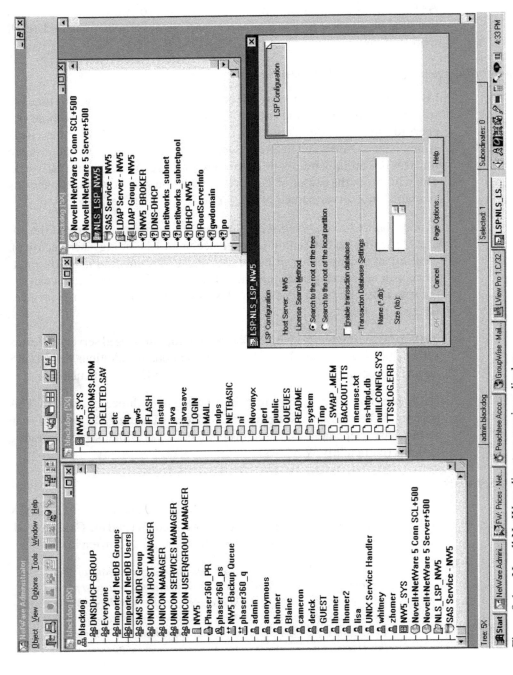

Figure 8-1: Novell NetWare directory services display

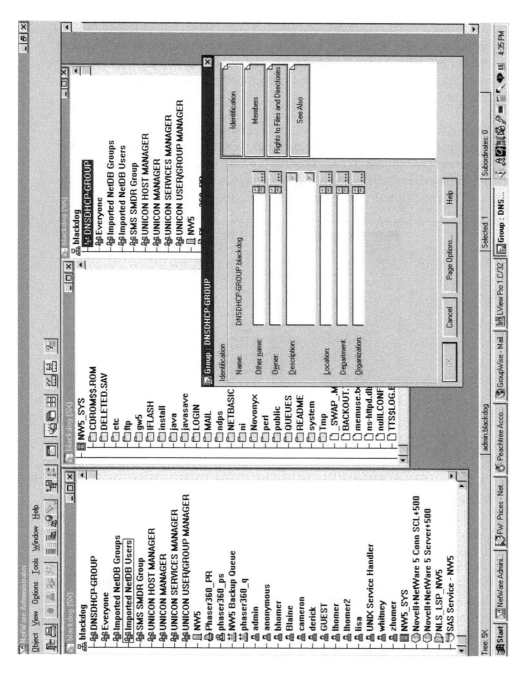

Figure 8-2: Novell NetWare users and groups display

161

Windows

Windows Server is the most widely used server operating system. Windows Server provides management services for servers, desktop computers, and network resources. It can handle clients running Mac OS X and some varieties of UNIX.

One of the primary resource management interfaces is the Active Directory Manager, which provides a hierarchical view of all user resources on the network. In Figure 8-3, for example, a group of users named Research is highlighted on the left side of the window. On the right, the network manager can see all users who are part of that group.

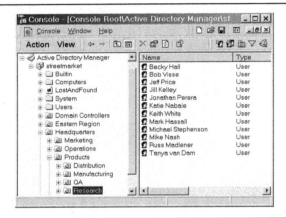

Figure 8-3:   Windows Active Directory Manager

Additional workstation and user management is provided by the Group Policy Editor (Figure 8-4). With this software a network administrator can deploy application software and automate management tasks such as operating system updates, application installation, installing user profiles, and locking down desktop systems to prevent users from changing them.

Hardware management is provided by the Computer Manager (Figure 8-5). The interface is very similar to that used by all Windows operating systems to configure system hardware. The overall intent is for Windows to provide network managers with a familiar GUI to make it easier for them to keep track of the organization of the network.

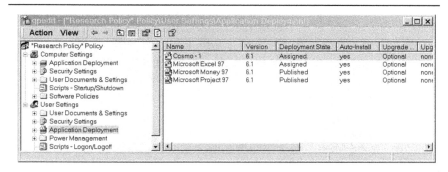

Figure 8-4:   Windows 2000 Group Policy Editor

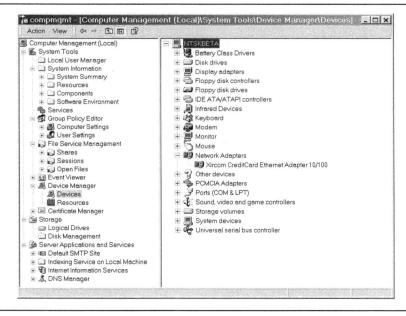

Figure 8-5:   Windows NT 2000 Computer Manager

Like most network computing environments today, Windows has moved toward providing significant support for Internet-based technologies. For example, in addition to supporting typical networked, shared printers, Windows also supports Internet Printing Protocol (IPP), which allows users to print directly to a URL. Other Web-related services include the following:

♦ *Active Server Pages* (ASP): Support for the development of web-based applications

♦ *CPU throttling*: CPU load balancing when multiple Web sites are being hosted on the same server

♦ *Microsoft Internet Information Server* (IIS): Web site hosting

♦ *Secure Socket Layer (SSL) support*: Support for secure Web sites

In addition, Windows Server provides extensive support for streaming audio and video.

UNIX/Linux

From its earliest days, UNIX has included networking capabilities. The TCP/IP protocols provide the basis for e-mail, file sharing, and file transfer. A UNIX server requires no special software to support ftp for file transfer or e-mail, for example.

There are many versions of UNIX. However, Linux is gaining considerable support in corporations, especially since major database vendors (for example, Oracle and IBM) have ported their products to that particular UNIX flavor. (The fact that it's open source and costs less than $100 for a distribution is, of course, another major factor in its popularity!) The remainder of the comments in this section therefore apply to using Linux as a server operating system. If you are working with another version of UNIX, then your particular software might differ.

Like all versions of UNIX, Linux's native networking protocol stack is TCP/IP. However, Linux also supports Service Message Block (SMB), also known as "Samba," to communicate with Windows computers. SMB serves as a replacement for NFS, the traditional UNIX file sharing protocol. Samba is easier to configure than NFS and is generally considered more secure.

The major drawback to using Linux as a file and print server is that setup of users, file sharing privileges, and print sharing is more difficult than with server operating systems that operate through a graphic user interface. Although there are several Linux GUIs, it is rare that you can use them for all server administration tasks. Some will need to be performed at the command line, including the editing to configuration files.

Although configuration of a Linux server may be more difficult than working with GUI-based server operating systems, there are several benefits to making the effort to do the setup.

◆ Linux is freeware. You may pay that small fee for a Linux distribution on CD-ROM, but the source code is available so you can customize your OS.
◆ Linux is cross-platform.
◆ Linux is extremely stable. Once you have the server up and running, crashes are extremely rare.

Maintenancec of a UNIX system typically requires more expertise than maintenance of either a Windows or Mac OS X server, which can be administered almost completely through a GUI. Even with the spread of Linux throughout businesses today, it is still more difficult to find a Linux networking expert than a Windows or Mac expert.

Mac OS X Server

Mac OS X Server is the server version of the desktop operating system that runs on most Macintosh computers today. It provides the typical file server features that you would expect, and can support clients running Windows and many varieties of UNIX. (Keep in mind that Mac OS X itself is a version of UNIX.)

As you can see in Figure 8-6, the services include print serving, directory support, network support (for example, DHCP), application serving, Web serving (via Apache), and e-mail serving. (Active services in Figure 8-6 have the darker radio buttons to their left.)

Because Mac OS X server can handle clients for all three major operating system platforms, it has become increasingly popular as a general-purpose server operating system, especially when bundled with Apple's X-Serve hardware. Like Windows, it has the advantage of a consistent, tightly integrated GUI for managing virtually all server functions.

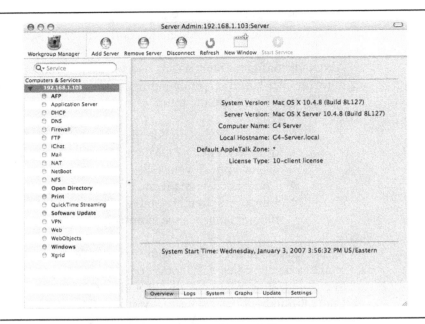

Figure 8-6:   Mac OS X Server services (list on left)

Web Servers

When it comes to setting up a Web server, you have three choices:

- ◆ Hire space on an external hosting service (my favorite choice because it's become so inexpensive and someone else does a lot of the work).
- ◆ Host a stand-alone Web server in-house.
- ◆ Allow personal Web sharing

The first two solutions are suitable for business Web sites. The third is really only suitable for small, personal Web sites, something you may not want to allow because they present significant security problems and are very difficult to manage.

Should you choose to host your Web site on your ISP's computers (or on some other remote commercial site), your responsibility—at most—lies in developing the Web content and uploading it to your site. You have little security vulnerability because there should be no Web traffic coming into your network. You also avoid associated hardware and software costs.

If you are determined to host your own Web site (and if you think I'm trying to discourage you from doing this, you're right!), then you will need the following:

- ◆ A static IP address for the Web server. This will almost certainly add to your Internet connectivity costs.
- ◆ A stand-alone machine to act as the Web server. In most cases, this will engender a single, up-front cost.
- ◆ Web server software. You can run Apache, which is shareware and runs more than half the world's Web servers. It's free and very stable. Anything else, such as Microsoft's IIS, costs money.
- ◆ An additional firewall to isolate the Web server from the internal network in what is known as a DMZ.
- ◆ Someone to design and develop the Web site.
- ◆ Someone to monitor and maintain the Web site. (This is not trivial, because Web sites, with their static IP addresses, are favorite targets for hackers.)

Personal Web sharing lets individual users set up a Web site on their desktop machines by opening up the software port for a Web server (for example, Apache) and placing documents for the Web site in a prespecified folder. This is fine if access to the personal Web site is going to be limited to your internal network. However, if the workstation has a static IP address, then the personal Web site can be opened up to the Internet, and then your internal network is open to serious security vulnerabilities. Given that there are other ways to share files interanlly, there is really no reason for an individual user to be running his or her own Web site. In my opinion, you shouldn't allow personal Web sharing at all.

Print Serving

Besides sharing an Internet connection, one of the most common uses of networking is to share printers. Most printers can be shared, even if they don't have built-in network connectivity. However, *print servers* (hardware to handle printer sharing over a network) are relatively inexpensive devices and many low-end workgroup printers come equipped with them.

Shared Printer Architectures

There is more than one way to connect a printer to a network:

- ◆ Connect a printer to a desktop computer and share that computer with other users.
- ◆ Connect a printer to a server and use that computer as a print sever.
- ◆ Connect a printer to the network, perhaps with a stand-alone print server as an intermediary.

Why do you need a print server? Because a printer is much slower than the network. Users can send print jobs to the printer much faster than the printer can print them. The solution to traffic jams on the way to the printer is *print spooling*, a technique in which the print server places copies of the print jobs on disk in a waiting area, known as a *print queue*. A print server is software, running either on a computer or on a small, stand-alone device, that manages the print queue. It takes care of adding jobs to the queue, sending them to the printer as the printer becomes available, and providing an interface for a system administrator to manage the queue.

The last printing option—a stand-alone print server—is the easiest to install and maintain. The printer server, which is usually no bigger than an eight-port unmanaged switch, attaches between the printer and the network. You then configure each workstation that will use the network-attached printer. (Windows machines typically need to have a printer driver installed before searching the network for the printer; Mac OS X machines usually won't need a driver but will still need to search the network to recognize and add the printer.)

The print-server has enough intelligence to accept print jobs from across the network. It requires no maintenance.

Occasional Printer Sharing

If you have printer that needs to be shared infrequently, then you may want to attach that printer to a workstation and share that printer through the workstation, rather than through a print server. To make it happen, the owner of the workstation has to turn on the printer sharing service.

Note: Every time you turn on an operating system service, you open a hole that a malicious hacker can sneak through. Although printer sharing through a workstation may be convenient, it may also be dangerous. Consider carefully whether you want to allow it because of the security exposure.

Windows

By default, current versions of Windows turn off printer sharing as a security measure. (It disables all remote access to a computer.) This means that you must first use the Network Setup Wizard to allow remote access before you can actually share the printer.

To allow other computers to share a workstation-attached printer:

1. Launch the Network Setup Wizard.
2. Continue to click the Next button until you reach the panel in Figure 8-7.
3. Complete the Network Setup Wizard, save the settings, and then restart the computer.

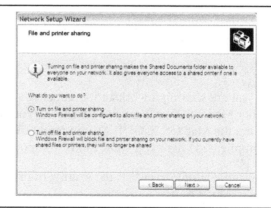

Figure 8-7:   Turning on Windows printer sharing

At this point you are ready to allow other users access to any printer connected to the computer:

1. Open the Control Panel.
2. Open Printers and Faxes.

3. Select the icon for the printer you want to share.
4. Click Share This Printer in the Printers task pane. The printer's property sheet opens, typically with the Sharing tab selected.
5. Click the Share This Printer radio button (Figure 8-8)
6. Click the OK button, and you're finished.

Figure 8-8:   Sharing a specific printer

Mac OS X

If you are sharing a workstation-attached printer running Mac OS X with other Mac OS X or Windows machines, you can perform the configuration using the Mac OS X GUI. As you might expect, things become a bit more complicated when you want Linux computers to share the printer.

It is quite simple to enable the sharing of printers from a single workstation using Mac OS X:

1. Open System Preferences.
2. Open the Sharing preferences panel.
3. If necessary, click the Services button.
4. Place a check in Printer Sharing. (See Figure 8-9.)
5. Click the Start button and you're done.

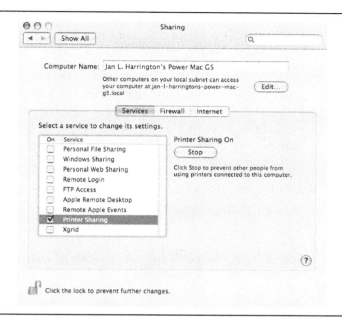

Figure 8-9:   Enabling Mac OS X printer sharing

The difference between this process and that for Windows is that you can't enable printer sharing for specific printers. It's an all-or-nothing service.

Linux

In the overall scheme of things, setting up a Windows or Mac OS X machine to share its attached printer over a network is fairly trivial. Linux, however, is a whole different situation. First, there are two major UNIX printer daemons—CUPS (Common UNIX Printing System) and *lpd*—either or both of which may be in use. Second, Linux's support for multiple GUIs means that there is no single user interface for doing the configuration; in fact, in some implementations you are probably better off working from the command line.

When you install Linux, the installer will take you through setting up any attached printers and will start the print queue for you. So far, so fairly easy. The trick at this point is to determine which printer daemon you are using and then to enable other machines on the network to see the appropriate print queues. It takes a different technique and different software for each OS to access the Linux machine's printer.

Linux-to-Linux Sharing

Assuming that your Linux machine is using CUPS, then you will need to instruct CUPS to broadcast the existence of the print queues across the network. (This is turned off by default on some Linux configurations.) You must also specify which IP addresses are allowed to browse your machine for print queues.

All of this configuration information can be found in */etc/cups/cupsd.conf*, excerpts from which can be found in Figure 8-10.

```
#
# Browsing: whether or not to broadcast and/or listen for CUPS printer
# information on the network.
#

Browsing On
.
.
.
#
# BrowseAllow: specifies an address mask to allow for incoming browser
# packets. The default is to allow packets from all addresses.
#
# BrowseDeny: specifies an address mask to deny for incoming browser
# packets. The default is to deny packets from no addresses.
#

BrowseAllow 127.0.0.1
BrowseAllow @LOCAL
BrowseDeny All
```

Figure 8-10:   Excerpts from the CUPS configuration file

If you are using *lpd*, you don't have to do anything special to configure a machine to share its directly connected printer. Just make sure that the *print-cap* file and *lpd* daemon are configured to print to the printer. You do, however, need to configure each machine that will be using the printer remotely:

1. Edit the file */etc/printcap*.
   a. Place a # at the left of each line of the *lp* entry to comment out the default values.
   b. Add a new line to identify the machine to which the printer is attached (*remotePrinter*):

      lp:rm=remotePrinter
2. Turn on the printer daemon:

   /usr/sbin/lpd

Sharing a Linux-Attached Printer with Windows and Mac OS X

Linux shares files and print resources with Windows and Mac OS X machines using SMB (Server Message Block, or Samba), an open source product. To enable printer sharing, you must first install and configure Samba. Assuming that it is present on your Linux machine, then you can proceed as directed in the rest of this section.

> *Note: If your Linux distribution doesn't include Samba, you can get it at http://us2.samba.org/samba/. You can also get the latest releases through this Web site.*

You can either create an account on your Linux machine for each user who should have access to the shared printer or set up a special account for anonymous printer access. To do the latter, use the following command to create the anonymous user:

/usr/sbin/adduser --system --disabled-password guestprinter

The result is a new account named *guestprinter*. (Well, the user doesn't have to be called *guestprinter*; the exact name is unimportant.) This user's home directory (*/home/guestprinter*, in this example) needs enough space for spool files. Also pay attention to security settings, restricting the access that the anonymous printing account has to other files and directories on the system.

The next step is to enable the printer driver to use the new account. For this example, we'll assume that you are using the CUPS driver. In that case, you would edit */etc/samba/smb.conf* (the Samba configuration file) so that it appears as follows:

[global]
    printcap name = cups
    printing = cups
    security = share
[printers]
    browseable = yes
    printable = yes
    public = yes
    create mode = 0700
    guest only = yes
    use client driver = yes
    guest account = guestprinter
    path = /home/guestprinter

Finish the process by restarting Samba with

/etc/init.d/samba restart

Printing through a Server

If the printer you want to share doesn't have a network interface (for example, it connects through USB only) or you don't have a stand-alone print server for a network-ready printer, then you can use just about any computer as a printer server. You can connect the printer to your file server, or even use an older, slower PC as a print server. You then need to set up a print queue and make it available to the network. Exactly how you do it, of course, depends on the operating system.

Windows

Setting up a print queue for sharing from a Windows server is a two-part operation. First, you configure the printer and then you share it. To set up the print queue:

1. Add the printer to the server as if you were adding a printer just for local use. This establishes a print queue on the local machine.

Note: Exactly what you see and the location of various commands varies among Windows versions. However, the procedures are essentially the same from Windows 2000 forward.

2. Locate the icon for the print queue (usually in Printers and Faxes).
3. Highlight the print queue that you want to share and choose "Share this printer" from the list of printer tasks The print queue's properties sheet appears with the Sharing tab visible (for example, Figure 8-11).
4. Give the print queue a name that network users can use to reference the printer.
5. Choose the "Share this printer" radio button and click the Apply button.

Figure 8-11:   Sharing a Windows print queue

Mac OS X

To set up a Mac OS X print queue, use the Server Admin application:

1. Choose the server in the list of servers so that the list of server services appears.
2. Click Print.
3. Click the Queues button at the bottom of the panel. Then click the + button to add a new print queue. System Admin shows a list of the printers it can find on the network (Figure 8-12).
4. Highlight the printer and click OK.
5. Click the Settings button at the bottom of the panel. Indicate the protocols that will be used by the shared printer (Figure 8-13) along with any other necessary settings. The print queue is now ready to use.

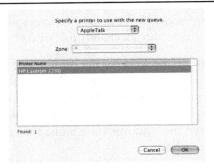

Figure 8-12:   Choosing a printer for a print queue

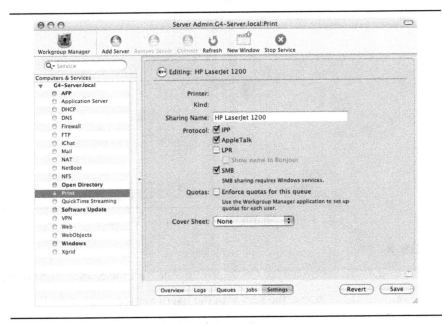

Figure 8-13:   Configuring the Mac OS X print queue

Linux

The process described earlier in this chapter for making a Linux-connected printer available to a network is the same as that used to set up a print server. In other words, when you configure a client machine to access a printer connected to a Linux computer, you automatically turn the machine to which the printer is connected into a print server.

9

Network Maintenance, Monitoring, and Control

Once you have your network up and running, you will probably want to monitor the traffic patterns on that network. Such monitoring can, for example, help you identify network segments that are under- or overloaded. With that information in hand, you may decide to reconfigure the network to balance the traffic more. Network monitoring can also help you find problems, including network devices that have gone down or are no longer accessible.

Network monitoring (often referred to as "network management") can be performed with any of a wide range of software packages. In this chapter you will be introduced to a sampling of those packages and the capabilities they provide.

> *Note: True network management is a lot more than simply collecting network traffic statistics and monitoring performance.*

It involves troubleshooting, user support, upgrade planning, performance tuning, and so on. Therefore, although much of this software is marketed as "network management" software, it is management at the hands-on day-to-day-operations level, rather than at the planning/strategic level.

Network monitoring software can also be used for *network discovery,* a process through which software traverses the network to discover its layout. This is of particular use when you inherit the management of a network that has grown without planning and you do not really know what devices are connected or how the network is configured. (It can also be very useful for finding things such as unauthorized wireless access points!) As you will see, some of the products discussed in this chapter can also be used for that purpose.

Note: Many of the screen shots in this chapter were taken from demonstration software provided free by the software developers. Typically, a demo version is fully functional but limited either in the amount of time for which it will work (for example, 30 days) or in the number of times you can launch the program. Most of these demos can be downloaded from the companies' Web sites, making it easy for you to test these packages before you decide which one you want to purchase. See Appendix B for contact information.

Command-Line Tools

The second section of this chapter will show you examples of full-featured, GUI-based network management tools. However, if you can't (or don't want to) use such software, you can use many of the individual tools that are part of your operating system to do some network monitoring and discovery from the command line. There are a number of such utilities, so we'll just touch on some of the more useful.

Note: All of the utilities discussed in this section can be used by hackers in attempts to crack your network. Although all have legitimate network management uses, you need to monitor their usage closely to prevent misuse.

netstat

The *netstat* utility is one of the most powerful programs in the command-line network arsenal. It provides a wealth of information about transport layer networking that can be used to discover and diagnose network problems. Because *netstat* is a UNIX utility, Linux and Mac OS X support full implementations; what you find in current versions of Windows works similarly but is somewhat limited in the options it supports. (Most of the omitted options are those that are less frequently used, so their omissions should have little impact on the majority of Windows users.)

When you issue the *netstat* command with a *-a* option, the output shows you all current active TCP connections along with the TCP and UDP ports on which the computer is listening. A sample of the first portion of the command's output appears in Figure 9-1. The IP address of the computer that produced the output was 192.168.1.102; the term *localhost* also refers to the computer producing the output. The ports on which the computer is listening are indicated by the syntax *IP address.port_number*. Therefore, 192.168.1.102.56695 refers to port 56695, which happens to be AOL Instant Messenger. The major use of this version of the command is to help you secure network devices to make certain that there are no unncessary open ports.

> Note: You'll find more about securing ports in Chapter 10, where we discuss network security.

The *netstat -s* command groups networking statistics by protocol. A portion of that output can be found in Figure 9-2. Notice that you can use this output to determine how many packets each protocol has sent and received since the machine was booted. Packets sent but not received, for example, is a good indication that the computer has lost contact with the network in some way.

Earlier in this book we discussed the routing tables that routers use to make routing decisions. Computers also maintain routing tables that are of most use if the machine has more than one network interface. You can use *netstat -r* to see the contents of a machine's routing table, producing output like that in Figure 9-3. The first section refers to IPv4 routing; the second covers IPv6.

```
Active Internet connections (including servers)
Proto Recv-Q Send-Q  Local Address            Foreign Address             (state)
tcp4       0      0  192.168.1.102.56695      64.12.25.105.aol            ESTABLISHED
tcp4       7      0  192.168.1.102.61057      game1.pogo.com.jabber-      CLOSE_WAIT
tcp4       0      0  *.lansurveyor            *.*                         LISTEN
tcp4       0      0  *.3971                   *.*                         LISTEN
tcp4       0      0  *.3831                   *.*                         LISTEN
tcp4       0      0  localhost.ipp            *.*                         LISTEN
tcp4       0      0  *.3793                   *.*                         LISTEN
tcp4       0      0  *.*                      *.*                         CLOSED
tcp4       0      0  *.*                      *.*                         CLOSED
tcp4       0      0  *.*                      *.*                         CLOSED
tcp4       0      0  192.168.1.102.commplex   *.*                         LISTEN
tcp4       0      0  *.*                      *.*                         CLOSED
tcp4       0      0  localhost.netinfo-loca   localhost.1017              ESTABLISHED
tcp4       0      0  localhost.1017           localhost.netinfo-loca      ESTABLISHED
tcp4       0      0  localhost.netinfo-loca   localhost.1019              ESTABLISHED
tcp4       0      0  localhost.1019           localhost.netinfo-loca      ESTABLISHED
tcp4       0      0  localhost.netinfo-loca   *.*                         LISTEN
udp4       0      0  *.*                      *.*
udp4       0      0  *.lansurveyor            *.*
udp4       0      0  *.snmptrap               *.*
udp4       0      0  *.itose                  *.*
udp4       0      0  *.49153                  *.*
udp4       0      0  *.4401                   *.*
udp4       0      0  *.49152                  *.*
udp4       0      0  *.59902                  *.*
udp4       0      0  *.ipp                    *.*
udp4       0      0  *.rockwell-csp2          *.*
udp4       0      0  *.*                      *.*
udp4       0      0  *.*                      *.*
udp4       0      0  192.168.1.102.49159      *.*
udp4       0      0  *.mdns                   *.*
udp4       0      0  localhost.49158          localhost.1022
udp4       0      0  localhost.49157          localhost.1022
udp4       0      0  localhost.1022           *.*
udp4       0      0  192.168.1.102.ntp        *.*
udp4       0      0  localhost.ntp            *.*
udp4       0      0  *.ntp                    *.*
udp4       0      0  localhost.49155          localhost.1023
udp4       0      0  localhost.1023           *.*
udp6       0      0  *.5353                   *.*
udp4       0      0  *.mdns                   *.*
udp4       0      0  localhost.netinfo-loca   *.*
icm4       0      0  *.*                      *.*
icm6       0      0  *.*                      *.*
```

Figure 9-1:   Partial output of *netstat -a*

```
tcp:
        690856 packets sent
                223201 data packets (27117554 bytes)
                302 data packets (116284 bytes) retransmitted
                0 resends initiated by MTU discovery
                332889 ack-only packets (9924 delayed)
                0 URG only packets
                1 window probe packet
                90622 window update packets
                43843 control packets
        755709 packets received
                255375 acks (for 26873622 bytes)
                19881 duplicate acks
                0 acks for unsent data
                468231 packets (335900663 bytes) received in-sequence
                3942 completely duplicate packets (2649393 bytes)
                20 old duplicate packets
                71 packets with some dup. data (50863 bytes duped)
                40966 out-of-order packets (40811051 bytes)
                34 packets (48219 bytes) of data after window
                0 window probes
                309 window update packets
                139 packets received after close
                1 discarded for bad checksum
                0 discarded for bad header offset fields
                0 discarded because packet too short
        22065 connection requests
        73 connection accepts
        0 bad connection attempts 0 listen queue overflows
        22107 connections established (including accepts)
        37541 connections closed (including 8546 drops)
                272 connections updated cached RTT on close
                272 connections updated cached RTT variance on close
                36 connections updated cached ssthresh on close
        13 embryonic connections dropped
        254629 segments updated rtt (of 255172 attempts)
        559 retransmit timeouts 20 connections dropped by rexmit timeout
        1 persist timeout 0 connections dropped by persist timeout
        117 keepalive timeouts
                0 keepalive probes sent 4 connections dropped by keepalive
        139673 correct ACK header predictions
        428274 correct data packet header predictions
        4 SACK recovery episodes
        0 segment rexmits in SACK recovery episodes
        0 byte rexmits in SACK recovery episodes
        14 SACK options (SACK blocks) received
        11216 SACK options (SACK blocks) sent
        0 SACK scoreboard overflow
```

Figure 9-2:   Partial output of *netstat -s*

```
Routing tables

Internet:
Destination          Gateway              Flags    Refs      Use   Netif Expire
default              192.168.1.1          UGSc     34          8   en0
127                  localhost            UCS       0          0   lo0
localhost            localhost            UH       12     284478   lo0
169.254              link#4               UCS       0          0   en0
192.168.1            link#4               UCS       1          0   en0
192.168.1.1          0:14:bf:5:b:84       UHLW     30          0   en0   1196
192.168.1.102        localhost            UHS       0          1   lo0

Internet6:
Destination          Gateway              Flags    Netif Expire
localhost            localhost            UH       lo0
                     localhost            Uc       lo0
localhost            link#1               UHL      lo0
                     link#4               UC       en0
jan-1-harringtons-   0:14:51:64:83:3f     UHL      lo0
ff01::               localhost            U        lo0
ff02::%lo0           localhost            UC       lo0
ff02::%en0           link#4               UC       en0
```

Figure 9-3:   Output of *netstat -r*

> *Note: For the complete nestat UNIX manual page, see*
> *http://man-wiki.net/index.php/8:netstat.*

ping

You use the *ping* commnad to determine whether a machine is responsive at a specific IP address. Each *ping* sends a packet to the target system and requests a response. For example, if you type *ping 192.168.1.1*, Windows will send four packets to IP address 192.168.1.1; UNIX systems continue to send packets until you stop the command with CTRL-Z.

> *Note: You can control the number of packets sent by adding the*
> *-n option with Windows or the -c option with UNIX. Follow the*
> *option by the number of times you want to ping.*

Sample output appears in Figure 9-4. Here, the recipient of the ping was the sender's default router, which sent a response to each received packet, indicating that the router was up and probably operating properly.

```
PING 192.168.1.1 (192.168.1.1): 56 data bytes
64 bytes from 192.168.1.1: icmp_seq=0 ttl=64 time=1.286 ms
64 bytes from 192.168.1.1: icmp_seq=1 ttl=64 time=0.873 ms
64 bytes from 192.168.1.1: icmp_seq=2 ttl=64 time=0.806 ms
64 bytes from 192.168.1.1: icmp_seq=3 ttl=64 time=0.807 ms
64 bytes from 192.168.1.1: icmp_seq=4 ttl=64 time=0.801 ms
64 bytes from 192.168.1.1: icmp_seq=5 ttl=64 time=0.782 ms
64 bytes from 192.168.1.1: icmp_seq=6 ttl=64 time=0.865 ms
64 bytes from 192.168.1.1: icmp_seq=7 ttl=64 time=0.790 ms
64 bytes from 192.168.1.1: icmp_seq=8 ttl=64 time=0.864 ms
64 bytes from 192.168.1.1: icmp_seq=9 ttl=64 time=0.863 ms

--- 192.168.1.1 ping statistics ---
10 packets transmitted, 10 packets received, 0% packet loss
round-trip min/avg/max/stddev = 0.782/0.874/1.286/0.141 ms
```

Figure 9-4:   Output of the *ping* command

Sample GUI-Based Tools

The tools that you read about in the preceding section require a knowledge-able user who can decide which tool is appropriate for a particular use. In addition, each tool must be used manually and its results interpreted manually. You can ease the task considerably, plus provide integrated displays of network information, by investing in a network management tool. This section looks at two examples to give you an idea of what such software can provide.

> *Note: The software discussed in this section was current at the time the book was written. But, like all other net-work things, network management software changes quickly. Please do your own research into software when you are ready to buy; the versions covered here may well have been superseded by newer versions with more fea-tures, and new products may well have appeared on the market.*

Freeware: Spiceworks

There is a lot of free software today, so it seems appropriate to start these examples with a suite of free network discovery and management tools. If you are willing to put up with a bit of advertising and an application that runs on the software developer's server as well as a local machine, you can use Spiceworks to monitor which devices are working properly and keep an inventory of hardware and software on your network.

Spiceworks must run on a Windows computer, but it can detect Windows, Linux, and Mac OS X computers, as well as a range of other devices. To obtain the portion of the Spiceworks application that runs locally, download it from *www.spiceworks.com*. After installing it on your Windows machine, you can instruct it to search for devices on your network. The result is a tally of what Spiceworks found, such as the display in Figure 9-5. Devices that Spiceworks detects but cannot identify can later be reclassified manually. Nonetheless, if Spiceworks doesn't find a device during a nework scan, the device is probably down.

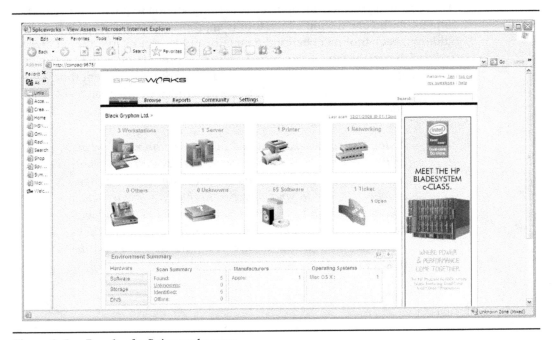

Figure 9-5:   Result of a Spiceworks scan

Note: Spiceworks needs access to an ssh account on UNIX machines (Linux and Mac OS X) to get more than minimal information from the machine. You need to supply a user name and password for each machine as part of the Spiceworks configuration.

A Spiceworks scan detects software as well as hardware. You can therefore also use the program to discover when essential network services have gone down.

Spiceworks is particularly well suited as a network inventory application. Even if a scan doesn't pick up all the information you want to store about a particular network device, the Spiceworks device database is editable, as in Figure 9-6.

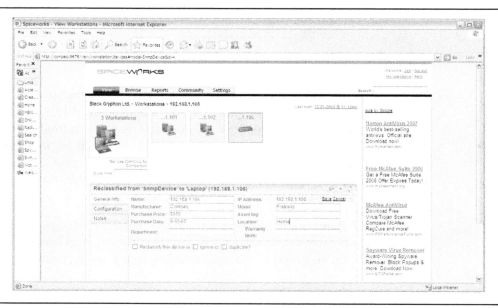

Figure 9-6:   Spiceworks information about a single device

As networks become larger, it can be difficult to remember which devices have which IP addresses, which operating system, which software, and so on. The Spiceworks Browse feature (Figure 9-7) lets you drill down from what information you do know to find a device or group of devices.

Figure 9-7:   Browsing the Spiceworks device database

In a network of more than just a few nodes, it becomes virtually impossible to keep track of the condition of each device manually. Software that can scan your network at predefined intervals and alert you to trouble conditions can save a great deal of time and effort. As you can see in Figure 9-8, Spiceworks supports tracking a variety of network trouble conditions. In addition, Spiceworks can manage network trouble tickets for you, making it easier to track problem resolutions.

There is one major drawback to Spiceworks: It relies on the Spiceworks Web site to operate. If *spiceworks.com* ever becomes unavailable, all the information you've stored in a Spiceworks inventory may be unavailable as well.

For Very Small Networks: Network Magic

Network Magic is a network discovery and management tool designed for the smallest of networks. In my opinion, it would be useful for a small, professional home network that has no more than 20 nodes or that has a traffic load small enough that it doesn't need traffic analysis features.

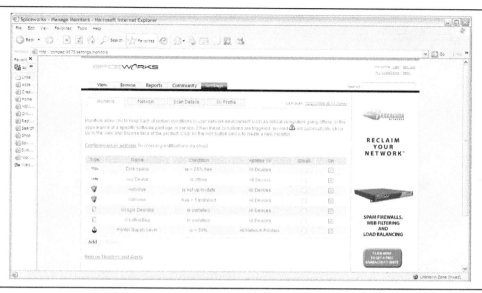

Figure 9-8:   Using Spiceworks to provide network alerts

Note: Network Magic equates network monitoring with recording when devices connect to and disconnect from the network. This is a very narrow, and in a business environment, not necessarily useful, view. Live network monitoring shows levels of traffic in real time and creates reports based on the those reports. However, for a small network, detecting that an intruder has connected to the network may be all you want to do.

Network Magic begins by scanning your network and creating a network map. (See Figure 9-9.) Like most network discovery and management software, it isn't terribly successful when dealing with unmanaged devices (e.g., those not running SNMP). For example, in Figure 9-9 there is an unmanaged Gigabit switch between the router and the rest of the network.

Note: The fact that most software can't pick up the inexpensive devices we typically use for small network innerconnectivity presents a bit of a conundrum: Do we stick with our $50 Gigabit switches that can't be managed remotely, or do we spend $250 for a switch of the same size and speed that includes management capabilities? The larger your network gets, the more you will benefit by being able to include all devices, including switches, in your troubleshooting activities.

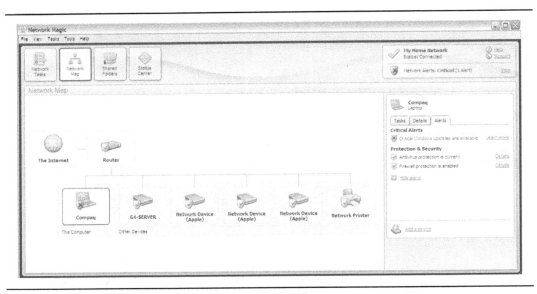

Figure 9-9:   A Network Magic map

In Figure 9-10 you will find the device control window that shows most of Network Magic's features, which include:

♦ Setting up peer-to-peer file sharing
♦ Setting up printer sharing
♦ Direct connection of Windows computers (although the software runs from either Windows or Linux and detects machines running Windows, Linux, and Mac OS X)
♦ Network mapping
♦ Wireless security, inlcuding intruder detection and setting up wireless encryption schemes
♦ Speed test
♦ Remote access over the Internet to internal network shared files
♦ Network sign-on log (time on and off for each user)

Several of these features—file sharing, printer sharing, wireless security, and remote access—are available directly from operating systems. However, Network Magic does make configuration and maintenance much easier.

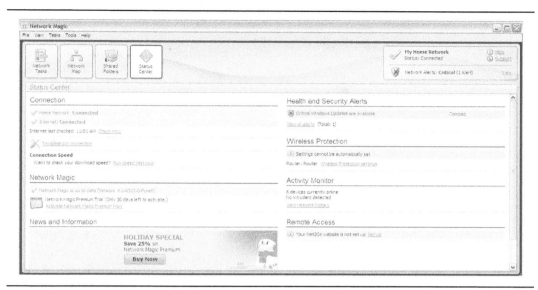

Figure 9-10:   Network Magic features

For Larger Networks: LANsurveyor

LANsurveyor is a commercial networking management and discovery tool. The software, which can run from either a Windows or Mac OS X machine, communicates with devices that run SNMP (SimpleNetwork Management Protocol), using a piece of client software known as a "responder." Once the responder is installed on a device, it can send a great deal of information about itself to the LANsurveyor application. Devices that run SNMP but not the responder (for example, a printer) or devices that don't run SNMP (for example, a switch or router) can still be detected by the software but without gathering as much information as it would if using the responder or SNMP.

The first step in using LANsurveyor is to ask it to generate a map of your network, such as that in Figure 9-11. The software uses *ping* to detect devices running TCP/IP (Figure 9-12).

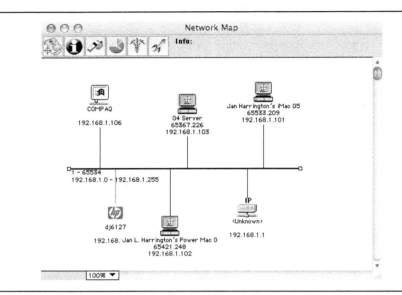

Figure 9-11:   A LANsurveyor network map

The four computers on the map are running the responder software. The printer cannot run the responder, but does include SNMP; the router (IP 192.168.1.1) cannot run the responder and does not run SNMP

Double-clicking a device's icon in the map displays whatever information the device can send. For example, you can see the information returned by a computer running the responder in Figure 9-13. The printer, which runs SNMP and not the responder, is a bit less verbose (Figure 9-14).

What can this map tell you? First, it can identify devices that shouldn't be on your network. In particular, look for devices such as wireless access points, hubs, switches, and routers that weren't installed by your staff. In terms of network security, such interconnection devices tend to be far more important than the occasional unauthorized laptop computer that someone brought in from home. The home laptop can certainly present a security threat, but it's just one machine; however, the interconnection devices can signal the presence of multiple unauthorized devices on the network.

Second, it can alert you to devices that should appear on the map but don't for some reason. A new network map can therefore identify downed nodes.

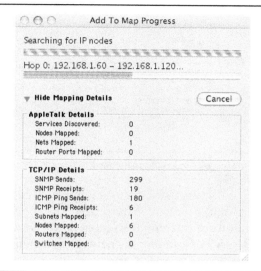

Figure 9-12:   Using *ping* to locate network devices

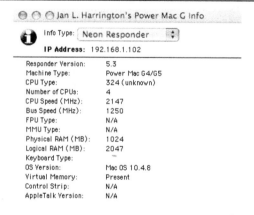

Figure 9-13:   Device information with an active LANsurveyor responder

Once you have a network map, LANsurveyor will let you manage a device
running a responder. From the computer running LANsurveyor, you can
shut down or restart a device, change its password, send files and folders
to the device, kill a process running on the device, run an application on
the device being managed, and so on.

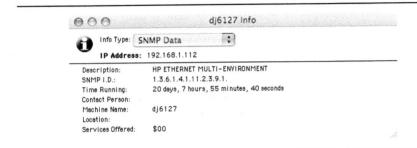

Figure 9-14:   Device information for an SNMP device without a responder

The software also creates a number of reports. Select the network nodes
you want to include in the report. Then you might prepare a report showing
a hardware inventory (essential if you are concerned about asset tracking),
OS services running on network machines (useful for finding machines
running unauthorized or uncontrolled network-accessible software or for
identifying locations where software that should be running isn't), or all
applications running on network machines (also useful for identifying unauthorized software or non-running software).

LANsurveyor will also monitor the IP traffic moving in and out of specific
network devices and poll devices to determine whether a device is responsive. For example, the poll list in Figure 9-15 indicates that three nodes are
up and responding and that a fourth is down.

Node Name	Poll Packets		Poll Time (ticks)			
	Sent	% Miss	Avg.	Last	Min	Max
COMPAQ	3	0.0%	.3	1	0	1
dj6127	3	100.0%	---	---	---	---
Jan Harrington's iMac G5	3	0.0%	.0	0	0	0
Jan L. Harrington's Power Mac G	1	0.0%	.0	0	0	0

Poll rate: 00:01:00   Last poll: 3:51:39 PM   Up: 3   Down: 1

Stop   Setup   Add   Delete   Locate   Reset

Figure 9-15:   A LANsurveyor poll list

Real-Time Monitoring and Packet Sniffing

The products we have used as examples to this point are missing two capabilities that you might want for monitoring your network: the ability to see real-time traffic loads of various network segments and the ability to capture and examine individual frames as they travel over the network. The latter is often known as *frame* or *packet sniffing*.

Real-time traffic monitoring can help you identify bottlenecks in your network as they occur. You may discover that loads on a specific segment are much heavier than you predicted, for example, and that a simple reconfiguring of a switch or two can relieve the congestion. Real-time monitoring can also lets you see security problems in progress, such as a denial-of-service-attack. (More on those in Chapter 10.)

Examining the content of frames means that you need to know the format of the frame you are examining so you know exactly where to look at what a value should be. Such activity can help you identify not only damaged frames, but frames whose address might have been changed by hackers.

Example: LANdecoder32

LANdecoder32 is a real-time network monitoring product that runs on a Windows host but can monitor a wide variety of network protocols and platforms. Its real-time outputs include the following:

♦ Which devices are communicating with each other, including the number of packets exchanged and the error rate during that exchange (Figure 9-16). Such data are useful for identifying high-traffic devices and for troubleshooting areas of the network that are susceptible to high error rates.

♦ The distribution of the size of packets on the network (Figure 9-17). These data are likewise useful for identifying high-traffic devices that, for example, might need be to upgraded from 10BASE-T to 100BASE-T to relieve a performance bottleneck.

♦ The percentage of network bandwidth being used over time (Figure 9-18). With these data, you can identify times of day

LANdecoder32 Monitor - ip [Mon Jun 29 14:40:37 1998]

File Monitor Log Format Settings Window Help

Conversations

Name[A]	Name[B]	Pkts[A»B]	Pkts[A«B]	Errs[A»B]	Errs[A«
Moby	Gateway				
Stingray	Brodcast				
Seahorse	Stingray				
Gateway	Brodcast				
<unknown>	Brodcast				
Moby	<unknown>				
<unknown>	Brodcast				
<unknown>	Todd				
Gateway	<unknown>				
Gateway	Hippo				
Hippo	Brodcast				
<unknown>	Stingray				

Figure 9-16:   LANdecoder conversation display

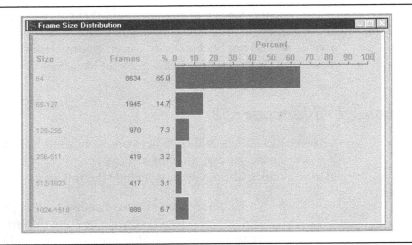

Figure 9-17:   LANdecoder packet size distribution display

when the network is heavily loaded and, if necessary, institute
upgrades or procedures that will help balance peak loads.

♦ An overview of network usage and performance ("vital signs"
in Figure 9-19). The dials represent network utilization, number of frames sent, number of octets (groups of eight bits) sent,
error rate, the amount of bandwidth being used, and the rate of
multicast packets sent.

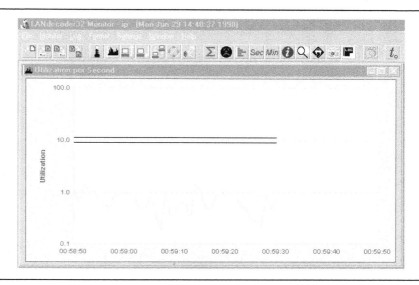

Figure 9-18:   LANdecoder network utilization graph

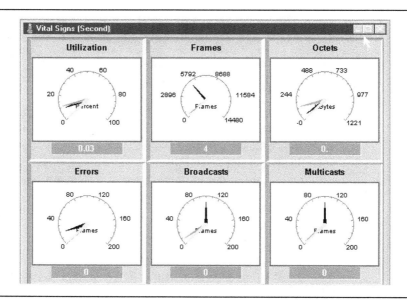

Figure 9-19:   LANdecoder network vital signs display

Remote Control

In addition to monitoring and discovery software, there is yet another class of software that provides multiplatform *remote control*. Such software allows a user on a network (or a user who has dialed into the network over a telephone line) to control or observe another computer in real time. The software also supports file transfer and real-time chatting between users. To enable remote control, both computers must be running the remote control software.

A major use of remote control software is troubleshooting. When a user is having a system problem, a network administrator can observe what the user is doing from his or her workstation, without needing to go to the user's location. The network administrator can also control the remote user's computer to make changes to the system.

A widely used example of remote control software is Timbuktu Pro from Netopia (formerly Farallon). Available for Windows and Macintosh platforms, the software works almost identically from either side. The Windows version supports connections using TCP/IP and IPX; the Macintosh version supports AppleTalk and TCP/IP. Both versions also support connections through a modem connected directly to the computer.

> *Note: If you have a Windows-only network, an alternative to Timbuktu Pro is PC Anywhere.*

To allow other users access to his or her computer, a Timbuktu Pro user first configures remote user permissions. As you can see in Figure 9-20, each remote user can be given a name and password along with user-specific access rights. In this case, the rights are an "all or nothing" affair: Either a remote user can or cannot perform an action.

Making a Connection

Timbuktu Pro is loaded into main memory at system start-up and runs in the background until a user needs it to access a remote computer. Regardless of what a remote user wants to do with a networked computer, he or she must first establish a connection with that machine. For a TCP/IP connection, the

Figure 9-20:   Configuring a Timbuktu Pro user

remote user must know the TCP/IP address of the computer, as in Figure 9-21 (Windows) and Figure 9-22 (Macintosh), or the network name of the computer if your network is running Domain Name Services (DNS). When working with AppleTalk, Timbuktu Pro is also able to provide a list of computers that are also running the software (see Figure 9-23).

Observation and Control

When a remote user is observing or controlling another computer on the network, the screen of the computer to which the remote user is connected appears in a window on the remote user's monitor. For example, in Figure 9-24 you can see a portion of the start-up monitor of a Macintosh appearing in a window on a Windows 95 desktop. You can find the opposite — a Windows 95 monitor in a Macintosh window — in Figure 9-25.

If observing, the remote user sees everything that occurs on the remote screen but has no control over that computer. If controlling, whenever the remote user's mouse pointer is over the remote window, the actions affect the remote computer, allowing the remote user to do anything his or her access rights allow with that remote machine.

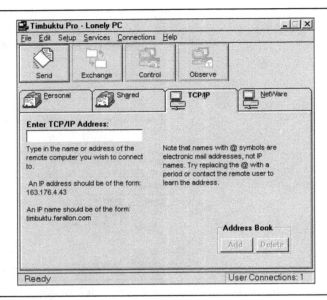

Figure 9-21:   Opening a new TCP/IP connection from a Windows PC

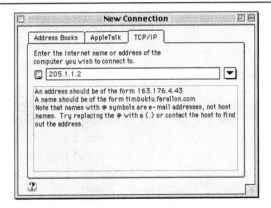

Figure 9-22:   Opening a new TCP/IP connection from a Macintosh

Note: If a Macintosh has multiple monitors, then Tim-buktu Pro shows only the start-up monitor — that is, the one containing the menu bar.

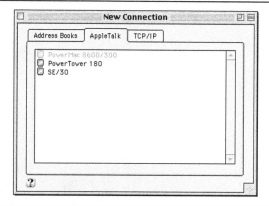

Figure 9-23:   Opening a new AppleTalk connection

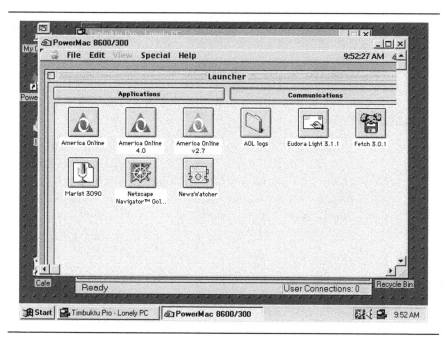

Figure 9-24:   A Macintosh screen in a Timbuktu Pro window on a Windows PC

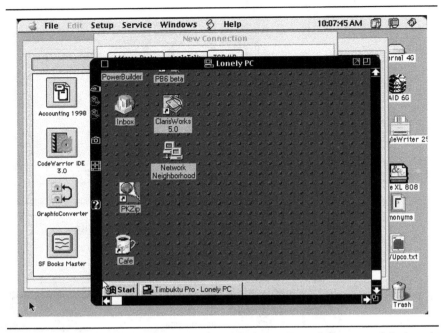

Figure 9-25:   A Windows 95 screen in a Timbuktu Pro window on a Macintosh

File Exchange

Timbuktu supports two types of file exchange, which it calls "sending" files and "exchanging" files. Sending a file transfers it to a single drop folder on the remote computer. Exchanging files gives the remote user complete control over where transferred files are placed, as in Figure 9-26. The interface for exchanging files from a Windows machine is identical to the Macintosh interface.

Messaging

Timbuktu Pro provides two ways to exchange real-time messages. The first is through a relatively standard chat room interface, such as that in Figure 9-27. A user can add himself or herself to a chat session, or a user can add a remote computer to a chat session (assuming that the remote user has the access rights to do so).

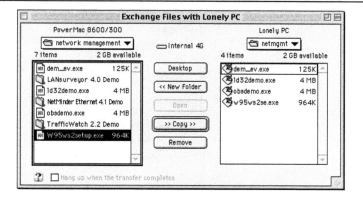

Figure 9-26:   Using Timbuktu Pro to exchange files

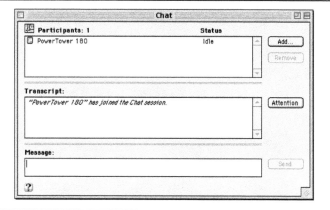

Figure 9-27:   Timbuktu Pro chat

If networked computers are equipped with microphones and speakers, Timbuktu Pro provides an intercom service that allows users to speak with each other (see Figure 9-28). This can be an alternative to a long-distance phone call when the remote user has dialed in to the network from some other location, perhaps using a dedicated line. (If the remote user is paying long-distance charges to connect to the network, of course there would be no savings.)

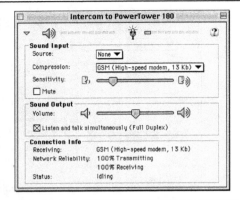

Figure 9-28:   Establishing a Timbuktu Pro intercom session

10

Security Issues

People, including yours truly, have written entire books on network security, and no single book can possibly cover the entire topic. But if you talk to professionals in businesses both large and small, their overriding concern today is network security. We would be horribly remiss if we didn't at least try to look at the major issues facing the operator of a network of any size and introduce you to some of the ways in which you can protect your network.

This chapter is an overview of both security threats and security fixes. It can't provide everything you need to know, but it will alert you to things you should watch and resources you should have at your fingertips.

Security Threats to Home and Small Offices

Is anyone really out there to get you, with your small network? Yes, they are. Well, not necessarily you in particular, but certainly the resources that your network can provide to help them with their larger attacks. You may also have content on your network that someone would want to steal. And just as important, there may be legal requirements for privacy that you must enforce.

From where does the danger come? Over the Internet and from your internal network. You have to be aware of dangers from both sources.

Malware

Malware is short for "malicious software," any software that could do something nasty to your network. There are several types of malware, each of which propagates differently and has a different goal:

- *Virus*: A virus is a self-propagating piece of software that runs as an executable program on a target machine. It is not, however, a stand-alone piece of software. It must piggyback on something else, such as a piece of e-mail or other application program, and is "installed" on a victim machine when the user accesses the host software. A virus's effect can be relatively benign—such as displaying a dialog box—or it can be seriously destructive, deleting files from a hard disk, causing a computer to reboot repeatedly, and so on. Some viruses are known to be *polymorphic*, meaning that they can change themselves as they propagate so that each copy looks a bit different from all others.
- *Worm*: A worm is a self-propagating piece of stand-alone software that has effects similar to a virus. It can cause of a denial of service attack or can damage items stored on a computer.
- *Trojan horse*: A Trojan horse is a piece of software that appears to be one thing, but is, in fact, another. Some Trojan horses are installed by crackers for their use as back doors into a system they have cracked. Others might record a user's keystrokes to a file that can be retrieved later by a system cracker.

♦ *Spyware*: Spyware originally was intended as a tool for share-ware authors to include advertising in their software as a way to raise revenue. The spyware (originally called adware) was to be installed with the shareware, show pop-up advertising, and—most important—send information about the computer on which it was running back to the advertiser. The idea was that the advertiser would collect only demographic information for use in targeted advertising campaigns. However, today spyware collects private information without the knowledge or consent of the person whose information is being collected and uses the victim's own Internet bandwidth to transmit the information.

Malware is easily disseminated. Not only can it be delivered through e-mail, but it travels quite nicely on removable media, such as floppy disks, CDs, DVDs, and USB flash drives.

Denial-of-Service Attacks

A denial-of-service (DoS) attack attempts to prevent legitimate users from accessing a computing resource. DoS attacks can take several forms:

♦ *Overwhelm a network*: The attack can flood a network with so many packets that legitimate traffic slows to a crawl.
♦ *Overwhelm a server:* The attack can flood a single server with so much traffic that legitimate users can't access the server.
♦ *Bring down a server*: The attack can cause a server to crash.

You can't prevent an attacker from launching a DoS attack, but you can detect one in progress and take steps to mitigate its impact. In addition, you can prevent hosts on your network from being unwitting parties to a distributed DoS, a DoS attack in which the source is multiple computers.

The earliest DoS attacks were launched from a single source computer. They are attractive types of attacks to system crackers because they don't require any account access. The attacker launches packets from his or her machine that compromise the victim by taking advantage of the victim's natural behavior to communication requests.

A distributed DoS attack uses multiple source computers to disrupt its victims. This does not mean that the attack is coming from multiple attackers, however. The most typical architecture, in fact, is a single attacker or small group of attackers who trigger the attack by activating malware previously installed on computers throughout the world (zombies).

In most cases, DoS attacks don't damage what is stored on a network's hosts, but they can cause major losses of business revenue because they prevent an organization from functioning normally. It is therefore important to monitor your network for DoS activity.

Authentication Vulnerabilities

For most networks, users are authenticated (identified as being who they say they are) by supplying a user name and password. Once an authorized pair is recognized by the computer, the human has access to all system resources available to that user name. But passwords aren't necessarily an adequate means of authenticating users. Poor passwords make it easy for a hacker to gain access to user accounts, which the hacker can then further manipulate to upgrade to a system administrator account.

General wisdom says that users should create strong passwords—more on strong passwords shortly—and that passwords should be changed every 60 days or so. New passwords should not use any portion of the preceding password. For example, users shouldn't take a word and simply add a different number at the end each time they recreate their password, nor should they be able to reuse passwords that have been used in the recent past. In addition, users should use different passwords for each account.

Certainly you want strong passwords, but should passwords be changed so frequently? The theory behind changing passwords frequently is that a moving target is much harder to decipher. At the same time, however, a password that is changed frequently is much harder to remember, and when users can't remember their passwords, they write them down. You might find a password on a sticky note stuck to a monitor or on a little slip of paper in the middle drawer of a desk. The problem, of course, is exacerbated when users are dealing with passwords for multiple accounts.

Current wisdom states that the best user authentication includes three things: something you know (the user name and password), something you have (a physical token), and who you are (biometrics, such as a fingerprint or retina scan). Although biometrics are moving slowly into the mainstream, physical tokens are becoming much more prevalent. In fact, U.S. banks are now required by law to provide a form of authentication beyond user names and passwords for large business customers to access online banking. (Once the banks have worked out procedures for large businesses, expect to see the same thing propagate down to the consumer level.)

Employees and Other Local People

A good portion of the attacks to which a network is subject today don't necessarily involve compromising your security with sophistcated electronic attacks. Some involve manipulation by employees and other local people.

What can your employees do? They're the ones who have legitimate access to the network. If they can be manipulated into revealing information about their accounts, then a hacker can log into your network. This type of attack is known as social engineering. (It is also the technique behind many attempts to gather information for identify theft.)

To understand social engineering, think "Mission Impossible" (the TV series) on a small scale. The person trying to obtain system access typically engages in a simple role play that tricks someone out of supposedly confidential information. Here's how such an escapade might play out when a CEO's secretary answers the telephone.

SECRETARY: Big Corporation. How may I help you?

CRACKER: Good morning. This is John Doe from Standard Software. We're the people who supply your accounting software. Your IT department has purchased a software upgrade that needs to be installed on your computer. I can do it over the Internet, without even coming into your office and disrupting your work.

SECRETARY: Say, that sounds terrific. Is there anything I need to do?

CRACKER: All I need is your user name and password. Then I'll upload the new files.

SECRETARY: Sure, no problem. My user name is Jane Notsmart; my password is Jane.

CRACKER: Thanks, Jane. The files will be on their way in just a couple of
  minutes.

The cracker then does exactly what he said he would do: He uploads files
to Jane's machine. But the files certainly aren't an upgrade to the accounting software. Instead, they give the cracker root access to the secretary's
computer. The cracker can come back later, log in to her machine, and
cruise through the entire corporate network.

Could it really be that easy? Are users really that gullible? Oh, yes, indeed.
We humans tend to be very trusting and need to be taught to be suspicious.
And it's just not the technologically unsophisticated who fall for such social engineering scams. Our tendency to trust anyone who says he or she is
in a position of authority provides an opening for clever crackers to trick
just about anyone.

> *Note: If you don't believe that humans trust most things said to
> them by someone who seems to be in a position of authority, visit
> the historical Web site http://www.age-of-the-sage.org/
> psychology/milgram_obedience_experiment.html. This Web page
> documents a classic psychological experiment conducted by Stan-
> ley Milgram in 1974 that revealed a very disturbing aspect of
> human behavior.*

An even more insidious form of social engineering is electronic. Social engineering can be done via e-mail as well as in person or over the telephone.
The intent is to trick the person into revealing information such as account
names and passwords, bank account numbers, or credit card numbers. This
is known as *phishing*.

One of the oldest types of phishing involves convincing a victim that he or
she has been selected to help transfer millions of unclaimed dollars from
an African bank and, as payment, will receive a significant percentage of
the funds. In Figure 10-1 you can find a typical e-mail that is intended to
scam bank account information from its victim. (This e-mail appears exactly as it was received, grammatical errors and all.) Like an in-person or
telephone social engineering attempt, it plays on the victim's gullibility
and, in this case, greed. Even though these scams are well known, people
fall for them repeatedly, sometimes losing hundreds of thousands of dollars when the scammer empties a victim's bank account.

FROM THE DESK OF, MR PETER NWA. EC BANK OF AFFRICA PLC. SEND YOUR REPLY TO
THIS EMAIL IF YOU ARE INTERESTED. nwa-peter@caramail.cm ATTN:MY FRIEND, I am
the manager of bill and exchange at the foreign remittance department of the EC
BANK OF AFRICA LAGOS, NIGERIA. I am writing following the impressive information
about you. I have the assurance that you are capable and reliable enough to
champion an impending transaction. In my department, we discovered an abandoned
sum of US$28.5m (twenty eight million and five hundred thousand US dollars), in
an account that belonged to one of our former customers who died along with his
entire family in a plane crash, in November, 1997. Since we received the
information about his death, we have expected his next of kin to come forward
and claim his money, as enshrined in our banking laws and regulations. So far
nobody has come forward, and we cannot release the funds unless someone applies
as the next of kin as stipulated in our guidelines.Unfortunately, we have
discovered that all his supposed next of kin or relations died alongside with
him in the plane crash, and effectively leaving nobody behind for the claim. It
is consequent upon this discovery that other officials and I in my department
decided to make this business proposal to you and release the money to you as
the next of kin or relation of the deceased person, for safety and subsequent
disbursement, since nobody is coming forward for it, and the mnoey is not reverted
into the bank's treasury as unclaimed. The bank's regulation stipulates that if
after five years, such money remains unclaimed; the money will be reverted to
the bank's treasury as unclaimed fund. The request for a foreigner as the next
of kin in this transaction is predicated upon the fact that the said customer
was a foreign national, and no citizen of this country can claim to be the next
of kin of a foreigner. We agree that 30% of the total sum we be given to you for
your assistance in facilitating this transaction. My colleagues and I are going
to retain 60% of the total sum, and 10% will be set aside for the expenses that
we may incur in facilitating the remittance. To enable us effect this remittance,
you must first apply as the next of kin of the deceased. Your application will
include your bank coordinates, that is, your bank name, bank address and telex,
your bank account. You will include your private telephone no. and fax no., for
easy and effective communication during this process. My colleagues and I will
visit your country for disbursement according to the agreed ratio, when this
transaction is concluded. Upon the receipt of your response, I will send to you
by fax,the text of the application. I must not fail to bring to your notice the
fact that this transaction is hitch free, and that you should not entertain fear
as you are adequately protected from any form of embarrassment Do respond to this
letter today through my email address(nwa-peter@caramail.com) to enable us
proceed with the transaction. Yours sincerely, MR PETER NWA. EC BANK OF AFRICA.

Figure 10-1   A typical money-stealing e-mail

The other typical phishing expedition involves fooling the e-mail recipient
into thinking he or she has received a legitimate e-mail from a trusted
source, such as eBay, PayPal, or the recipient's ISP. The e-mail (for example, Figure 10-2) directs the recipient to a Web site (see Figure 10-3)
where—in this case—the user is asked to enter everything but his or her
driver's license number! When you click the Continue button at the bottom

of the Web page, you receive an error message (see Figure 10-4). You can bet, however, that all the text entered on the preceding page was stored somewhere where the thief could retrieve it.

```
Dear eBay membber ,

Since the number of fradulent eBay account take-over has increased
with 100K in the last 4 weeks , eBay Inc. has decided to verify
all eBay account owners and their personal information in order
the claify all accounts satus .
This is the only time you will receive a message from eBay security
theam, and you are to complete all required fields shown in the
page displayed from the link below .

Click the following link and complete all required fields in order
for a better account verification :

http://update-secuire-ebay.com

Account confirmation is due : If you refuse to coperator you dont
leave us any choice but to shut-down your eBay account.

thank you for your cooperation
```

Figure 10-2:   A user ID/password stealing e-mail

Note: The Web page in Figure 10-3 (pages 212–214) has been broken into three parts so that it could be reproduced in this book in a size that you could read. However, when viewed on the Web, it was a single page.

As with "live" social engineering attempts, the best defense against phishing is good user education. It can be difficult for users who aren't technologically savvy to look at the routing information of an e-mail or the URL of a Web page and determine whether the addresses are legitimate. Therefore, it is often more effective to stick with behavioral rules, such as "Never give your user ID and password to anyone" and "Never follow links in e-mails."

Is phishing a big problem? According to the Anti-Phishing Working Group (APWG at http://www.antiphishing.org), it's a very big problem and it's getting worse. Consider the following: APWG found that 5 in 100 people respond to phishing e-mails, while only 1 person in 100 responds to spam

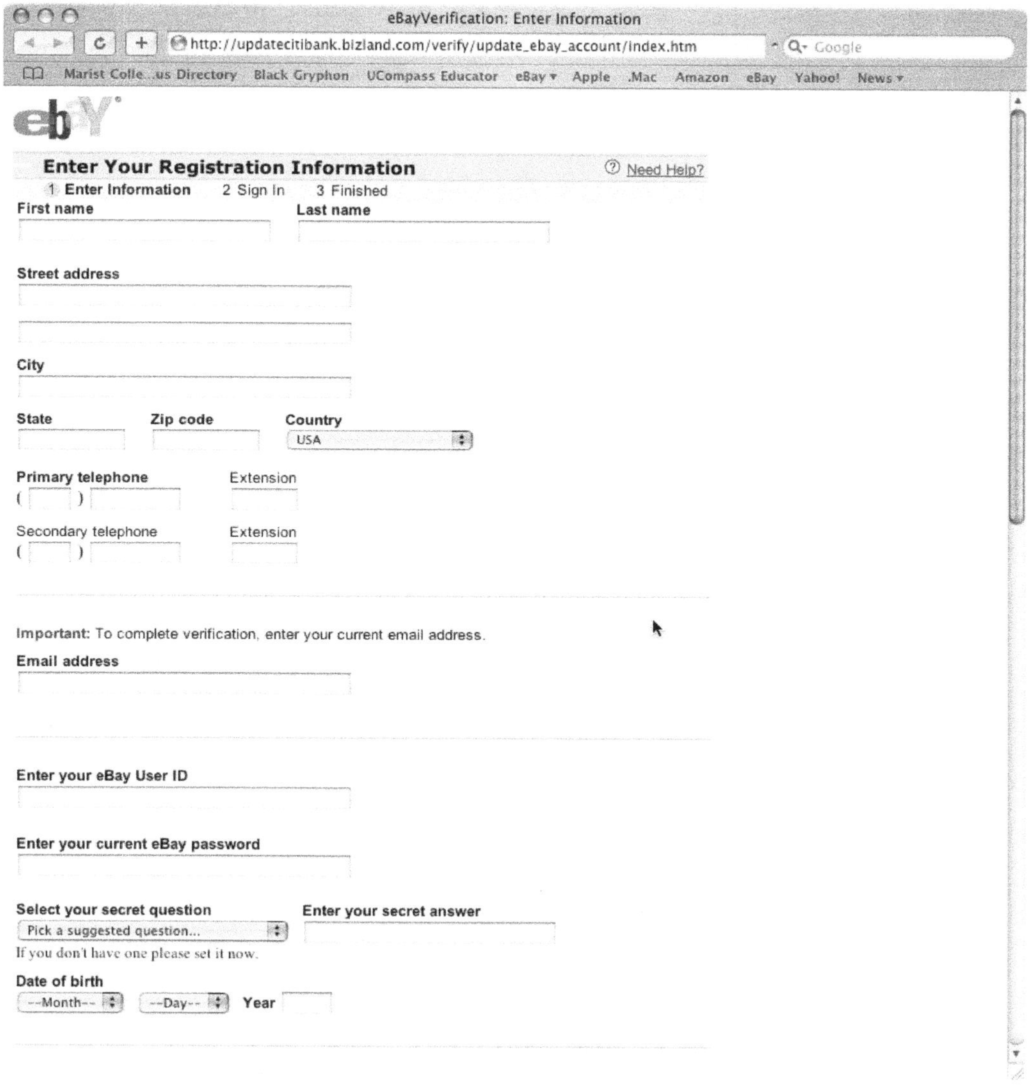

Figure 10-3: A phishing Web page (continues)

e-mail. Add that to its data for 2004, which shows a steady increase in the number of phishing sites from 192 in January to 407 in December. The result is a serious challenge to end-user confidence in the e-mails they re-

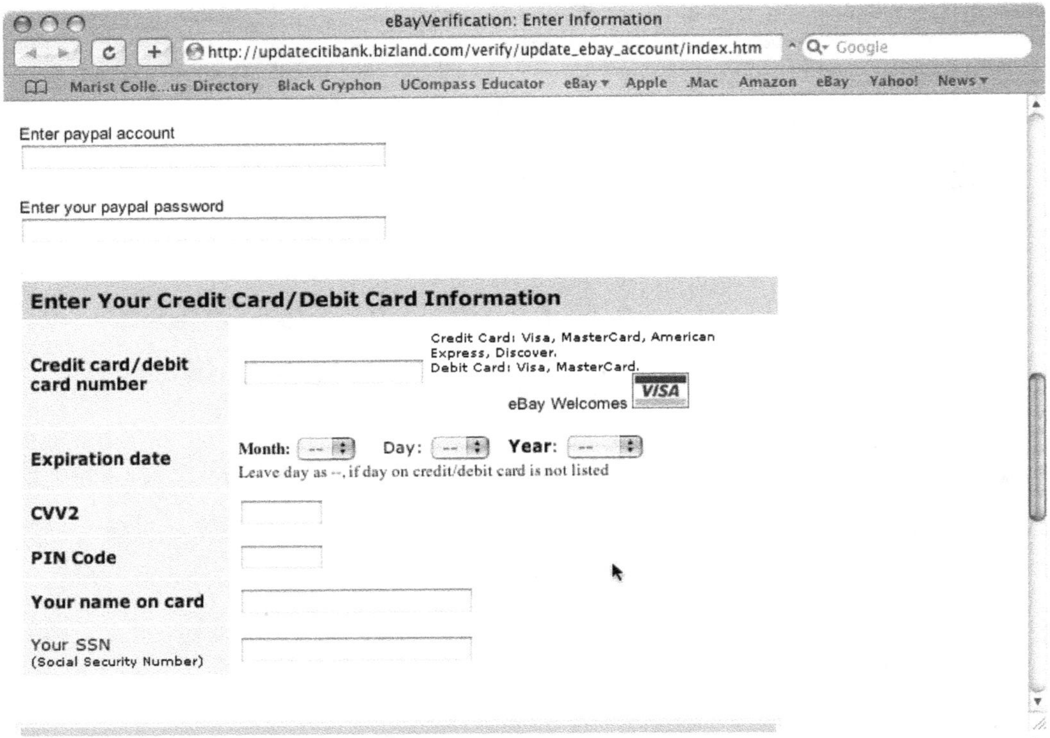

Figure 10-3:   A phishing Web page (continues)

ceive. Some observers believe that users will become so afraid of e-mails from commercial sites that e-commerce will be seriously crippled. Although such a prediction may well be too extreme, it does highlight the seriousness of phishing attempts that prey on human fears, such as having an account canceled.

It's not unusual for an attack to combine multiple techniques. For example, Web spoofing relies on social engineering to draw victims to the spoofed site. In the case of distributed DoS attacks, client malware needs to be installed on an intermediate system before the DoS attack can be launched. This often means that the attacker must gain root or administrative access to the machine to install the client, change system configuration files (if necessary), hide the modifications, and erase traces of his or her activity.

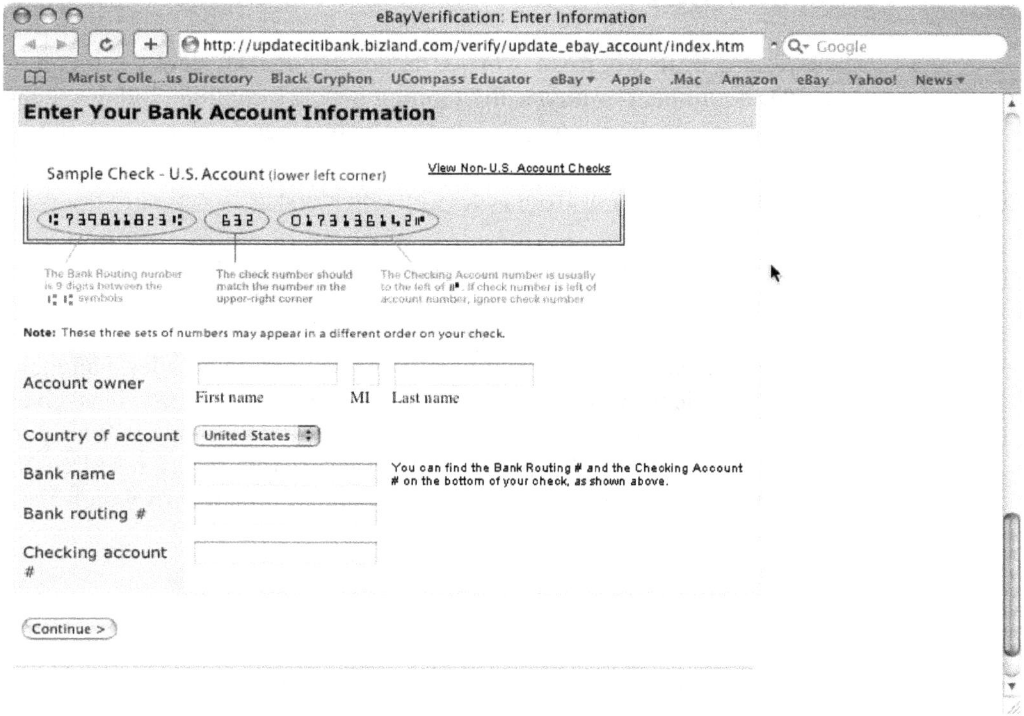

Figure 10-3:   A phishing Web page (continued)

Figure 10-4:   The result of sending information to the phished Web site

Physical Vulnerabilities

There was a time when we worried about people physically damaging computer equipment or physically tapping network cabling. Today's technology, especially the access provided by the Internet, has largely eliminated such threats. However, there are still some very good reasons to secure your network equipment from access by outsiders:

- ◆ Servers are often left logged in by administrators. A knowledgeable hacker can walk up to a server and have administrator access without ever having to hack an account.
- ◆ Hackers can plug laptop computers or even smaller, handheld devices into open ports on switches and routers. This gives them instant access to the network (although they still have to authenticate themselves to gain access to network resources).
- ◆ Hackers can install malware on any computer to which they can gain physical access.

Basic Defenses

In this section we'll look at things that you should do to provide basic protection for your network. Although most cost a bit of money, none are beyond the range of most businesses, regardless of how small. The good news is that if you implement these basic protections, you can protect yourself against all but the most sophisticated network attacks.

Virus Detection Software

Because viruses were the first malware, the software that detects and removes malware is still known as "virus" software, although such programs have been upgraded over time to handle all types of malware. At one time, there were many virus detection software packages available. As with most software arenas, however, time has shaken out the marketplace, leaving several leading products that have shown to have staying power.

You can perform malware detection at two places: on each host or on your servers. In particular, it is well worth the investment to purchase an e-mail server that includes malware detection. Because malware can enter a computer through a vehicle other than e-mail, you should also have virus checkers installed—and preferably set to run automatically—on all computers.

> *Note: Some of your users may be savvy enough to disable the running of a virus checker that has been configured to run when a computer is booted. If you want to prevent this, consider running the checker whenever the computer connects to your network. The college where I teach has a rather Draconian—but effective—means of enforcing virus scanning. Any machine that attempts to connect to the network and hasn't been connected in the past week is scanned for viruses by a network server. The machine isn't allowed to use the network unless it passes the virus check. This way, if a user chooses to disable local virus detection and doesn't pass the network-based virus check, the onus is on the user to clean up his or her own machine. At least other machines on the network won't be infected.*

Host-Based Virus Detection Software

The simplest type of virus detection software is host-based. Its job is to scan a single computer, looking for any malware that is stored on the host's hard disk, either as separate files or embedded in other files. Such software is usually reasonably priced and, in most cases, should be configured to run automatically whenever the computer is booted.

> *Note: Because new and improved malware is constantly appearing, virus checking software goes out of date rapidly. If a virus checker doesn't provide constant and free updates to its malware-recognition database, then the product isn't worth your money. The major vendors provide automatic update options: When configured properly with a live Internet connection, the software checks the vendor's Web site at predetermined intervals and downloads any virus detection information.*

Symantec

Symantec is one of the oldest developers of virus detection software. Having acquired Norton Software, they now market the Norton AntiVirus line for individual desktop machines. When installed on an end system, the software detects worms, viruses, and Trojan horses; it will remove them automatically. It also detects viruses in e-mail attachments, spyware, and keystroke logging programs. In addition, it can scan file archives (for example, ZIP archives) for malware before files have been extracted.

Like all good virus checking software, Norton AntiVirus provides a simple user interface that even those who aren't technologically savvy can use (see Figure 10-5). All the user needs to do to start a scan is to click the Scan Now button. At the end of the scan, the software presents its results (see Figure 10-6).

Like any worthwhile virus checking software, Norton AntiVirus can update itself automatically from the vendor's Web site (see Figure 10-7). When choosing antivirus software, be sure to look into whether the updates are free or require a subscription. Also find out how often updates are made available (for example, as needed to handle new virus threats or on a predetermined schedule).

McAfee

McAfee VirusScan is the major competitor to Norton AntiVirus. As you can see in Figure 10-8, the software can detect spyware as well as the more traditional viruses and Trojan horses. As with any good virus checker, it alerts the user to the presence of any suspicious files and—unless configured for automatic removal—takes no action until the end user directs it to do so (see Figure 10-9). VirusScan also detects malware in incoming and outgoing POP3 e-mail attachments.

Note: Automatic updates require a yearly subscription fee.

Note: VirusScan is a Windows application; the McAfee product for the Macintosh is the venerable Virex.

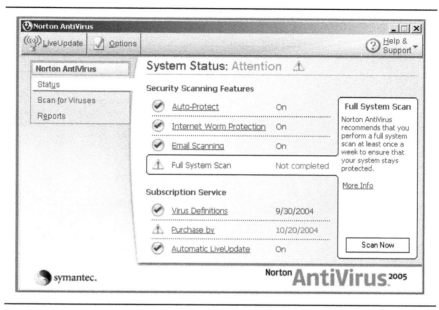

Figure 10-5: The Norton AntiVirus user interface

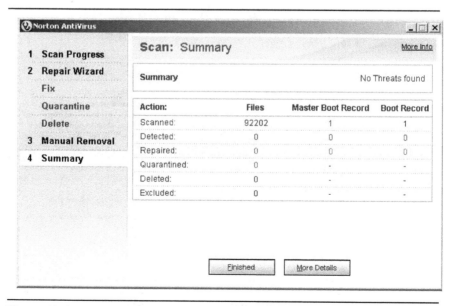

Figure 10-6: The results of a Norton AntiVirus scan

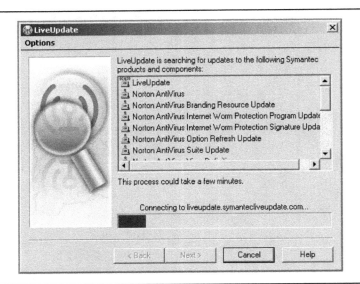

Figure 10-7: Getting virus definition updates for Norton AntiVirus

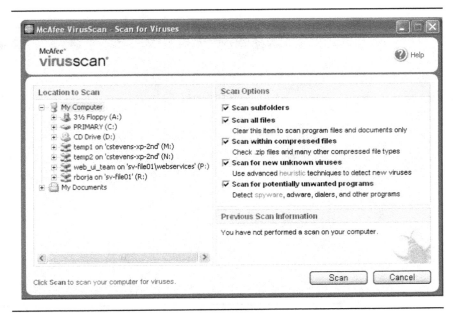

Figure 10-8: Configuring McAfee VirusScan

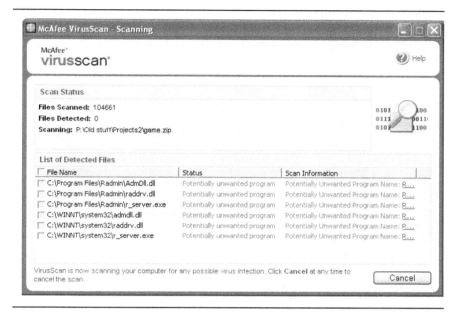

Figure 10-9: The results of a malware scan performed by McAfee VirusScan

Sophos

Although not as well known to end users as Symantec and McAfee, Sophos provides a heavy-duty suite of products for protecting end-user systems. Its simple user interface (see Figure 10-10) makes it suitable for users who aren't terribly technologically savvy.

Network- and Server-Based Virus Detection Software

All the vendors discussed in the preceding section provide network- and server-based malware control software. Network-based virus detection software centralizes malware detection. The beauty of server-based control is that it prevents malware from getting onto individual machines. It means that you don't have to rely on users either running their own virus checking software or avoiding risky behavior (for example, downloading and opening questionable e-mail).

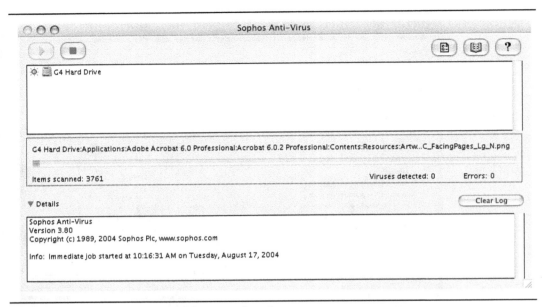

Figure 10-10: The Sophos Anti-Virus user interface

Symantec

Symantec's AntiVirus is intended to protect an entire network. It provides centralized management of software that scans servers as well as end-user systems. Like Norton AntiVirus, it handles worms, viruses, Trojan horses, and spyware as well as scans incoming and outgoing e-mail attachments. The major difference between the "Symantec" label and the "Norton" label is the ability to control all copies of the software from a single computer. This ensures that all copies are configured in the same way and makes it easier to propagate updates. It also makes it easier to determine whether an end user is attempting to avoid using malware detection software.

Large networks, however, may want software that works directly on specific server software. For example, Symantec Mail Security for SMTP works directly with a variety of SMTP-based mail servers, providing malware detection and spam control. Symantec also provides application-specific products that add malware security to Web servers.

McAfee

Like Symantec, McAfee provides a product (McAfee Active VirusScan SMB Edition) that centralizes both end-user and server malware detection and control. It detects and stops viruses, worms, Trojan horses, and spyware. It can also scan file archives without decompressing them and handles both MAPI and POP-3 e-mail attachments. In addition, the product scans Web transfers for malware.

McAfee's enterprise-level product (McAfee VirusScan Enterprise) isn't directed so much at specific servers, but instead adds more overall network security features to malware detection. In particular, it protects against known buffer overflow problems in specific software products and also looks for unknown software that might creep onto a network. (Such unknown software could be part of a *root kit* that gives a system cracker access to administrative functions on your computer, for example.) Finally, VirusScan Enterprise provides features to combat a virus, worm, or DoS attack in progress.

> *Note: McAfee also provides a specific product for handling malware on Linux systems — LinuxShield — and another for Novell Netware (NetShield for Netware).*

Sophos

Sophos Anti-Virus for networks, like the offerings of the previously mentioned vendors, is a network-based solution for end-user systems and servers. It provides the same centralized control as its competitors and works with a wide range of platforms (all versions of Windows, NetWare, OS/2, various flavors of UNIX, Mac OS, and OpenVMS).

Sophos's PureMessage Small Business Edition is designed to protect Exchange and SMTP e-mail servers, controlling both malware and spam. Its control panel (see Figure 10-11) provides an overview of e-mail traffic to give you quick information about the state of your e-mail.

> *Note: Most enterprise-level virus detection products scan e-mail attachments, but they are limited in the languages they "understand." For example, Sophos PureMessage Small Business Editions works with English and Japanese only (and the antispam feature is effective for English only). This can be a major roadblock for organizations with heavy international e-mail traffic.*

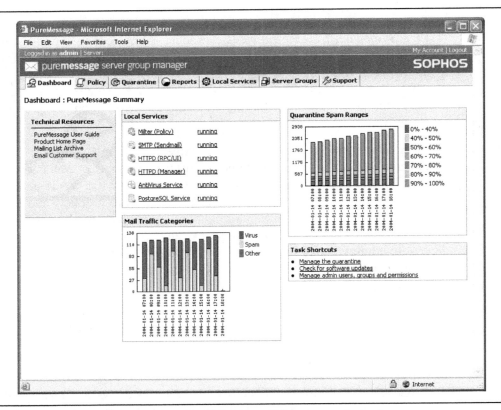

Figure 10-11: Sophos PureMessage Small Business Edition control panel

Firewalls

A firewall is a piece of software—running on a computer, a router, or a stand-alone applicance—that prevents unwanted packets from gaining access to your network. It can block packets destined for specific software ports, filter traffic based on IP addresses, or even block packets destined for specific applications. Because firewalls are so important to network security, this section looks at the types of firewalls and how they work.

First and foremost, a firewall is software. It can run on a workstation, a server, a router, or a stand-alone piece of hardware (the aforementioned firewall appliance). The type of hardware on which a firewall is running is generally independent of the type of traffic filtering the firewall provides. The following discussion therefore focuses on the actions of firewall software rather than specific hardware.

In addition to blocking dangerous traffic, firewalls usually log traffic, either all traffic or blocked traffic (depending on software configuration). Such logs contain the source IP address of the blocked packet, the destination address, the date and time the packet arrived at the firewall, the port for which the packet was destined, and the disposition of the packet (transmitted or blocked). Some firewalls also assign a threat level to each packet. Firewall logs therefore provide a valuable source of information about the traffic attempting to enter a network and can provide substantial clues to system-cracking attempts in progress. (You will find more about using firewall logs and other system logs throughout this book.)

Packet Filtering Firewalls

Packet filtering firewalls work at levels 3 and 4 of the TCP/IP protocol stack, filtering TCP and UCP packets based on any combination of source IP address, destination IP address, source port, or destination port. The simplest packet filtering firewalls filter only incoming packets and block those destined for ports that have been "closed." More sophisticated varieties allow an administrator to define rules that combine criteria. For example, a rule might allow Web traffic (port 80) onto the network only if packets have the destination IP address of the organization's Web server. Any other Web traffic would be blocked.

Note: For a listing of well-known TCP ports, see Appendix B.

Packet filtering firewalls, especially those running on routers or on stand-alone appliances, also provide network address translation (NAT). An edge router presents a single IP address to the Internet (or internet or intranet). As packets arrive, the firewall examines the packet to determine the port to which the packet is directed. The firewall then uses an internal table to map the port to the internal IP address of the host on which the port is open. The internal IP addresses are usually nonrouteable addresses that are then hidden from the Internet.

Almost all personal firewalls, those designed to run on and protect a single workstation, are packet filtering firewalls. They differ only slightly from those that run on routers designed for home networks. Typically, personal firewalls have better logging capabilities than those found on home network routers, and, of course, don't provide NAT.

> *Note: If you want to install a personal firewall on the workstations on your network, you don't necessarily have to spend money on one, at least if your computers are running Windows. Download the free version of ZoneAlarm from www.zonelabs.com. Its logging features are certainly not as comprehensive or easy to use as the commercial version of the software, but the price is right.*

Stateful Firewalls

There are two major limitations to packet filtering firewalls. First, they don't examine the payload of a packet, and second, they don't keep track of what happens to a packet once it gets through the firewall.

Does it matter what a packet does once it's been approved by the firewall? Indeed it does. Some system crackers can design packets that change the port to which they are destined after they pass through a firewall. For example, a packet might be addressed to port 80 so that it can pass through a firewall that has port 25 (SMTP) closed. Once the packet is onto the local network, it changes its port so that it can access the e-mail server and leave a virus or other malware behind.

A stateful firewall keeps track of the state of communications sessions. It monitors the incoming and outgoing packets in each TCP connection. For example, when a packet originates within the local network, the firewall keeps track of the destination address and allows traffic from the destination addressed to the source back onto the local network. By the same token, a packet that appears to be a response to a request by an internal host but that doesn't correspond to an existing TCP session can be blocked. In addition, a stateful firewall monitors the port used by packets once they enter the local network and blocks packets that attempt to change their ports.

Like packet filtering firewalls, stateful firewalls work at levels 3 and 4 of the TCP/IP protocol stack and are therefore relatively independent of the application to which packets are destined.

Application Proxy Firewalls

Application proxy firewalls take a different approach than the two previously mentioned types. They work at the application layer of the TCP/IP protocol stack, providing proxy service for specific applications. Each application proxy sits between the internal network and the world outside. There is no direct communication between the internal computer and the other end of the conversation, as there is with packet filtering and stateful firewalls. Instead, packets travel between the external system and the proxy. The proxy examines the packets and determines which packets should be passed on to the application.

Application proxy firewalls provide a high degree of security and excellent logging features. However, the need to have a separate proxy for each application to be protected is a major limitation, especially if proxies aren't available for some of the software that you need to protect.

Comparing Types of Firewall

As you would expect, each type of firewall has its pros and cons. You can find a summary of them in Table 10-1. Notice that there is increasing price and effectiveness as you move from packet filtering to application proxy firewalls.

However, before you rush out and purchase an application proxy firewall, don't forget that you must have a proxy program for each application you want to protect. The protection for each application that has a proxy is excellent, but applications for which proxies aren't available won't be protected; you'll need some other type of firewall to handle them.

All three types of firewall are effective at stopping a good portion of unwanted network traffic. Home network and small business network users will be well served by packet filtering firewalls, for example. Whatever you do, at least install a firewall where your network connects to the Internet. Nothing else will give you as much protection for the money.

Table 10-1: Comparison of Firewalls

	Packet Filtering	Stateful	Application Proxy
Price	Least expensive	Moderately expensive	Most expensive
Speed	Fast	Fast	Slower
Ease of configuration	Easy	Moderate	Moderate
Application independence	High	Moderate	Low. Must have a separate proxy program for each application for which traffic is to be filtered.
Amount of packet examined	Header information only	Header and contents	Header and contents
Sophistication of filtering rules	Low	Moderate	High
User authentication	None (uses IP addresses)	None (uses IP addresses)	High
Network exposure	Both ends of allowed communication connected directly through the firewall unless NAT is in effect	Both ends of allowed communication connected directly through the firewall unless NAT is in effect	Ends of conversation isolated from each other by application proxies
Packet types filtered	TCP and UDP	TCP and UDP	Generally TCP only (although a few do handle UDP)
Effectiveness	Lowest	Moderate	Highest

Software Patching

Many attacks take advantage of bugs in software, letting hackers install and run their own software on a victim computer. When such software holes are known to the software developer, the developer usually rushes to issue a patch, a software update that modifies the application program or operating system to eliminate the bug. To avoid attacks through known software holes, you need to patch your software regularly.

Operating system patches, the most important patches for most networks, are made available in a variety of ways:

- ◆ *Over the Internet*: This is the best source for Linux patches.
- ◆ *At the vendor's Web site*: If you are running Windows, www.microsoft.com is your best source.
- ◆ *Through automatic software updates*: Mac OS X's Software Update utility searches the Apple Web site for all Apple brand-ed software patches and gives you the opportunity to download and install them.

Backup

Many people don't think of backup as a security measure, but if something happens to destroy your network—a fire, a flood, a server hard disk crash—then good backup copies may be the only way you can restore functionality.

Backup used to be easy: you copied your data files to floppy disk and put the disks in a drawer. Times have changed considerably. To put it more precisely, storage capacities have increased. When we have hard disks that store hundred of gigabytes, we need equally large backup devices. And the proverbial desk drawer just isn't a very safe place for backup copies to reside!

The Backup Plan

Effective backup takes some planning. First, what needs to be backed up? Just your data files, or data files and applications? In many cases, applications can be restored from their original distribution media. Although it takes longer to recover when you have to reinstall your applications, back-ups will be faster and take up less storage space.

How much should you back up? If you need to back up everything, then you do a full backup. Full backups ensure that the contents of the backup media are complete. Because the backup contains the most recent copy of each file, restoring from a full backup is also faster than any other type of restore. On the other hand, copying every file to backup media is the slowest type of backup. You therefore might want an incremental backup, during which you copy only those files that have been changed since the last backup (archival or incremental). Because an incremental backup involves only a subset of the files, it can be performed much faster than a full backup. However, restoring from incremental backups is more difficult because you must find the most recent copy of each file before restoring it.

As files age and sit unused, you may decide that you no longer need them online. If you nonetheless need to retain the files (for legal or other reasons), then you will want to create an archival backup, during which you copy the files to some type of removable media and then delete them from online storage. The backup media are then stored in a safe place where they can be accessed if ever needed.

How often should a backup be made? Perhaps you need a complete archival backup daily (or even more frequently), or perhaps you need an archival backup once a week, with incremental backups done daily. Given that it takes longer to recover from a set of incremental backups than from a single archival backup, but that making a complete archival backup takes longer than making incremental backups, what is the best mix of archiving and incremental backups for your organization? How quickly do you need to be back up and running after a system failure? How volatile are your files (how quickly do they change)? How much modified data are you willing to lose?

Can you make backups while the network and/or servers are in use? Are there application programs that must be shut down to make backups of the data files they use? If you must bring some machines and/or applications off-line, when can you do so with minimal impact on your users?

Who will perform the backups? Usually making backups is the responsibility of system operators, but you need to ensure that the backups are actually being performed.

How many "generations" of backups will you keep? Conventional wisdom states that you should keep three sets of backups, each one backup period older than the preceding. When time comes to create a fourth backup copy, you reuse the media from the oldest of the three existing backup copies. The idea is that if the first backup is damaged, you have two more to fall back to.

The three-generation backup is good in theory, but beware: In some cases you can end up with all three backup copies being damaged. This is particularly true if a system has been infected by a virus or worm that isn't detected immediately, or if a file is corrupted by being written to a bad disk sector or some other similar problem. (You won't detect the latter until someone attempts to read the file, by which time it may be too late to recover a clean copy of the file.)

Where will you store the backups? It's convenient to have the backups close at hand—somewhere on site—but if your physical facility is damaged, your backup media might be damaged as well. Therefore, you probably want to keep at least one backup copy offsite. Which site will you use? Do you want to pay simply for offsite storage, or do you want a true "hot site," where you can run your software until your facility is restored? A good storage site is secure from environmental extremes (heat, cold, fire, and water) and is easily and readily accessible. You will need 24/7 access to your offsite backups, in all kinds of weather. A mountain-top cave may be cool and dry and safe from flooding, but it could be too hard to reach in the winter.

Backup Media

During the period when your files were so small they would fit on a single floppy disk, choosing backup media was easy. Floppies were cheap and easy to store, and they provided random access for quick file restores. However, to accommodate today's large file sizes, we have a variety of options.

Tape

The first medium used for large system backup was magnetic tape. Initially running on reel-to-reel tape drives, tape provided the capacity to hold large files for mainframe systems. Although not particularly fast, tape backups can often be run in the background with other processing and therefore may have minimal impact on system performance.

Even today, tape provides the highest backup capacity for the lowest cost. However, tape is a sequential access medium—to reach a specific file, you must read past all preceding files on the tape. To make matters even more inconvenient, many tape drives can't read backwards. That means that if you need a file that precedes the tape's current location, the tape must be rewound and read again from the beginning.

Nonetheless, if you are backing up large files or storing backups offsite, then tape may be your only feasible option. The other media described in this section probably will be too costly or won't have enough storage capacity. Keep in mind, however, that hard disk storage sizes often outstrip tape capacities and that backing up extremely large files may still require more than one tape.

Tape cartridges for desktop systems come in a wide range of formats, with in capacity up to about 160 gigabytes. This is considerably smaller than many of today's hard drive storage. You may therefore need to allocate more than one tape for each archival backup.

CD and DVD

As soon as CD burners became affordable, many computer users looked at them as a replacement for floppy disk or tape backup. Certainly the media are more durable—a CD stores hundreds of times more than a floppy disk—and provides random access to the contents of the disc. However, hard disk capacities have rapidly outstripped the less than 700 Mb capacity of a CD, making them ill-suited for server backup.

For a time, DVDs looked to be the best alternative, but even when double-layer, double-sided recordable DVDs are available, the maximum capacity will be only around 14 Gb. This clearly isn't enough to back up today's hard disks without a lot of media swapping.

DVD blanks are much cheaper than tape cartridges. They are also easier to store and longer lasting. Coupled with their random access capabilities, they are limited primarily by their low storage capacity. Nonetheless, CD and DVD may be reasonable backup choices for individual desktop or laptop computers.

Hard Disk

The highest capacity device available for use as a backup medium is a hard disk. This isn't a low-cost solution, but it has several advantages:

♦ A hard disk provides fast, random access recovery of individual files.

♦ If an entire hard disk becomes unreadable, the backup disk can replace the damaged primary disk almost immediately.

♦ RAID software or hardware can be used to control writing to the backup drive each time something is written to the primary drive (disk mirroring). This alternative ensures that an up-to-date backup copy is always available, although it does slow down writing to the disks.

Which costs more, tape or hard disk? It depends on your overall backup scheme. As an example, consider the trade-off for a desktop network server: If you are keeping three generations of backups, then you will need three backup hard drives. Assuming that your backup drive is large enough to store all files that need backing up, three hard drives (for example, external FireWire drives) will cost about the same as a high-capacity cartridge tape drive. Add in the cost of tape cartridges, and the initial investment in the tape drive is more than the three backup hard disks.

The tape drive, however, is not limited in capacity. If you upgrade the size of the hard disk in the server, you don't necessarily need to replace the tape drive; you just need to get more cartridges. Unfortunately, the backup hard drives may no longer be large enough to be useful and will need to be replaced. In the long run, tape can be much cheaper.

There are situations in which the cost of using a hard disk as a backup medium isn't an overriding factor. If you need a system that is always available and you can't afford to lose any data, then your best choice is another hard disk. You should consider setting up disk mirroring or even setting up a shadow computer, a machine that is identical to your primary server that can become the primary server if the current primary goes down for any reason.

The Internet

Some organizations use servers connected to the Internet to store backup copies. The organization uses the Internet to transfer files that should be backed up, usually employing FTP transfers. The biggest benefit to this solution is that the organization doesn't have to maintain its own backup facilities; it doesn't have to purchase backup hardware or software, or worry about upgrading the platform as storage needs increase.

However, there are several drawbacks. First, the Internet isn't terribly fast or reliable for the transfer of extremely large files. Second, the organization is placing all its backup copies in the hands of another company. If that company goes out of business, the backup copies will be inaccessible and the security of the data they contain will be suspect. Third, backing up over the Internet may not be cost-effective.

In-house Backup

Another major question you need to answer about backup is where you will perform and store the backups. Most organizations make and retain their own. If you are going to do so, then you need to answer the following two questions, in addition to those discussed earlier in this chapter:

♦ Who will be responsible for ensuring that backups are being made as scheduled? Typically, computer operators or network administrators make the backups. There should be, however, a supervisor who monitors compliance with backup policy and procedures.
♦ How will you secure the backup copies? Assuming that you are keeping three generations, where will each one be stored? At least one copy should be in some type of fireproof and waterproof storage, such as a fireproof filing cabinet. You should seriously consider off-site storage. (For more information on off-site storage, see"Hot Sites" on the next page)

Outsourced Backup

An alternative to handling your own backup is to contract with an outside firm to perform the backups. The company you hire generally will access your servers either over the Internet or via a dedicated leased line. It will make the backup copies and store them on its own premises. The difference between this solution and the use of the Internet discussed earlier in the section on backup media is that the organization whose data are being backed up is not actually performing the backup. If you outsource, the company you hire does all the work. You provide the access to your servers and step aside.

Outsourcing completely frees an organization from having to deal with backup. However, it is subject to the same drawbacks as using an Internet server as a backup medium. In addition, you must also give the company you hire access to your servers.

Hot Sites

An organization of almost any size should seriously consider keeping a backup copy off-site. Fires, flood, earthquakes—all manner of natural and unnatural disasters—can render your data processing facility unusable. Many organizations use hot sites, companies in the business of providing off-site storage for backup copies. Hot sites also keep hardware on which you can load your backups and run your business should your hardware become unavailable.

One of the best-known hot sites is Iron Mountain (*www.ironmountain.com*). Originally located in a worked-out iron mine in upstate New York, Iron Mountain now provides secure storage throughout the United States. The services provided by this company are typical of what you can expect from a hot site:

- ◆ Storage for records in any format, including paper files.
- ◆ Secure document shredding.
- ◆ Off-site storage for backup copies, including the pickup and delivery of media on a regular schedule. You make the backups and Iron Mountain stores them.
- ◆ Outsourced backup. Iron Mountain makes and stores the backups.
- ◆ Outsourced archival storage for all types of electronic records, such as e-mail and images.
- ◆ Hardware on which you can run your business should your hardware become unusable.

Passwords

As we discussed earlier in this chapter, passwords can be a Catch-22 when long, but strong passwords become hard to remember. You can handle the problem in several ways:

- ◆ Don't insist that passwords be changed frequently. If users pick strong passwords, this may be acceptable.
- ◆ Insist that passwords be changed frequently and stress good password behavior. If you believe that your users will not write passwords down, then this is a good alternative.
- ◆ Provide users with host-based password management software and insist that the master password is changed frequently and never written down. This strategy has the advantage of requiring users to remember only a single password, while changing passwords as recommended, and can therefore be a good solution to the problem of multiple Internet account passwords.
- ◆ Use software that provides single sign-on at the network level. This allows users to authenticate themselves once and then gain access to all resources they have on a network, providing a solution to the problem of multiple local network logins. Its major drawback is that because a single password unlocks all network resources for a user, the overall security level for a user drops to the level of the least secure system to which the user has access.

Note: The last two solutions in the preceding list are certainly not mutually exclusive.

Enhancing Password Security with Tokens

It is possible to equip your users with devices that they must have in their possession to be authenticated for network access. One of the most widely used—SecurID from RSA Security—provides a typical adjunct to password security.

Although there are many devices that work with RSA SecurID software, RSA sells the device in Figure 10-12, which generates a new, one-time use password every 60 seconds. The device is small enough to fit on a user's keychain and is supplied with a lifetime battery.

Figure 10-12:   The RSA SecurID device that generates a one-time use password

There are three major advantages to a system of this type:

♦ Users are authenticated by two factors: something they have (a one-time password from the SecurID device) and something they know (a PIN).
♦ The one-time use password eliminates some problems with password management because users don't need to remember or change their own password, although users do need to manage their PINs, just as they would any other password.
♦ Authentication using the hardware token requires no software on the desktop, although it does require authentication server software. The server software, as you might expect, is the most complex component of the system.

On the down side, unless the network provides single sign-on capabilities, a user will need a separate SecurID device for each account to which he or she has access.

If a company chooses, it can use software SecurID tokens instead of hardware devices. The SecurID client software (for example, Figure 10-13) works like the hardware, generating a one-time password that the user enters when signing on to network resources. The software is available for Windows computers, Palm handhelds, Blackberry handhelds, and many mobile phones.

Note: For more information on RSA's SecurID system, see http://www.rsasecurity.com/node.asp?id=1156.

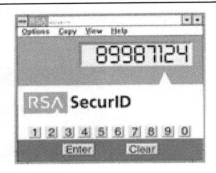

Figure 10-13:   SecurID software

User Education

There is really only one defense against social engineering: good user ed-ucation. You will need to warn users about the types of social engineering attacks that can occur and include instructions about how to report such at-tempts. Such types of employee training sessions often include role-plays that try to ensnare the participants with examples of social engineering.

Handling DoS Attacks

If you notice significant network congestion, receive reports of your Web site becoming inaccessible, or systems begin crashing without explana-tion, then you should look for evidence of a DoS attack.

The best way to detect such an attack is to check your firewall's log. If you see a lot of packets coming repeatedly from the same sources, then you've probably identified a DoS attack. As an example, consider the small log ex-tract in Figure 10-14. The system under attack was a single host using a dial-up connection! Notice that the attack packets, using port 4313, are coming rapidly from just a few source systems. (What was the attacker's aim? Given that the attack was against a single system, the attacker was probably a teenager out to make mayhem. However, the number of packets was so small that it was only a chance look at the system log that detected the attack; processing never slowed down because the bandwidth usage

```
6/25/03 2:11:09 PM    Denied Unknown  4313  TCP    24.191.100.133    l-
18bf6485.dyn.ptnline.net
6/25/03 2:11:10 PM    Denied Unknown  4313  TCP  24.191.100.133 l-
18bf6485.dyn.ptnline.net
6/25/03 2:11:10 PM    Denied Unknown  4313  TCP  208.63.162.145 adsl-63-162-
145.mb.bellsouth.net
6/25/03 2:11:11 PM    Denied Unknown  4313  TCP  24.191.100.133 l-
18bf6485.dyn.ptnline.net
6/25/03 2:11:19 PM    Denied Unknown  4313  TCP  204.131.27.6    crwcd-
ntserver.crwcd.gv
6/25/03 2:11:20 PM    Denied Unknown  4313  TCP  24.191.26.231  l-
18bf1ae7.dyn.ptnline.net
6/25/03 2:11:22 PM    Denied Unknown  4313  TCP  204.131.27.6    crwcd-
ntserver.crwcd.gv
6/25/03 2:11:23 PM    Denied Unknown  4313  TCP  24.191.26.231  l-
18bf1ae7.dyn.ptnline.net
6/25/03 2:11:24 PM    Denied Unknown  4313  TCP  172.136.60.3
ac883c03.ipt.al.cm
6/25/03 2:11:27 PM    Denied Unknown  4313  TCP  68.81.136.107
pcp01328601pcs.chrstn01.pa.cmcast.net
6/25/03 2:11:27 PM    Denied Unknown  4313  TCP  172.136.60.3
ac883c03.ipt.al.cm
6/25/03 2:11:27 PM    Denied Unknown  4313  TCP  69.0.120.136
69.0.120.136.adsl.snet.net
6/25/03 2:11:28 PM    Denied Unknown  4313  TCP  204.131.27.6    crwcd-
ntserver.crwcd.gv
6/25/03 2:11:29 PM    Denied Unknown  4313  TCP  24.191.26.231  l-
18bf1ae7.dyn.ptnline.net
6/25/03 2:11:29 PM    Denied Unknown  4313  TCP    68.81.136.107     Unknown
6/25/03 2:11:30 PM    Denied Unknown  4313  TCP    69.0.120.136      Unknown
6/25/03 2:11:33 PM    Denied Unknown  4313  TCP    172.136.60.3      Unknown
6/25/03 2:11:34 PM    Denied Unknown  4313  TCP    68.81.136.107     Unknown
6/25/03 2:11:36 PM    Denied Unknown  4313  TCP    69.0.120.136      Unknown
6/25/03 2:11:41 PM    Denied Unknown  4313  TCP    67.86.181.180     Unknown
6/25/03 2:11:45 PM    Denied Unknown  4313  TCP    172.136.60.3      Unknown
6/25/03 2:11:45 PM    Denied Unknown  4313  TCP    67.86.181.180     Unknown
6/25/03 2:11:48 PM    Denied Unknown  4313  TCP    137.21.88.157     Unknown
6/25/03 2:11:49 PM    Denied Unknown  4313  TCP    24.166.75.20      Unknown
6/25/03 2:11:51 PM    Denied Unknown  4313  TCP    24.166.75.20      Unknown
6/25/03 2:11:51 PM    Denied Unknown  4313  TCP    67.86.181.180     Unknown
6/25/03 2:11:53 PM    Denied Unknown  4313  TCP    68.185.149.239    Unknown
6/25/03 2:11:55 PM    Denied Unknown  4313  TCP    65.33.46.46       Unknown
6/25/03 2:11:56 PM    Denied Unknown  4313  TCP    68.185.149.239    Unknown
6/25/03 2:11:57 PM    Denied Unknown  4313  TCP    24.166.75.20      Unknown
6/25/03 2:11:58 PM    Denied Unknown  4313  TCP    65.33.46.46       Unknown
6/25/03 2:12:00 PM    Denied Unknown  4313  TCP    68.57.124.77      Unknown
6/25/03 2:12:01 PM    Denied Unknown  4313  TCP    68.185.149.239    Unknown
6/25/03 2:12:03 PM    Denied Unknown  4313  TCP    68.57.124.77      Unknown
```

Figure 10-14: An excerpt from a firewall log showing a distributed DoS in progress

6/25/03 2:12:04 PM	Denied	Unknown	4313	TCP	65.33.46.46	Unknown
6/25/03 2:12:09 PM	Denied	Unknown	4313	TCP	68.57.124.77	Unknown
6/25/03 2:12:19 PM	Denied	Unknown	4313	TCP	12.207.17.128	Unknown
6/25/03 2:12:21 PM	Denied	Unknown	4313	TCP	68.49.152.132	Unknown
6/25/03 2:12:09 PM	Denied	Unknown	4313	TCP	67.100.17.120	Unknown
6/25/03 2:12:13 PM	Denied	Unknown	4313	TCP	68.99.19.118	Unknown
6/25/03 2:12:13 PM	Denied	Unknown	4313	TCP	67.100.17.120	Unknown
6/25/03 2:12:16 PM	Denied	Unknown	4313	TCP	68.99.19.118	Unknown
6/25/03 2:12:16 PM	Denied	Unknown	4313	TCP	165.24.250.47	Unknown
6/25/03 2:12:17 PM	Denied	Unknown	4313	TCP	67.100.17.120	Unknown
6/25/03 2:12:18 PM	Denied	Unknown	4313	TCP	68.49.152.132	Unknown
6/25/03 2:12:19 PM	Denied	Unknown	4313	TCP	165.24.250.47	Unknown
6/25/03 2:12:22 PM	Denied	Unknown	4313	TCP	12.207.17.128	Unknown
6/25/03 2:12:22 PM	Denied	Unknown	4313	TCP	68.99.19.118	Unknown
6/25/03 2:12:25 PM	Denied	Unknown	4313	TCP	165.24.250.47	Unknown
6/25/03 2:12:26 PM	Denied	Unknown	4313	TCP	12.207.17.128	Unknown
6/25/03 2:12:28 PM	Denied	Unknown	4313	TCP	68.49.152.132	Unknown
6/25/03 2:12:43 PM	Denied	Unknown	4313	TCP	68.210.107.135	Unknown
6/25/03 2:12:47 PM	Denied	Unknown	4313	TCP	12.250.130.200	Unknown
6/25/03 2:12:47 PM	Denied	Unknown	4313	TCP	68.210.107.135	Unknown
6/25/03 2:12:48 PM	Denied	Unknown	4313	TCP	137.21.88.157	Unknown
6/25/03 2:12:50 PM	Denied	Unknown	4313	TCP	12.250.130.200	Unknown
6/25/03 2:12:52 PM	Denied	Unknown	4313	TCP	68.210.107.135	Unknown
6/25/03 2:12:54 PM	Denied	Unknown	4313	TCP	66.26.68.208	Unknown
6/25/03 2:12:54 PM	Denied	Unknown	4313	TCP	68.185.149.239	Unknown
6/25/03 2:12:55 PM	Denied	Unknown	4313	TCP	63.229.25.180	Unknown
6/25/03 2:12:56 PM	Denied	Unknown	4313	TCP	12.250.130.200	Unknown
6/25/03 2:12:57 PM	Denied	Unknown	4313	TCP	68.185.149.239	Unknown
6/25/03 2:12:57 PM	Denied	Unknown	4313	TCP	66.26.68.208	Unknown
6/25/03 2:12:58 PM	Denied	Unknown	4313	TCP	63.229.25.180	Unknown
6/25/03 2:13:03 PM	Denied	Unknown	4313	TCP	68.185.149.239	Unknown
6/25/03 2:13:03 PM	Denied	Unknown	4313	TCP	66.26.68.208	Unknown
6/25/03 2:13:04 PM	Denied	Unknown	4313	TCP	63.229.25.180	Unknown
6/25/03 2:13:24 PM	Denied	Unknown	4313	TCP	155.201.35.53	Unknown
6/25/03 2:13:29 PM	Denied	Unknown	4313	TCP	155.201.35.53	Unknown
6/25/03 2:13:29 PM	Denied	Unknown	4313	TCP	24.49.99.191	Unknown
6/25/03 2:13:33 PM	Denied	Unknown	4313	TCP	155.201.35.53	Unknown
6/25/03 2:13:38 PM	Denied	Unknown	4313	TCP	24.49.99.191	Unknown
6/25/03 2:13:50 PM	Denied	Unknown	4313	TCP	67.84.72.191	Unknown
6/25/03 2:13:58 PM	Denied	Unknown	4313	TCP	64.252.7.27	Unknown
6/25/03 2:13:58 PM	Denied	Unknown	4313	TCP	67.84.72.191	Unknown
6/25/03 2:13:59 PM	Denied	Unknown	4313	TCP	67.84.72.191	Unknown
6/25/03 2:13:59 PM	Denied	Unknown	4313	TCP	65.105.166.186	Unknown
6/25/03 2:14:01 PM	Denied	Unknown	4313	TCP	64.252.7.27	Unknown
6/25/03 2:14:02 PM	Denied	Unknown	4313	TCP	65.105.166.186	Unknown
6/25/03 2:14:02 PM	Denied	Unknown	4313	TCP	68.34.220.31	Unknown
6/25/03 2:14:05 PM	Denied	Unknown	4313	TCP	68.34.220.31	Unknown
6/25/03 2:14:07 PM	Denied	Unknown	4313	TCP	64.252.7.27	Unknown

Figure 10-14: An excerpt from a firewall log showing a distributed DoS in progress *(continued)*

```
6/25/03 2:14:08 PM    Denied  Unknown  4313  TCP    65.105.166.186   Unknown
6/25/03 2:14:11 PM    Denied  Unknown  4313  TCP    68.34.220.31     Unknown
6/25/03 2:14:14 PM    Denied  Unknown  4313  TCP    68.193.145.171   Unknown
6/25/03 2:14:14 PM    Denied  Unknown  4313  TCP    68.74.69.12      Unknown
6/25/03 2:14:15 PM    Denied  Unknown  4313  TCP    68.198.53.157    Unknown
6/25/03 2:14:17 PM    Denied  Unknown  4313  TCP    68.193.145.171   Unknown
6/25/03 2:14:17 PM    Denied  Unknown  4313  TCP    68.74.69.12      Unknown
6/25/03 2:14:18 PM    Denied  Unknown  4313  TCP    68.198.53.157    Unknown
6/25/03 2:14:20 PM    Denied  Unknown  4313  TCP    192.104.254.78   Unknown
6/25/03 2:14:23 PM    Denied  Unknown  4313  TCP    68.193.145.171   Unknown
6/25/03 2:14:24 PM    Denied  Unknown  4313  TCP    68.198.53.157    Unknown
6/25/03 2:14:27 PM    Denied  Unknown  4313  TCP    192.104.254.78   Unknown
6/25/03 2:14:23 PM    Denied  Unknown  4313  TCP    68.74.69.12      Unknown
6/25/03 2:14:23 PM    Denied  Unknown  4313  TCP    192.104.254.78   Unknown
6/25/03 2:14:50 PM    Denied  Unknown  4313  TCP    80.134.177.56    Unknown
6/25/03 2:14:54 PM    Denied  Unknown  4313  TCP    216.158.45.214   Unknown
6/25/03 2:14:54 PM    Denied  Unknown  4313  TCP    80.134.177.56    Unknown
6/25/03 2:14:57 PM    Denied  Unknown  4313  TCP    216.158.45.214   Unknown
6/25/03 2:14:57 PM    Denied  Unknown  4313  TCP    141.157.64.226   Unknown
6/25/03 2:14:59 PM    Denied  Unknown  4313  TCP    141.157.64.226   Unknown
6/25/03 2:14:59 PM    Denied  Unknown  4313  TCP    68.164.7.217     Unknown
6/25/03 2:14:59 PM    Denied  Unknown  4313  TCP    80.134.177.56    Unknown
6/25/03 2:15:02 PM    Denied  Unknown  4313  TCP    68.164.7.217     Unknown
6/25/03 2:15:03 PM    Denied  Unknown  4313  TCP    216.158.45.214   Unknown
6/25/03 2:15:05 PM    Denied  Unknown  4313  TCP    68.164.7.217     Unknown
6/25/03 2:15:05 PM    Denied  Unknown  4313  TCP    141.157.64.226   Unknown
6/25/03 2:15:07 PM    Denied  Unknown  4313  TCP    65.41.187.130    Unknown
6/25/03 2:15:11 PM    Denied  Unknown  4313  TCP    80.134.177.56    Unknown
6/25/03 2:15:11 PM    Denied  Unknown  4313  TCP    68.164.7.217     Unknown
6/25/03 2:15:11 PM    Denied  Unknown  4313  TCP    65.41.187.130    Unknown
6/25/03 2:15:14 PM    Denied  Unknown  4313  TCP    68.164.7.217     Unknown
6/25/03 2:15:15 PM    Denied  Unknown  4313  TCP    24.118.45.103    Unknown
6/25/03 2:15:16 PM    Denied  Unknown  4313  TCP    65.41.187.130    Unknown
6/25/03 2:15:17 PM    Denied  Unknown  4313  TCP    24.118.45.103    Unknown
6/25/03 2:15:32 PM    Denied  Unknown  4313  TCP    24.118.45.103    Unknown
6/25/03 2:15:32 PM    Denied  Unknown  4313  TCP    68.164.7.217     Unknown
6/25/03 2:16:08 PM    Denied  Unknown  4313  TCP    24.44.145.104    Unknown
6/25/03 2:16:08 PM    Denied  Unknown  4313  TCP    68.164.7.217     Unknown
6/25/03 2:16:18 PM    Denied  Unknown  4313  TCP    24.44.145.104    Unknown
6/25/03 2:16:18 PM    Denied  Unknown  4313  TCP    38.72.192.220    Unknown
6/25/03 2:16:20 PM    Denied  Unknown  4313  TCP    68.8.4.173       Unknown
6/25/03 2:16:20 PM    Denied  Unknown  4313  TCP    38.72.192.220    Unknown
6/25/03 2:16:23 PM    Denied  Unknown  4313  TCP    68.8.4.173       Unknown
6/25/03 2:16:26 PM    Denied  Unknown  4313  TCP    38.72.192.220    Unknown
6/25/03 2:16:29 PM    Denied  Unknown  4313  TCP    68.8.4.173       Unknown
6/25/03 2:16:42 PM    Denied  Unknown  4313  TCP    219.57.16.49     Unknown
6/25/03 2:16:44 PM    Denied  Unknown  4313  TCP    198.107.58.66    Unknown
6/25/03 2:16:45 PM    Denied  Unknown  4313  TCP    219.57.16.49     Unknown
```

Figure 10-14: An excerpt from a firewall log showing a distributed DoS in progress *(continued)*

6/25/03 2:16:47 PM	Denied Unknown	4313	TCP	198.107.58.66	Unknown
6/25/03 2:16:49 PM	Denied Unknown	4313	TCP	64.203.194.247	Unknown
6/25/03 2:16:51 PM	Denied Unknown	4313	TCP	68.82.71.109	Unknown
6/25/03 2:16:51 PM	Denied Unknown	4313	TCP	219.57.16.49	Unknown
6/25/03 2:16:52 PM	Denied Unknown	4313	TCP	64.203.194.247	Unknown
6/25/03 2:16:53 PM	Denied Unknown	4313	TCP	198.107.58.66	Unknown
6/25/03 2:16:54 PM	Denied Unknown	4313	TCP	68.82.71.109	Unknown

Figure 10-14: An excerpt from a firewall log showing a distributed DoS in progress *(continued)*

wasn't high enough.) The log shows that the attacking packets were dropped at the firewall's external interface and that the attack had no effect on the intended victim system.

What can you do if you or your software determines that your network (or a host on your network) is the victim of a DoS attack? The easiest solution is to shut down the affected host or network. (It may not be enough to isolate the network from the Internet if malware is propagating packets around the network.) That may sound extreme, but it is just about the only way to stop the attack. Shutting down will give you time to examine your computers to see if any DoS client software has been installed.

There are less extreme alternatives, of course. One alternative is to close down the TCP connections to the source(s) of the packets involved in the DoS attack. This is certainly practical for a single-source attack but may require too much bandwidth for a distributed DoS. In addition, you need to regain control of your network, and the only sure way is to cut it off from the source of the attack. In other words, shut down Internet access! (If the attack is coming from an internal source, you will need to shut down the local network as well.)

The next step is to make a backup of any computers that have been involved in the attack. This will give you something to analyze even after you have restored the network. It will also give you evidence for any legal investigations that might occur once the attack is over.

At this point, you can begin examining involved network hosts for software used in the attack. Look for DoS attack clients and agents/daemons, network sniffers (software that grabs network packets and deciphers them), and backdoor software that gives an attacker access to a host. To detect these files, look for unauthorized modification to system files and for user files that neither the system administrator nor the user can identify.

Once you've identified which hosts on your network have been compromised, you can recover. You'll need to

- ◆ Install a clean copy of the operating system.
- ◆ Install all vendor patches.
- ◆ Disable unused services.
- ◆ Use all new passwords.

Be very careful if you choose to restore data files from a backup: The backups may be compromised, depending on how long an attacker's software has been on a host.

Advanced Defenses

The defenses you've read about to this point can provide significant security protection for reasonable amounts of money. If, however, you need for even stronger security—perhaps you are protecting patient information or a new product under development—then you may want to invest in additional security. One major piece of software to consider is an *instrusion detection system* IDS), which can identify denial-of-service attacks as well as other attempts to penetrate your network. If you have remove users accessing your network over the Internet, you can secure their access with a VPN, an effective (but not necessarily inexpensive) solution.

Intrusion Detection Systems

For the most part, IDSs work by looking for patterns of network and/or host activity. One part of the IDS logs network events (or looks at existing system logs). The analyzer then examines the event log to determine if suspicious activity is occurring. The rules that the analyzer uses are based on knowledge of previous attacks and known system vulnerabilities.

> *Note: As you might guess, the "heart" of an IDS is its event analyzer. The better it is at detecting unusual activity — without generating false positives — the more effective it is.*

If you are running an IDS, the IDS should be configured to alert you when the software detects evidence of a DoS attack. You will then need to examine the IDS logs to determine exactly what is occurring so that you can stop the attack or at least minimize its effects.

As an example, consider the part of an IDS log in Figure 10-15 (generated by GFI LANguard). The specific events that are logged are determined by filters created by the software administrators. The software also keeps additional detail about each recorded event that you can display as needed (for example, Figure 10-16).

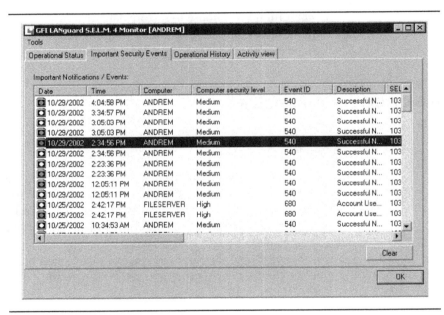

Figure 10-15:   An IDS event log (from GFI LANguard)

IDSs are generally quite effective at detecting DoS attacks that consume network resources such as bandwidth. Along with a firewall, they are your best line of defense against DoS attacks. However, if an attacker knows that an IDS is in place, he or she can launch DoS attacks that attempt to disable the IDS. The following techniques have been known to work:

> ◆ An attack can tie up CPU cycles on the hardware running the IDS by sending packets that cause the IDS to check large numbers of packets. For example, the attacker might send fragments

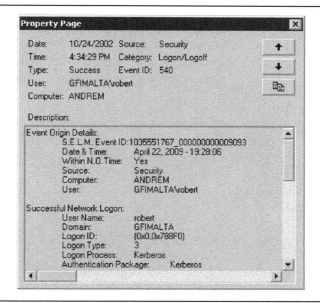

Figure 10-16:   IDS event detail

of many messages that the IDS would attempt to assemble into complete messages.

♦ An attack can consume the RAM on the hardware running the IDS. Each message fragment that the IDS encounters, for example, requires a RAM-based message queue to save the parts of the message until the entire message is assembled. Therefore, the attack mentioned in the previous bullet can be used to tie up RAM as well as CPU cycles.

♦ An attack can send events to the IDS that need to be stored on disk. A flood of such events can consume all available disk space.

♦ An attack can overwhelm network bandwidth by flooding the network with meaningless packets. (This kind of attack is certainly a double whammy because it affects not only the IDS but all hosts on the network as well.)

♦ If an IDS is capable of reacting automatically to DoS attacks, it can be susceptible to "false positives," attacks that repeatedly cause it to react to a nonexistent attack. An IDS may take many types of action, but usually it will shut down the TCP communication with the source of packets used in a DoS attack; each time it does this, it must send traffic over the local network. The IDS therefore becomes the middle man in a DoS on its own network. Because many IDSs are vulnerable to this type of problem, you may want to configure an IDS to trigger alarms only, rather than to take attack countermeasures on its own.

The bottom line is that an IDS is as vulnerable to a DoS attack as any other software on your network. A good practice is to use an IDS to trigger alarms to which a network security professional will respond. In many cases, only a human can determine the best reaction in a specific situation, whether it be shutting down TCP connections or shutting down the entire network.

Virtual Private Networks

If you need to have users gain secure access to your internal network over the Internet, then you will probably want to use a *virtual private network*, or VPN. The intent behind a VPN is to allow geographically removed users to send data over an existing WAN—most commonly the Internet—in a secure fashion. The basic technique provides a secure transmission path known as a *tunnel* between two systems. The tunnel can connect two systems or two networks.

Currently there are at least four competing VPN technologies, each of which has drawbacks and benefits when used for remote access.

IPSec VPNs

As originally defined, the TCP/IP protocol stack is very weak in terms of security. IPSec is a group of protocols that were added to IP to provide encryption for data traveling over the Internet. Because IPSec works at the network layer of the protocol stack, it is independent of any specific application program. One of its biggest advantages, therefore, is that applications don't need to be written specifically to take advantage of it.

> *Note: According to some sources, the original protocol name was written IPsec. However, current common usage tends to write it IPSec, which is what I'm using in this book.*

When used for a VPN, IPSec establishes a tunnel between a client machine running IPSec client software and an IPSec server located at the destination end of the connection (tunnel mode, as illustrated in Figure 10-17).

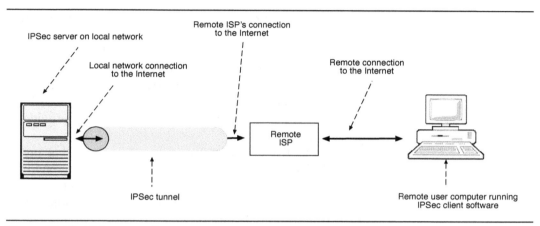

Figure 10-17: IPSec tunneling

In tunnel mode, IPSec's encryption is in place only as data travel over the Internet. It does not encrypt data on the local network or between a remote host and its connection to the Internet. Therefore, if you have a remote office that needs to access the home office LAN on a regular basis, IPSec is a good VPN solution. You can place an IPSec server at either end of the connection, alleviating the need for each client machine at the remote office to run IPSec client software. You can then use an Internet connection to share the VPN tunnel among the remote office users.

> *Note: IPSec servers generally are sold as hardware appliances rather than as software you add to an existing network machine.*

IPSec can provide end-to-end (host-to-host) encryption—when it is running in transport mode. However, to use transport mode, you must have control over the entire length of the transmission, something that isn't supported with a VPN that requires users to connect to the Internet using an ISP provided by some other organization.

If you need to connect mobile or widely scattered remote users securely, an IPSec VPN may not be the best solution:

♦ IPSec allows users to access the destination LAN as if they were connected directly to that LAN. This may not be desirable for some remote users (for example, customers or other business partners who aren't employees).

♦ Most intermittent remote users must connect to an ISP before they connect to the Internet, and data are not subject to IPSec protection as they move from remote user to ISP.

♦ IPSec tunneling is not compatible with most firewalls and can't make its way through a router using *network address translation* (NAT). To ensure compatibility with firewalls and NAT, you'll need to purchase hardware that specifically provides such capabilities.

♦ IPSec requires that client software from the vendor that supplied the IPSec server (or software from a compatible vendor) be installed on each remote host. This is fine if all your remote users are working with computers owned by your organization, such as laptops for users who are traveling. However, remote users may need to use hardware that you don't own, such as the Internet access provided in a hotel room or Internet cafe. An IPSec VPN isn't accessible in such environments.

PPTP VPNs

One alternative to an IPSec VPN for remote access is to use a protocol based on a dial-up protocol, such as *point-to-point tunneling protocol* (PPTP). This VPN solution avoids some of the problems with using IPSec for remote access, including the issue of firewall and NAT incompatibility. (NAT compatibility requires an editor for PPTP packets, however.) And because PPTP VPN support is part of operating systems by Microsoft and Apple, you don't need to purchase extra client software. Network operating systems from both vendors also provide PPTP server software.

PPTP has been designed as a wrapper for *point-to-point protocol* (PPP), the protocol used by most dial-up connections between the client computer's modem and an ISP's modem. It takes the PPP frame, encapsulates the frame using *Generic Routing Encapsulation* (GRE), and then encapsulates it once more into an IP packet.

PPTP encrypts the data in the PPP frame. However, the encryption doesn't begin until after the PPP connection is established. This means that the exchange of authentication information—in particular, the user name and password—is sent in the clear.

PPTP also can't authenticate hardware, although hardware authentication isn't being widely practiced. On the other hand, PPTP doesn't require certificates of authority (CAs), which simplifies its implementation.

L2TP/IPSec

IPSec and PPTP work only with TCP/IP networks. If the WAN over which remote traffic will be traveling uses another protocol (for example, X.25, Frame Relay, or ATM), then neither IPSec nor PPTP is a viable solution. *Layer 2 Tunneling Protocol* (L2TP), which is suppported by both Microsoft and Apple, functions over the alternative WAN protocols, as well as IP. When used with IP, it provides tunneling over the Internet.

In contrast to PPTP, which uses TCP, L2TP uses UDP datagrams to control its tunneling. Each PPP frame is encapsulated by L2TP, then by UDP, and finally by IP.

L2TP can work with IPSec to provide end-to-end security. The combination—known as L2TP/IPSec, uses IPSec encryption to encode the PPP data field. Because IPSec establishes an SA before beginning transfer of any message packets, the encryption is in place prior to the beginning of PPP user authentication. This ensures that the user name and password are encrypted, rather than being sent in the clear as they are with PPTP. However, the IPSec authentication does require that mechanisms for CAs be in place.

L2TP has problems getting through routers with NAT. However, if both the client and VPN server are running *IPSec NAT traversal* (NAT-T), then NAT will function.

SSL VPNs

The final major VPN alternative is *secure socket layer* (SSL), which made its debut as a protocol for securing Web browser traffic. For applications with a Web browser interface, SSL supports VPN access using any browser on a client machine. It also avoids problems with NAT by incorporating proxies that direct a VPN connection to a specific application.

Many vendors advertise their SSL VPN solutions as "clientless." However, SSL VPNs avoid client software only when the application to be used through the VPN has a Web browser interface. To access non-browser-enabled applications, the SSL VPN server must be able to handle proxies to pass browser traffic through to the needed applications. In addition, most SSL VPN vendors also supply client software that provides access similar to that provided by an IPSec VPN, where the client computer has full access to the local network.

Windows and Mac OS X provide built-in VPN clients. Their server software can be configured to act as a VPN server. However, many vendors (for example, Cisco) who make stand-alone VPN server appliances do require that clients run software specific to the manufacturer's hardware.

> *Note: Linux parovides significant support for VPNs, but setting up a Linux machine as a VPN client or server, especially if it's behind a firewall and a router using NAT, isn't trivial. Nonetheless, you can find a good tutorial at http://www.tldp.org/HOWTO/VPN-Masquerade-HOW-TO.html.*

Security Resources

Network security is the proverbial moving target. No matter what you do, some miscreant is out there trying to get past your defenses. This means that you need to stay up-to-date on security issues, including the discoveries of new malware threats and the issuing of relevant software patches.

To help, here are some resources you can use to get much of the information you need.

Professional Security Update Sites

There are two major Web sites that monitor system cracker activity across the Internet:

- *http://www.cert.org*: CERT (located in the Carnegie Mellon Software Engineering Institute) is a federally funded security research and development center. The CERT site posts security alerts, papers on the result of security research, and security tips for end users. Documents on the site identify threats, describe how they work, and suggest remedies. CERT also offers professional training courses.
- *http://isc.sans.org*: SANS is a training institute that also monitors Internet security threats. Its Internet Storm Center site also presents an analysis of various threats over the recent past.

Other professional sites include:

- *http://www.auscert.org.au/render.html?cid=1*: The Australian Computer Emergency Response Team.
- *http://ciac.llnl.gov/cgi-bin/index/bulletins*: Computer Incident Advisory Capability (CIAC) from the U.S. Department of Energy.
- *http://www.secureroot.com/*: A wide variety of links to descriptions of types of attacks, current security advisories, forums, exploits categories by platform, and so on.
- *http://www.antiphishing.org*: The site of the Anti-Phishing Working Group, which monitors phishing attempts and provides advice on how to avoid being trapped by them.

Other Sites of Interest

- *http://www.staysafeonline.info/*: The National Cyber Security Alliance provides security tips for small business and home end users. The information there may be useful as part of a user education program.
- *http://securityresponse.symantec.com/*: Symantec, a developer of security software, provides updates on the most recent viruses. The page includes links to other security advisories, as well as free malware removal tools.
- *http://us.mcafee.com/virusInfo/default.asp?cid=10371*: McAfee, another developer of security software, provides information on current virus threats and removal tools.

- *http://www.sophos.com*: Sophos is another security software developer whose Web site contains information about the latest virus threats.
- *http://www.antionline.com/*: AntiOnline is a place to meet others concerned with computer security. Answers to security questions on message boards are rated.
- *http://csrc.nist.gov/*: The Computer Security Resource Center (CSRC) of the National Institute of Standards and Technology (NIST) provides information on standards, testing, research, and so on.
- *http://www.microsoft.com/athome/security/protect/default.aspx*: Microsoft's Protect Your PC site.
- *http://www.infosyssec.com/*: InfoSysSec is a portal to a wide variety of security resources.

11

Network Design and Simulation Software

It's unfortunate for their owners and operators, but many of today's LANs have grown without overall planning. When it is unclear how a network is configured, network discovery software provides a way for a network administrator to map the hardware and software on his or her network. If, however, you have the luxury of being able to plan an entire network *before* it is implemented—as you might if your company was moving to a new location—then you can take advantage of some powerful software to help you do so. Such network design and simulation software can also let you test the network under different traffic loads and under a variety of failure conditions.

Network Design Tools

Network design and simulation software typically provides the following capabilities:

- Modeling networks of many sizes, from global to within a single floor
- Tools for diagramming a network's physical layout, including the ability to place vendor-specific hardware and software
- The ability to layer network diagrams, collapsing and expanding smaller units, such as a wiring closet, within a larger unit (for example, a floor)
- Storage for customized network configuration documentation, including quotes from vendors, equipment speeds, and so on
- The ability to specify traffic loads through specific nodes on the network and to use animation to simulate the performance of the network under those assumptions
- Simulation of failures of any network device and viewing animated simulations of how routers and switches can reroute traffic

In addition, network simulations can help identify potential design trouble spots, such as loops or cascades that are too long.

At its heart, network design software is a specialized drawing program. Most such programs let you arrange icons for hardware and software and then link those icons into a network. You may also find that you can nest larger objects, such as floors within a building, expanding them as needed to see the network detail within a containing object.

The examples in this chapter come from two software packages, Net-Cracker Designer and ConceptDraw NetDiagrammer. The first is a Windows-only package and provides network traffic simulation capabilities; the second runs on both Windows and Mac OS X. and provides basic network discovery features. Why confuse you with two products? (They certainly aren't the only ones available.) In my opinion, NetCracker Designer is best suited for diagramming larger networks while ConceptDraw Net-Diagrammer works welll for smaller networks and more general diagramming needs, such as floor plans. Both, however, are full-featured programs with some capabilities that you may never use. For example, you may never want to program using ConceptDraw's programming language.

The Network Hierarchy

Most business networks involve more than one room and often more than a single floor. To help you organize a network design based on a hierarchy of physical subunits, network design software usually provides objects—known as *containers* with NetCracker Designer—that can be collapsed within one another. This nesting can greatly simplify the design of a large network. It can also help manage such a network by providing a variety of levels at which the network's configuration can be viewed.

The network that will be used to demonstrate the use of a diagramming and simulation tool is contained in several rooms on a single floor. As you can see in Figure 11-1, an icon for the floor appears in a window named "Top," indicating that it is the top level in the network. The small rectangle drawn around the icon indicates that it is a container and that it can be expanded to show detail. The tree structure in the pane at the left of the window shows the overall container hierarchy.

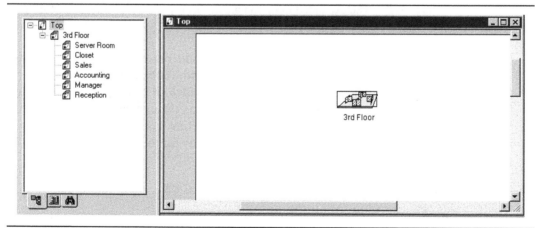

Figure 11-1:   The top level of the sample network

Note: Given that this network occupies only one floor, it is not strictly necessary to include an icon for the floor. However, if the network ever expands beyond a single floor, creating the diagram in this way will make diagramming the expansion much easier.

When expanded, the floor icon provides a window for the contents of the floor (Figure 11-2). Although it may be difficult to see in the illustration, each icon in Figure 11-2 is surrounded by a boundary rectangle, indicating that all of them are also containers.

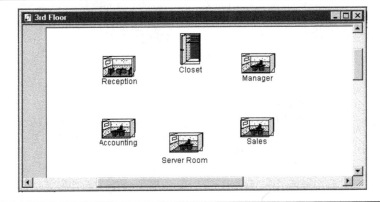

Figure 11-2:   The expanded floor container, displaying five rooms and a wiring closet

In contrast, NetDiagrammer doesn't provide expandable containers. It does, however, support hyperlinks. You could, for example, create a starting diagram containing a floor, just as we did with NetCracker. Then you would create a hyperlink to the file containing the expanded floor diagram (in Figure 11-3, an actual floorplan). A hyperlink from the label identifying each room can then open individual diagrams for the rooms.

Choosing and Configuring Network Devices

Both of the products we are using as examples in this chapter provide large databases of images to place in diagrams. As you design your network, you can place devices on the diagram. NetCracker Designer devices will go inside appropriate containers, with each container's contents appearing in a

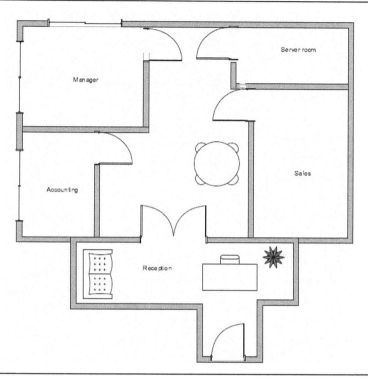

Figure 11-3:   A ConceptDraw NetDiagrammer floorplan

separate window. If you are using NetDiagrammer, then you'll either place devices on a floorplan, on a logical diagram without room boundaries, or in separate documents connected by hyperlinks.

> *Note: Which should you use — a floor plan depicting devices and wiring in their intended physical locations or a logical diagram where physical location isn't an issue? It depends on the target audience of the diagram. As you will see, placing too much information on a floorplan can be confusing, but some people do prefer to see where everything will be placed.*

In Figure 11-4 you can see the NetCracker Designer work area. The scrolling list at the left of the window contains categories of network hardware and software. The icons available within a category appear in the icon well at the bottom of the window. You can drag icons from the well into the work area to add them to the network.

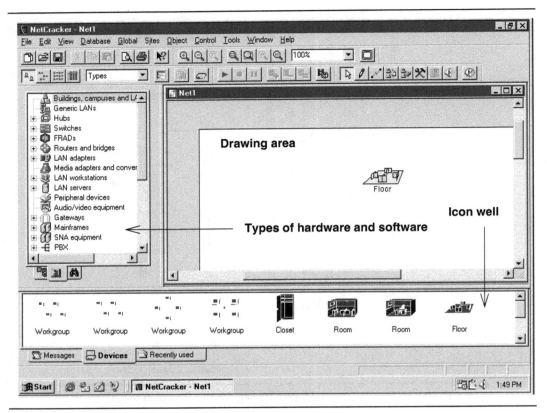

Figure 11-4:   The NetCracker Designer work area

Icons for network devices and software can be generic, as they appear in Figure 11-5. Alternatively, you can choose from a database of specific devices. For example, in Figure 11-6, the icon well contains hubs from 3Com's SuperStack line.

If you cannot find an icon in the program's database that matches the hardware or software you need, you can custom-configure your own devices, which are then stored in a user database for use wherever needed. (You will read more about this shortly.)

The ConceptDraw libraries are presented somewhat differently (see Figure 11-7), but provide similar options. The drawing surface is a separate window, much like what you'd find in a general-purpose drawing program.

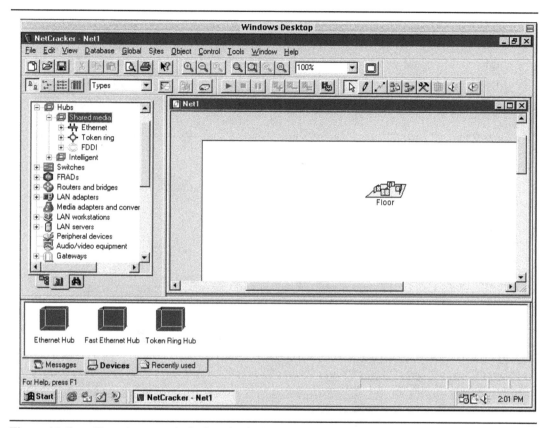

Figure 11-5::   Generic network devices in the icon well

Device Properties

The NetCracker device icons serve multiple purposes. Not only do they indicate network devices in a graphic representation of the network layout, but they can be used to document a great deal of information about each device. For example, in Figure 11-8 you can see the General properties for a stackable hub. This particular panel provides information such as the manufacturer, model number, and catalog number of the device.

Specific purchase quotes can be stored in the Price/Support Properties panel (Figure 11-9). As you can see, this makes it possible to store complete information about a device along with the network layout diagram.

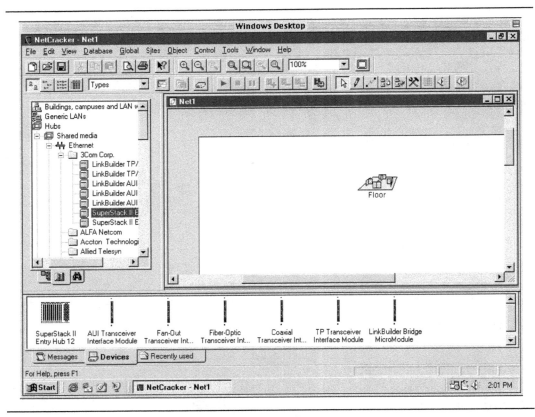

Figure 11-6:   Vendor-specific devices in the icon well

One of the most important parts of a network device are its ports. Device properties therefore include a separate listing of all ports supplied with or added to a device, as in Figure 11-10. Each port can then be configured individually (see Figure 11-11).

ConceptDraw doesn't include predefined device properties sheets. However, you can define any number of "custom" properties to apply to specific device icons. For example, in Figure 11-12 you can see the setup for the custom properties of a network interconnection device. The definitions produce the dialog box in Figure 11-13. Once defined and given values, custom properties are accessible to ConceptDraw's programming language and can therefore be included in any variety of reports, including network inventories and bills of materials.

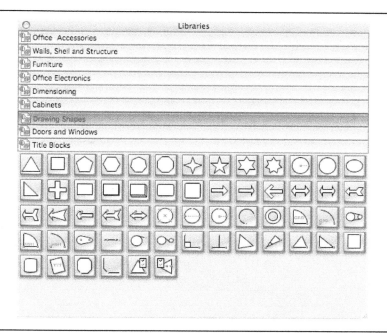

Figure 11-7:   ConceptDraw image libraries palette

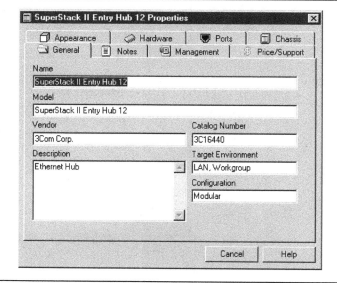

Figure 11-8:   General device properties

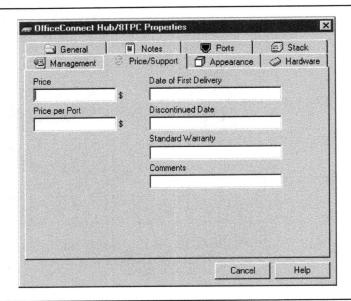

Figure 11-9:   Price/support properties

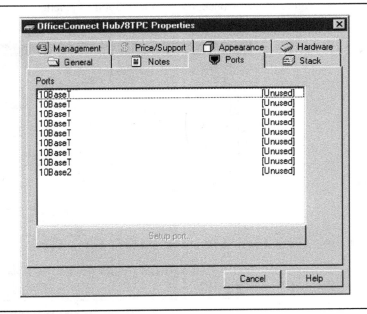

Figure 11-10:   Device port list

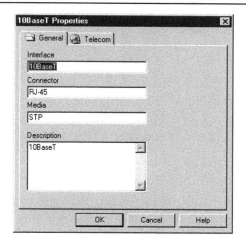

Figure 11-11:   Port properties

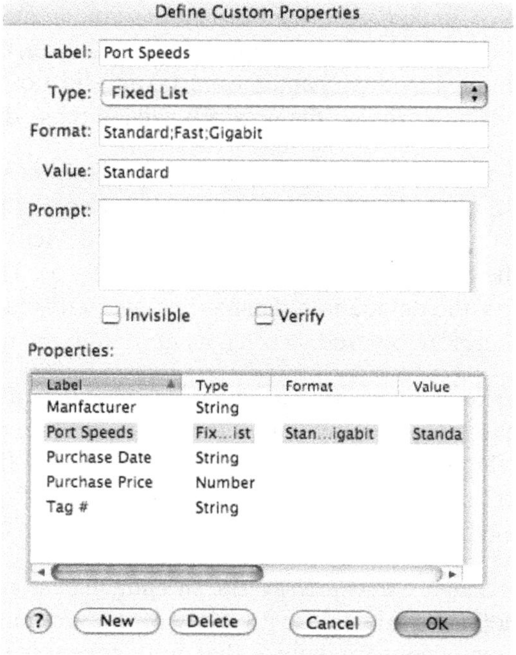

Figure 11-12:   Creating custom properties

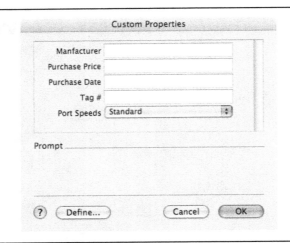

Figure 11-13:   A dialog box for entering custom property values

Custom-Built Icons

NetCracker's Device Factory lets you create devices that do not appear in the database. For example, NetCracker 1.5, the version from which the examples in this chapter were taken, did not include any Gigabit Ethernet NICs. However, the network needed those devices in its servers.

The Device Factory is actually a Windows Wizard that takes you through the process of configuring a new device. For the Gigabit Ethernet NIC, you would begin by choosing the type of device (Figure 11-14) and then giving the custom device a name (Figure 11-15). This name will be used to identify the device in a database of user-created devices. The new device can therefore be used as often as needed in the network design.

What happens after a device is named depends on the type of device. In the case of a NIC, the only other configuration necessary is the type of bus in which the card will fit (see Figure 11-16). If, however, you are creating a PC or workstation, you will need to specify ports, hard drives, removable media drives, RAM, and so on.

Because ConceptDraw doesn't attach custom property sheets to images by default, you can use a variety of the program's generic drawing shapes to create icons for devices that don't appear in the libraries. If you have a custom icon that you need to use repeatedly, you can add it to an appropriate library to make it accessible throughout the program.

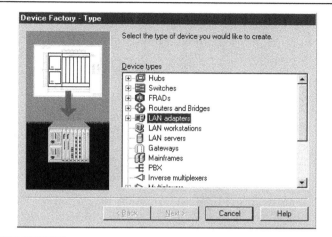

Figure 11-14: Choosing the general type for a custom device

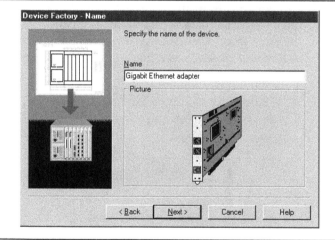

Figure 11-15: Giving a custom device a name

Linking Network Devices

Because NetCracker is basically container-oriented, it uses a method for setting up links between network devices that is somewhat different from that of ConceptDraw. To establish links between NetCracker network devices, you click on a pair of devices to be linked with a linking tool. If the

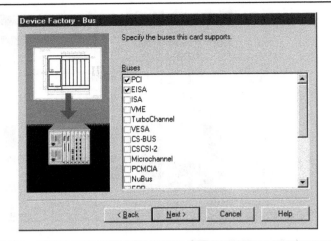

Figure 11-16:   Choosing bus types for a custom NIC

two devices are within the same container, then the process is simple: You click twice and then configure the link. However, if the two devices are in different locations—such as a workstation in a specific room and a switch in a wiring closet—then linking is a four-step process:

1.   Click on the containers in which the devices to be linked are found. The software draws a dashed line between the containers to indicate that there is an incomplete link (Figure 11-17).

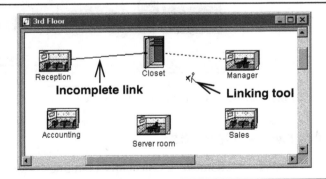

Figure 11-17:   Linking containers

2. Open one of the containers. You will see a small square that represents the link. Click on the square and the device being linked with the linking tool. Because the link is still incomplete, the line between the square and the device is dashed (Figure 11-18).

3. Open the second container. Click on the square representing the link and the device being linked with the linking tool.

4. The Link Assistant dialog box appears (Figure 11-19). The software chooses a pair of compatible ports for the link. If there are other compatible ports, you can change the selection. Then you click the Link button and close the dialog box. Because the link is complete, all lines representing the link are now solid, as in Figure 11-20.

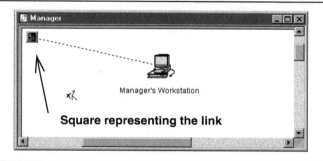

Figure 11-18:   Setting the first half of the link

The colors of the link lines represent the type of media. Although this book is printed in black and white, in Figure 11-21 one of the lines is labeled "yellow." This is the fiber optic link to a Gigabit/Fast Ethernet switch in the server room. (The switch has Gigabit Ethernet ports for the servers and a Fast Ethernet port to connect to the switch in the wiring closet.) The remainder of the links are blue, indicating UTP wiring.

Although this particular software does not allow you to customize a label for the square representing the links, each square contains a small icon of the type of device to which the link is connected. For example, in Figure 11-21 the link to the switch in the server room has what appears to be a thick line in it; this is actually a tiny drawing of a switch. The remaining squares have small PCs in them because each link goes directly to a PC. In addition, holding the mouse pointer briefly over a square brings up a hot tip with the name of the device and its container.

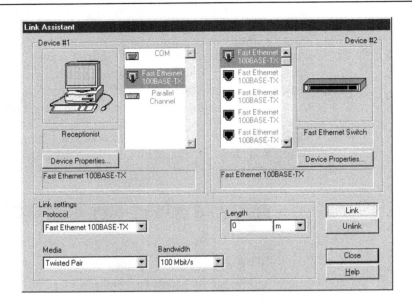

Figure 11-19:   Configuring a link

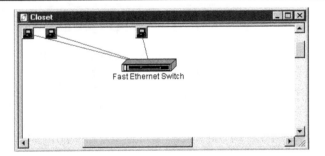

Figure 11-20:   Completed links

In Figure 11-22 you can see ConceptDraw's connectors, both in use and waiting to be placed. The "in use" connectors link the manager's desktop computer to the wall outlet using UTP cabling and the wall outlet to the wiring closet. (Because this is an exploded view of the managers office, hyperlinked to the original floor plan, the link to the wiring closet isn't shown completed but simply points in an appropriate direction.) At the top are two links whose ends can be dragged to necessary places on the diagram.

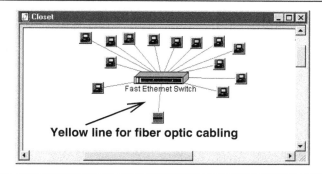

Figure 11-21:   Completed links to switch in wiring closet

The right angle link, which creates a straight line connection, has hot spots on either end that "stick" to objects in the diagram ("smart links"). If the linked object is moved on the diagram, the link moves with it. The arced connector is also a smart link with hot spots on either end, but it produces a curved line.

Simulating Network Traffic

One of the most useful things network design software can do is to simulate network traffic using animation so that you can identify potential problems. For example, a traffic simulation can help you identify bottlenecks that slow up traffic, indicating that you perhaps need to further segment your network.

Note: ConceptDraw NetDiagrammer does not provide traffic simulations, in my opinion because it is a more general-purpose drawing program than NetCracker Designer, which is dedicated to networking. The following example therefore comes solely from NetCracker Designer.

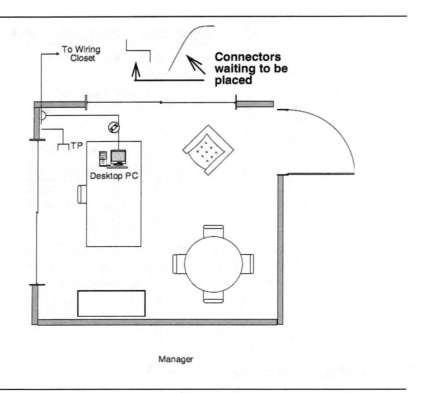

Figure 11-22:   ConceptDraw connectors

Assigning Traffic Loads

To be able to simulate network traffic, software needs to know the type of traffic that will be traveling between any two devices. The number of packets that travel between any two workstations, for example, will generally be far less than traffic between a database server and a workstation.

Before you can animate traffic, you must therefore set up traffic flows. Using Netcracker Designer you click on the two devices that will be communicating with the set traffic tool. Then, you assign a traffic profile, as in Figure 11-23.

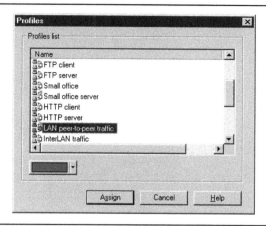

Figure 11-23:   Assigning a traffic profile

Each preconfigured traffic profile represents a typical conversation of a given type. For example, peer-to-peer traffic will be more sporadic than workstation-to-database server traffic. It is therefore probably a major understatement to say that the usefulness of a simulation rests in appropriate choices for the traffic profiles! It is also true that you are relying on the of the software developer to provide realistic estimates of the characteristics of network traffic. Only your knowledge of your own network traffic loads (or estimated loads, if you are designing a new network) and experience with a given network simulation product can determine how closely a simulation matches what occurs in the actual network.

> *Note: An enhanced version of this product — NetCracker*
> *Professional — lets you create your own traffic profiles.*

The colored rectangle in the lower left of the dialog box controls the dropdown color menu that sets the color with which the flow of packets will be illustrated. While the animation is running, the color is assigned to a small shape that indicates the protocol in use. In the example you will see, all the packets are rectangular, indicating that they are TCP/IP packets.

Packet characteristics for the entire network are configured separately. As you can see in Figure 11-24, the sliders provide relative settings for intensity (the rate at which packets are generated), speed (the speed at which an individual packet travels), and packet size.

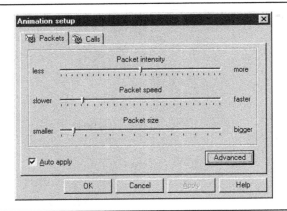

Figure 11-24:   Configuring packets for animation

Running Simulations

After assigning traffic flows, you simply start the animation. The animation appears in all windows that contain data flows, and you can switch between windows to view the traffic at various levels in the network hierarchy.

As an example, in Figure 11-25 you can see the data flow between a workstation and a printer. Although the two devices are in the same room, the network connection between them is in the wiring closet. That is why the flow is not connected directly. This is one drawback to using containers to organize a network: Viewing the contents of a container does not necessarily indicate how two devices within the container are connected.

If you move to the window showing the entire floor, however, there is both more and less information (Figure 11-26). It is clear that there is traffic among the Sales, Reception, and Manager's offices, but it is not clear exactly which devices are communicating.

One of the reasons the animation gives less information than we might like is the design of this network. Because the network is very small (only about 15 nodes), all workstations are connected to the same switch in the

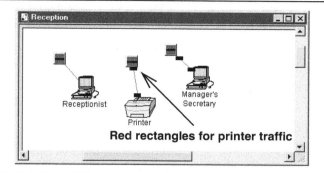

Figure 11-25:   Traffic flow between a workstation and a network printer

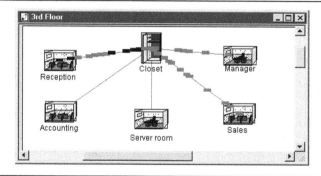

Figure 11-26:   Traffic flow within an entire floor

wiring closet. However, if each room was a workgroup with its own hub, which in turn was connected to a switch in the wiring closet, then the animation would be able to show traffic flows through each hub, providing a more complete view of peer-to-peer traffic. As you will see as you read through the network design examples in the following chapters, network animation becomes more effective with larger networks.

> *Note: It goes without saying that you should not design your network around the animation provided by network design software.*

Documenting the Network Design

As you read earlier, network design software allows you to store information that you can use to document network device purchasing plans. Network design software therefore provides a variety of reports that include information stored in device configuration/properties dialog boxes.

NetCracker Designer, for example, provides the preconfigured reports in Figure 11-27. The summaries can be generated for any level in the hierarchy or for the entire network. Reports can include sublevels in the hierarchy and provide grouping by container.

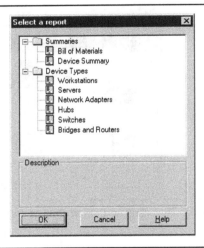

Figure 11-27:   Available reports

As an example, take a look at the partial Device Summary report that appears in Figure 11-28. This report lists each device along with its manufacturer and model. For a "shopping list" of network components, you would use the Bill of Materials report. The reports grouped by device type provide shopping lists for specific categories of hardware.

As you might imagine, the reports are only as thorough as the information entered into the network design. If a designer does not bother to include vendor and price information in the device properties, then that data will not show up in the reports.

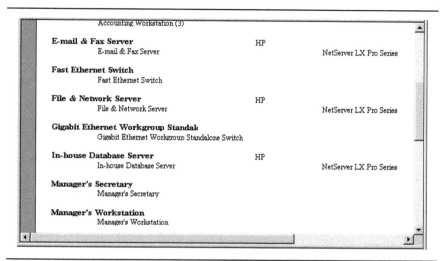

Figure 11-28: A portion of the Device Summary report, showing device, manufacturer, and model

Part Four

Ethernet Solution Examples

In this final part of the book you will read about the Ethernet networks designed for three businesses: a professional home network, a small real estate office, and a medium-size law firm. These fictional organizations will illustrate many of the concepts discussed throughout this book and give you a perspective on how network solutions change with the size of the company. In addition, you will see some of the factors that influence the decisions that a network designer might make.

> Note: The designs for the networks that you see in this part of the book are definitely the author's opinion on how the networks should be configured. Feel free to disagree! The point is for you to understand why the decisions were made as much as to show you specific solutions.

12

Network Example 1: Professional Home Network

There was a time not so long ago when the idea of a network in a home seemed ludicrous. Even though you might be running a full-time business from your home office, a network was something only people with separate office premises could do. Of course, if you've read this far in this book, you know that it's not so difficult to network a home for the professional home office. The biggest hurdle is the up-front planning.

Assume, for example, that you are running a graphics design business from the bonus room over your garage. You have two employees, both of whom split their time between the office and client premises. When they are out of the office, the employees use laptops. In the office, they use desktop computers, for a total of three desktops and two laptops.

The three of you often work together on design projects. You would therefore like a file server to act as a central repository for the files on which you are collaborating. You also need to share an Internet connection, primarily for e-mail accounts that are supplied by your ISP.. The laptops your employees use in the field typically don't connect to the network unless they are present in the office.

The choices you will make before setting up the network include:

- *Type of Internet access*: For most very small businesses, regardless of whether they are running from a home or from a separate office, the choice is between cable access or DSL. A satellite link is also a choice, but because of the uplink delay and its vulnerability during heavy rain, this should be considered only when nothing else is available. A leased line generally is too expensive (and probably overkill in terms of bandwidth); dial-up is simply unacceptable for professional use. For this example, we'll choose DSL, but there's no reason that cable access wouldn't work as well. It all depends on what's available in your area.

- *Wireless versus wired connections*: As discussed earlier in this book, wireless connections are problemmatic for several reasons, including performance and security. Stationary equipment (in this example, everything except the two laptops) can be wired. The laptops, however, tend to come and go and although you can certainly leave patch cables dangling to connect them when necessary, it will be easier to allow them to connect wirelessly as needed. (Those dangling patch cables will be stepped on; you can count on it!)

- *Type of cabling*: Fiber optic cabling supports fast transmissions, but it is hard to work with. Given that you can support Gigabit Ethernet over UTP cabling, there is little reason in a network this small to use anything else. You will want to use Cat 5e or better wiring to support high-speed links.

- *Interconnection hardware speeds*: Do you want Gigabit Ethernet or will Fast Ethernet be fast enough? Certainly the traffic coming from the Internet isn't fast enough or heavy enough to warrant Gigabit Ethernet. That means that a router that supports Fast Ethernet should be fast enough. However, because this is a graphics design business that transfers large files internally, you may want Gigabit Ethernet capabilities to access the file server. The easiest way to do this is to use a Gigabit switch that in turn connects to the router, giving you an architecture something like that in Figure 12-1.

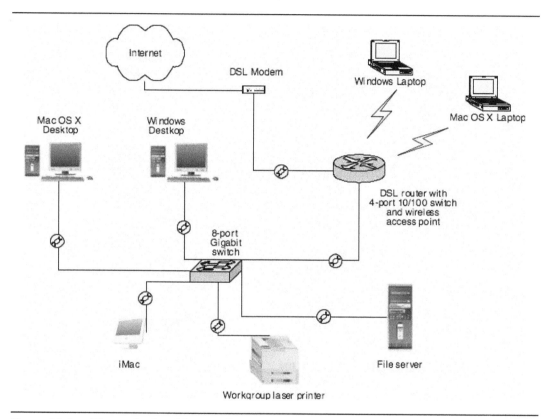

Figure 12-1:   The professional home office network architecture

In addition, you will need to give some serious thought to network security. There are two major sources of vulnerability: the shared Internet connection through the router and the wireless connections for the laptops.

Because you're not running an in-house Web server, you don't need to open many ports into your network. In fact, the firewall supplied with the router can shut down most unwanted incoming traffic. Coupled with firewall services provided by your ISP, you will be in fairly good shape, especially if you add virus protection software to each machine. (Personal firewalls certainly won't hurt but might be overkill in this scenario.) Be sure to keep track of the patches available for the desktop and file server operating systems as well. Apply them as they become available.

To secure the wireless connections, you will need to do those very basic things discussed earlier in this book: change the service set ID from the default to something known only to your employees and turn off the broadcast of the service set ID. If you want to be even more secure, turn on whatever encryption your router/access point makes available. We know that WEP isn't perfect, but it's certainly better than nothing.

The final—and perhaps most important thing—to do in terms of security is to educate your two employees on good security practices. Talk to them about password security, phishing, social engineering, safe downloading, and so on. Make them aware of security with everything they do. That will go a long way toward keeping the network free of viruses and other malware, as well as protecting your private files.

13

Ethernet Example 2: Small-But-Growing Real Estate

Small-But-Growing Real Estate (SBG) is an independent real estate brokerage that represents both buyers and sellers of homes and property. Established in 1985, the business is run as a sole proprietorship by Gregory Banks. In this chapter you will read about the introduction of a new network into an established, very small business. The choices that the business makes are related not only to its size and current needs but also to the potential for further growth.

Business Overview

Mr. Banks originally worked alone from his home. In 1989 he hired his first employee (another certified real estate broker). By 1992, he had three employees (another broker and a clerical assistant), at which point he moved from his home to his current storefront location in a strip mall.

Today, SBG employs six brokers and two clerical assistants in the same strip mall location. Each clerical assistant is equipped with a stand-alone PC that is used primarily for word processing and the preparation of specialized real estate documents. The office also has two workstations that are connected by dedicated dial-up lines to a multiple-listing service and a PC used for e-mail and faxing. All five computers have their own dot-matrix printers.

The only Internet access at this time is a dial-up connection from the e-mail computer. Employees must physically go to the computer to sign on to their e-mail accounts (hosted by a local ISP), receive e-mail, and respond to it. The floorplan of the office looks something like Figure 13-1.

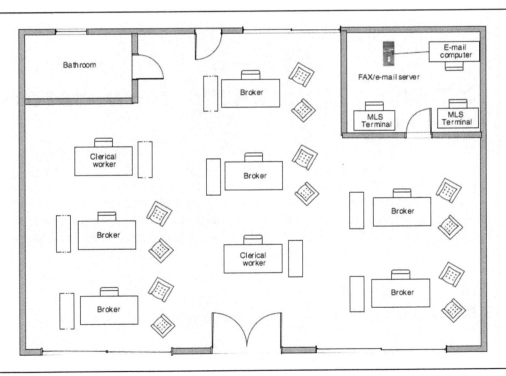

Figure 13-1:   The SBG floorplan

The office floor is carpeted and all electrical wiring runs under the carpets. Whatever network cabling SBG uses eventually can also be run under carpeting. (The office does not have dropped ceilings.)

Needless to say, the brokers are unhappy with not having e-mail and access to the multiple-listing services at their desks. Mr. Banks has been slow to adopt technology in the past, but he has finally come to the realization that networked computers are essential if he is going to continue to be successful in his field. And he has actually become somewhat enchanted with what the Internet can bring into his business.

Network Plans

As the next step in promoting his business, Mr. Banks would like to give his firm an Internet presence. He has seen the Web sites prepared by other real estate offices and believes that the sales of properties listed through his office would increase significantly if he could reach the wide audience of the Internet. After talking with a computer consultant, Mr. Banks realizes that there is a lot more to an Internet presence than some fancy graphics. He knows that the time has come to put a networked PC at each employee's desk and that he needs a broadband Internet connection. The clerical assistants will get new desktops; the brokers will get laptops that they can take into the field. Mr. Banks also wants to add a single, networked printer (and get rid of the old dot-matrix printers).

The brokers will be trained to use digital cameras and to upload photos of newly listed properties to a file server, where they can be accessed by the firm's employees. The brokers will also prepare most documents (for example, binders and mortgage qualifications) on their laptops, using forms prepared for them by the clerical workers.

Mr. Banks makes contact with a local college that has an IT major. The students are often looking for small businesses that need IT work; these "live" clients become the focus of a required IT project. Mr. Banks is therefore able to take advantage of the expertise of these students to set up and maintain an in-house Web site. He may not be able to afford a full-time IT professional, but the students are very talented and will be able to create an excellent Web presence for this firm.

Note: E-mail will be handled through the ISP. Having the Web site in-house makes life easier because files don't have to be maintained on a remote Web server. However, Mr. Banks loses nothing by having the e-mail hosted by his ISP.

The company's network will therefore consist of the following hosts:

♦ Two desktop workstations (one for each clerical assistant)
♦ Six laptops (one for each broker, including Mr. Banks)
♦ One network printer and its print server
♦ One file server
♦ One fax server
♦ One Web server

The location of Mr. Banks's office is not served by DSL, although cable Internet service is available. Mr. Banks therefore decides to use the business service available throught the cable provider. This service provides the static IP addressing that is needed for the in-house Web server.

Network Design Considerations

The design for SBG's network has two major goals: It must support a Web server and it must support the internal network. The internal network must be protected from Web traffic and from security threats that may come in through the Internet.

You can find a diagram for the top portion of the network in Figure 13-2. Notice that the Web server is connected directly to the edge router and therefore isolated from the core switch that acts as a gateway to the internal network. Hardware firewalls block incoming Web traffic from the internal network but permit it to travel to the Web server.d

The remainder of the network hosts need to be connected to workgroup switches that in turn connect to the core switch. There are currently 11 devices, 8 of which are end-user machines and 3 of which are servers. The fax and print servers work with slow devices (a fax modem and printer, respectively) and therefore don't need particularly fast network connections.

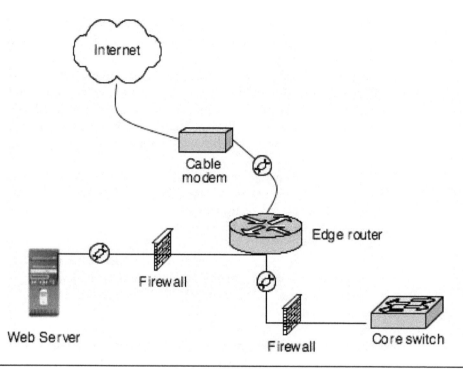

Figure 13-2:   Top of the network hierarchy for SBG

On the other hand, the file server will see a lot of use and therefore should have a fast connection.

The initial design breaks the network into three segments: two Fast Ethernet segments for workstations and slower devices and one Gigabit segment for the file server. The intent is to make it easy to expand the network without purchasing additional equipment. The core switch has 10/100/1000 autosensing ports and can therefore scale up to Gigabit Ethernet throughout the network when the time comes to upgrade workstations to Gigabit Ethernet.

How big should the router and switches be? In other words, how many ports should they have? For the foreseeable future, the router will connect only to the Web server and the core switch. A large number of ports aren't necessary, although having the LAN ports support Gigabit Ethernet would extend the life of the router.

The switches in the current design support four and six workstations and one file server. The server switch may eventually support a group of file servers and should therefore have at least eight Gigabit Ethernet ports. The workgroup switches should have 10/100 ports at a minimum (and Gigabit if affordable). Although the workgroup switches could be small (say, eight ports each), it is inevitable that the number of hosts on the network will grow. Therefore, 16-port switches would allow reasonable growth.

The laptops will use wired connections to the network. Why? Primarily for performance reasons. The brokers will be uploading large graphics files to the file server and wireless transmissions currently are relatively slow. An all-wired network will also be more secure.

> *Note: The next generation of wireless equipment —*
> *802.11n — should eventually have the throughput to han-*
> *dle high-resolution photographs, but at the time this book*
> *was written, 802.11n hadn't come to market.*

The design of the internal network (from the core switch) can be found in Figure 13-3. All of the cabling is UTP. There won't be enough server traffic to warrant fiber optics at this point and UTP is significantly easier to install and maintain. The patch cables for the laptops will run under carpeting to the brokers' desks and then run up the desk legs to the desktops, held in place with plastic cable ties. The cables therefore will be protected from damage even when not connected to computers.

There are no hard and fast rules about how to divide the network hosts into network segments. The SBG network is organized primarily around usage patterns. The clerical workers do most of the printing and faxing. It therefore makes sense to have the fax server and the shared printer on the same network segment as the clerical workers' workstations, keeping most of the fax and printer traffic out of the core switch. Should the brokers start to do more than occasional printing, it may make sense to add a second printer on their segment rather than have printer traffic go through the core.

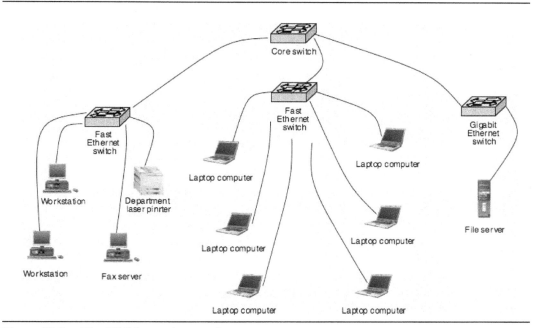

Figure 13-3:   The SBG internal network

Decisions of this type can be made, however, only after the network has been up and running for some time. Performance bottlenecks don't necessarily show up early in a network's life. As users become more comfortable with what the network can do, they tend to use it more and more.

Note: The tendency of network usage to go up over time is an example of the "superhighway effect," which was first observed (and named for) road usage. A new road is put in and estimated to handle traffic without significant backups for X number of years. Everything looks fine at first, but word gets out that the road is good, and more and more people use it. The road capacity is filled in X/2 years (or something significantly less than the original estimate). The same thing tends to happen with the bandwidth of computer networks. As users discover all the things they can do with the network, they use up the available bandwidth much more quickly than estimated and the network needs expansion sooner than its designers anticipated.

The physical placement of equipment doesn't necessarily mirror the logical network arrangement. The router, the firewalls, and the switches will be mounted in a single rack that is placed in the current equipment room. The file server and fax server can also be placed in the equipment room. At least one, and perhaps two, of the desks that currently support stand-alone PCs can be removed. (One might be needed for the file server and another for the fax server.)

What about security? Now that users can access e-mail and the multiple-listing services from their desktops, the equipment room can be locked. It can be secured with a smart-lock that uses an entry code. Only those involved in maintaining the hardware should have access to that room.

The two hardware firewalls (specialized appliances running firewall software) provide significant protection. As mentioned earlier, the firewall that isolates the Web server admits Web requests but the firewall that isolates the internal network does not. (The internal network's firewall lets Web requests go out and admits responses to requests from the internal network, however.)

Despite the firewalls, the file server should be protected with passworded user accounts. Because users on the internal network will be downloading e-mail, some of which will have attachments, they should have up-to-date virus and malware protection software, as well as personal firewalls. And, as always, user education about safe downloading, avoiding social engineering threats, and other secure behaviors is essential.

Network Example 3: Small Law Firm

Small Law Firm (SLF) is a 55-year-old law firm that will be moving from offices on three floors of an old building into two floors of an office tower currently under construction several blocks away from its current location. SLF has been given the opporunity to wire its floors for telecommunications while construction is still in progress.

SLF has 30 attorneys (10 of whom are partners), 20 legal secretaries, one office manager, one bookkeeper, and one receptionist. Each partner has his or her own legal secretary; the remaining legal secretaries work for two attorneys each.

In its current location, SLF has a 10Base-T Ethernet network that gives all clerical workers access to an e-mail server and a file server. Some of the attorneys also have PCs in their offices that they use for e-mail.

The file server contains templates for common legal forms. When a form is needed, a legal secretary loads a copy of the form from the server and fills it in. The form is then printed and copied. All printed document copies are retained in filing cabinets.

SLF sees the move to new quarters as an opportunity to upgrade its network and data processing in general. First, the attorneys would like to move away from the slower 10Base-T Ethernet to at least Fast Ethernet, with the possibility of using Gigabit Ethernet for the network backbone (in other words, for the connection between floors). Second, they would like to move to permanent electronic storage of documents and the retrieval of those documents over the network. This will involve placing document images on high-capacity network attached storage devices. The network consultant working with the firm estimates that the initial document database will require two terabytes of storage and will grow by at least a half a terabyte a year.

Third, SLF would like to consider an online subscription to a law book service that could also be available over the network through a shared Internet connection. In the long run, this would save the attorneys considerable money, given that SLF will need only one subscription to each law book series, rather than relying on attorneys to purchase their own hard copies. The idea is to eventually move to an all-electronic law library, including online access to legal search services such as Lexis from all offices rather than just from the library.

> *Note: SLF understands that there may be some attorneys who purchase their own hard copies of law books anyway, given that they like the "look" of all those books on their office shelves.*

There are two ways to begin designing a network of this type. One is from the "bottom up," where you start with the workstations and other end-user devices and then collect them into workgroups. You connect the workgroups with switches and then connect the entire network through some sort of backbone. Alternatively, you can work from the "top down," where you begin with the backbone, moving to workgroups in general and finally to the individual end-user devices.

Most successful information technology projects today are designed using a nominally top-down approach. In truth, you cannot design a network without considering the end-user devices as you specify backbones, routers, and switches. At the very least, you must have some idea of how many end-user devices (workstations and printers, for example) you will have and how they will interact.

The Internet, the Backbone, and Equipment Rooms

Because SLF is not occupying an entire building, it does not have the option of locating its main equipment room in the basement; the main equipment room must be somewhere on one of the two floors occupied by the law firm (the fourth and fifth floors of the building).

> *Note: In theory, SLF could negotiate with the building owners to allow them to place wiring in the basement. However, this presents major security problems. The equipment room, the location where Internet access enters the building, is beyond the control of the firm's network administrators. SLF wouldn't have the right to restrict access to the basement and therefore securing an equipment room there would present a considerable challenge. In addition, there would be a long run of cable from the basement to the firm on the fourth and fifth floors. It would then be difficult to secure the cables as they ran through spaces not occupied by SLF.*

The reception desk, the office manager's office, and the bookkeeper's office are to be located on the fourth floor. The attorneys and the legal secretaries are distributed throughout both floors, resulting in more room on the fifth floor for computer equipment. There will therefore be an equipment room on each floor, but the fourth floor will be a relatively small wiring closet while the fifth floor will have a much larger server room.

Note: The physical entrance to the business will be on the fourth floor. This means that there will be much less foot traffic on the fifth floor and only employees will be able to go there unescorted. The fifth floor is therefore more secure than the fourth and makes a better location for physically sensitive servers.

The network designer needs to make several choices when designing the backbone running between the two floors and the connection to the Internet:

♦ *Type of Internet access*: A business of this size might choose to use DSL or cable access. However, given that SLF plans to subscribe to law books online and also provide access to legal search services over the Internet, neither DSL nor cable access may have enough bandwidth for the entire firm. Therefore, a T1 line to a local ISP is probably the best choice. The ISP can also provide e-mail serving, which relieves SLF of one IT chore. In addition, should SLF decide to set up a Web site, the ISP can be used for hosting, rather than SLF managing the Web server in-house.

♦ *Type of Internet interconnection hardware*: SLF will almost certainly want an edge router to provide Internet connectivity. For security purposes, it should also consider a stand-alone firewall between the router and the internal portion of the network.

♦ *Number of subnets on each floor and how they will connect into a hierarchical structure*: SLF could use a single edge router and a hierarchy of switches, but to achieve better performance in a network of this size, SLF will probably want a router on each floor. The routers can then connect to a group of workgroup switches.

♦ *Speed to the interconnection hardware*: The backbone will certainly run Gigabit Ethernet and run a Gigabit Ethernet line to the server farm, but Fast Ethernet will be adequate for the desktops. It is true that many desktop computers are now shipping with Gigabit Ethernet on the motherboard, but Gigabit switches of more than eight ports are relatively expensive, and if the firm needs to cut financial corners at any point, sticking with Fast Ethernet equipment could help.

♦ *Type of cabing to use for the backbone and other interconnection runs*: Legally, SLF must use a minimum of Cat 5 plenum cabling in the drop ceilings and between floors. However, fiber optic cabling is also a viable choice between the two floors given that this vertical riser cable will be carrying traffic from the server farm.

In addition, SLF will need to contract with a company to scan and index existing hard copy documents for the electronic archive. This process will start with the most recent documents and proceed backward in time, stopping when SLF feels those documents most likely to be referenced have been scanned. Recent documents that have been prepare electronically will also need to be added to the document collection. SLF will need to choose hardware and software for maintaining the documents and their index. This will include upward of 4 to 5 terabytes of hard disk space. (Remember that the initial storage will use about 2 terabytes and that growth of about a half a terabyte a year is expected. Given what we know about the superhighway effect, growth will likely exceed the initial estimate!)

Between the Floors

SLF's connection to the Internet and backbone interconnections can be found in Figure 14-1. Notice that the routers to each floor connect directly to the edge router. This means that Internet traffic will be split relatively evenly between the two routers (assuming that workstations are allocated relatively evenly between the floors), which should improve performance.

In adidtion to the link from the edge router to each floor router, there is a link between the two floor routers. The purpose of this cable is to allow internal traffc, especially that from the fourth floor to the server room, to travel directly to its destination, without being handled by the edge router. This will not only improve internal performance, but should provide additional security for internal traffic, since in most cases such packets won't go outside the firewalls.

The routers can handle the resulting loop structure (although switches cannot without the spanning tree protocol), and the loop also provides fault tolerance should one of the links from the edge router go down.

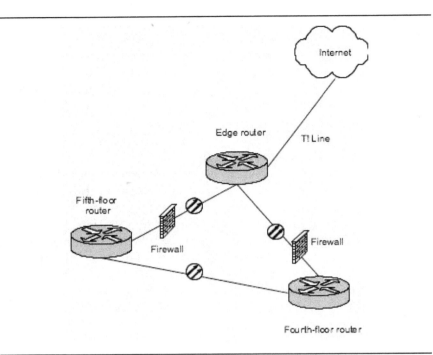

Figure 14-1:   SLF's top-level network inteconnections

The Fifth-Floor Server Room

As mentioned earlier, the fifth floor provides an excellent location for the server room. It has the physical space to house the server farm and is more secure than the fourth floor. The server room must house a file server and the document database server with the NAS storage arrays. This area will also contain a rack for the edge router, the fifth-floor router, and workgroup switches used on the fifth floor.

> *Note: The T1 line to the Internet enters the building through the basement, along with all the other utilities. We'll look at securing this line at the end of this chapter.*

The servers and NAS are organized into their own network segment, using a Gigabit switch. Because they are close together, using fiber optic cabling to connect them to their switch (and the switch to the fifth-floor router) is relatively easy. This will provide the best performance possible for these high-traffic machines.

The connections in the server room are diagrammed in Figure 14-2. The one aspect of this layout that might seem unusual is that the disk arrays for the document database are not connected directly to the database server, but instead attached to the network. This allows the database server to take advantage of the Gigabit Ethernet connection to access the storage devices, as well as providing fast access for end users.

The Fourth-Floor Wiring Closet

The fourth-floor wiring closet only needs to provide one or more work-group switches for the fourth floor. It will therefore contain the fourth-floor router and switches in a single rack. As you would expect from what you have seen already, there are two fiber optic cables running to the fifth floor, one to the fifth-floor router and one to the edge router.

Connecting End-User Devices

Once the floor interconnections are designed, SLF needs to decide how to organize the end-user devices, which are primarily desktop workstations and printers.

> Note: Some of the lawyers have laptops that they use at home, but all laptops have docking stations at the office that are wired to the network. There is no wireless access needed or wanted for this network.

SLF could use one of two basic strategies to connect its end-user devices to the network. It might create a collection of small network segments (for example, 8 to 16 devices) connected with switches. Each small segment would be connected to the floor router in the wiring closet. Alternatively, all workstations can be connected directly to a single, large switch.

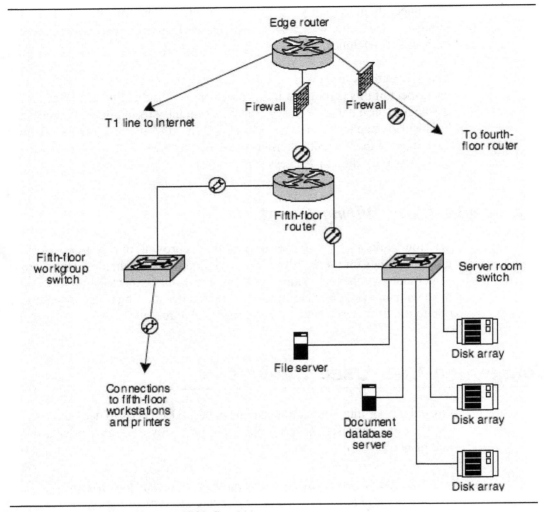

Figure 14-2:   The server room (fifth floor)

Note: In either case, SLF will want twice the number of
ports as end-user devices to allow for future expansion.

As you might expect, there are benefits and drawbacks to both strategies.
Using small network segments makes the network more fault tolerant. If
one of the switches in the hierarchy goes down, the other network segments can continue to function. Small network segments will have better

performance under heavy loads if most traffic is between the devices on a single subnet because there will be less traffic contending for the floor router in the wiring closet and for the backbone. However, performance will suffer if a large portion of the traffic requires access to the servers or is between subnets. Small network segments will make the network design more complex: The network will be more difficult to manage and problems will be more difficult to troubleshoot.

SLF decides to use two 24-port workgroup switches on each floor. This provides enough ports for workstations and printers, only four switches to be managed, and have enough excess capacity to make small changes in configurations easy to handle.

End-user network devices use Fast Ethernet with UTP Category 5e wiring.

Security Considerations

A network such as SLF's is subject to both legal and ethical constraints on the disclosure of information. It is particularly essential that the document database remain secure because it contains information that legally must remain private. Although it is hidden behind the firewalls that isolate the internal network, there are nonetheless vulnerablilities to which the network administrators need to respond, including the following:

 ◆ *Physical security*: The location of the the servers in the fifth floor server room and the lock on the door provides a significant degree of protection against those who could exploit physical access to server consoles.
 ◆ *Denial-of-service attacks*: Because this network is connected to the Internet, it is vulnerable to denial-of-service attacks. Careful log monitoring and instrusion detection software will help.
 ◆ *Malware*: Because there will be so much e-mail passing in and out of this network, malware is a major threat. Good virus checking software on each server and workstation is the best automated protection.

♦ *User authentication*: The primary goal of a hacker is to gain access to at least one user account on the network, and to then promote that access to administrator status. The network will therefore need to authenticate users carefully; simple user names and passwords probably aren't enough. A second factor such as a fingerprint or one-time password generated by a small device carried by the user will add significant security.

♦ *Social engineering*: Because the network will be technically hardened against intrusions, many hackers will attempt to gain entry by conning information out of employees, especially clerical employees. Employee education is therefore essential so that employees can recognize attempts to trick them into revealing sensitive information.

A

Older Ethernet Standards

Although prices for Fast (100 Mbps) Ethernet have decreased dramatically, 10BASE-T Ethernet can still be found in existing small networks. Even older types of Ethernet—10BASE5 (thicknet) and 10BASE2 (thinnet)—still exist in legacy installations. This appendix gives you an overview of the three older standards so that you will be familiar with their limitations should you ever encounter them.

All three Ethernet standards discussed in this appendix are rated at a maximum of 10 Mbps. Both 10BASE5 and 10BASE2 use the original bus topology; 10BASE-T, which can use a hub or a switch, is a true bus when using a hub (although the bus wiring is hidden in the hub) but is little different from Fast Ethernet (except in speed) when configured with a switch.

Thick Coaxial Cable (10BASE5)

The original Ethernet standard and the first IEEE standard (10BASE5) was written for thick coaxial cable, such as that in Figure A-1. Although a single piece of cable can be up to 500 meters long without running into signal problems, thick coax is physically hard to bend, simply because it is so thick. In fact, its diameter is about a half-inch. Although you can't tell from the black-and-white illustration, its typical bright yellow outer coating has given thick coax its nickname of "frozen yellow garden hose."

Figure A-1:   Thick coaxial cable (Courtesy of Belden Wire & Cable Co.)

The basic technique for creating 10BASE5 networks was to install a *drop cable* made of a single, unbroken stretch of thick coaxial cable. Then, each device was equipped with a NIC that had an AUI to which a transceiver cable was attached. The other end of the transceiver cable was attached to the transceiver, which in turn clamped onto the drop cable.

In early implementations, the transceiver actually cut through the outer wrappings of the drop cable to make physical contact with the copper mesh layer and the copper wire at the center (a "vampire clamp," such as the one used by the transceiver in Figure A-2). This meant that if you disconnected a transceiver from the drop cable, you were left with a break in the cable's shielding.

Because 10BASE5 is so difficult to work with, it is not being used in new networks. However, there are still some 10BASE5 *backbones* (networks to which other networks are connected) in use in office parks and college campuses, and it is possible to get replacement parts (cables and transceivers) for such networks.

Figure A-2:   A 10BASE5 transceiver that uses a vampire clamp to tap into thicknet cable (Courtesy of Allied TeleSyn)

Thin Coaxial Cable (10BASE2)

Prior to the relatively popularity of 10BASE-T and UTP wiring, most Ethernet networks were constructed using thin coaxial cable (thinnet or 10BASE2), such as that in Figure A-3. Although it looks like the cable you use to connect your VCR to your TV set, the electrical characteristics of the cable and the connector are different.

Figure A-3:   Thin coaxial cable (Courtesy of Belden Wire & Cable Co.)

As you can see in Figure A-3, coaxial cable is made of several layers. A copper wire runs down the center, surrounded by a sheath of plastic insulation. The plastic is covered by a foil shield, which in turn is covered by a braided-copper mesh. The outer covering is plastic, which protects the cable from the elements. The connectors placed on the end of the cable make contact with both the inner copper wire and the braided-copper mesh.

10BASE2 does not require a hub or switch like 10BASE-T. Instead, devices are connected to the network using transceivers and a transceiver cable, as in Figure A-4. The transceiver is a separate unit (see Figure A-5).

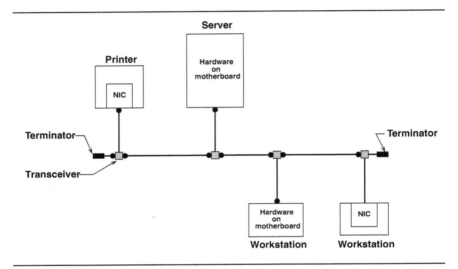

Figure A-4:   Connecting devices to create a 10BASE2 network

Figure A-5:   A 10BASE2 transceiver (Courtesy of Allied Telesyn)

Thinnet networks typically use BNC connectors such as that in Figure A-6. The outer sleeve of the connector rotates to snap into place, making a firm connection between the cable the transceiver or NIC to which it is being attached (see Figure A-7). (Many RGB monitors also used BNC connectors to connect individual red, green, and blue cables.)

Figure A-6:   BNC connector (Courtesy of Belkin)

Note: There seems to be some disagreement over what BNC stands for. Some people think it means British Naval Connector, and others think it means Bayonet Neill-Concelman. (Neill and Concelman designed the connectors.) And still others insist that the meaning is Barrel Nut Connector. Take your pick ...

A 10BASE2 network is made of short segments of cable. The bus is assembled by connecting lengths of coax with BNC tee connectors (see Figure A-8). You need one tee connector at each point to which a device is connected to the network. A piece of network cable attaches at each end of the tee's crossbar; a transceiver cable connects to the "leg" of the tee.

10BASE2 network segments also require *terminators* at each end (see Figure A-9). A terminator prevents the unwanted reflection of signals from the ends of the bus back down the network medium. You can either put a separate terminator on each end of the cable or purchase tee connectors that are self-terminating and use the self-terminating tee connectors for the last device on each end of the cable.

Thin coax is relatively inexpensive and, as you might guess by its name (10BASE2), can handle segment lengths of up to 200 meters. It also bends easily and therefore lends itself to being installed in walls, ceilings, and across floors to be connected directly to network devices. In addition, it has the benefit of not requiring a hub.

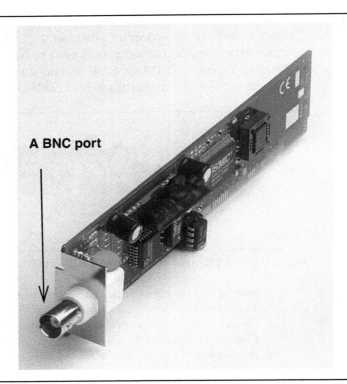

Figure A-7:   A BNC port on a NIC (Courtesy of Farallon Corp.)

Figure A-8:   A BNC tee connector (Courtesy of Belkin)

Figure A-9:   10BASE2 cable terminator (Courtesy of Belkin)

However, the flexibility of UTP wire and the ability to use existing wiring resulted in fewer and fewer new 10BASE2 networks being installed once UTP cabling was widely available. Thin coax is also limited to 10 Mbps, while UTP wiring can carry at least up to 1000 Mbps.

10BASE-T

The arrival of UTP cabling to carry Ethernet seignals created a great change in networking: The hardware was significantly easier to install and maintain and it was much cheaper than any other type of installation. Networking could be used by much smaller businesses. Hubs and patch cables made it possible to have a true "plug and play" network. It's no wonder that the bulk of our Ethernet today looks much like an upgrade of the original 10BASE-T.

Creating 10BASE-T Network Segments with a Hub

Simple 10BASE-T networks almost always used a hub like that in Figure A-10, producing what looked like an external star configuration. Keep in mind, however, that a hub is a passive device that contains internal bus wiring. It makes no routing decisions but can only broadcast all received signals out all ports.

An RJ-45 connector snapped into place in the hub just like an RJ-11 telephone connector. Connecting a small 10BASE-T network therefore required nothing more than snapping cables into the network interfaces of
the devices to be connected to the network and snapping the other ends of
those cables into the hub's ports.

Figure A-10:   10BASE-T hub (Courtesy of 3Com Corporation)

If a NIC or the Ethernet hardware on a motherboard didn't have an RJ-45
port, but instead had either an *AUI* (attachment unit interface) or *AAUI*
(Apple attachment unit interface) port, you could still use that device on a
10BASE-T network by connecting the device first to a 10BASE-T transceiver such as that in Figure A-11.

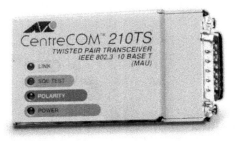

Figure A-11:   A 10BASE-T transceiver (Courtesy of Allied Telesyn)

The transceiver, connected to the device via a transceiver cable, acted as a
converter between the AUI or AAUI port and an RJ-45 port. It also ensured
that the device received the same type of signal, regardless of the type of
Ethernet cabling in use.

Note: Most RJ-45–equipped NICs did not require external transceivers because the circuitry contained in a transceiver was built into the NIC.

In Figure A-12 you will find a summary of the ways in which you would typically attach devices to a 10BASE-T hub. Notice that some devices use a NIC, some use a NIC and a transceiver, while still others have all networking hardware (including the transceiver) built onto the motherboard.

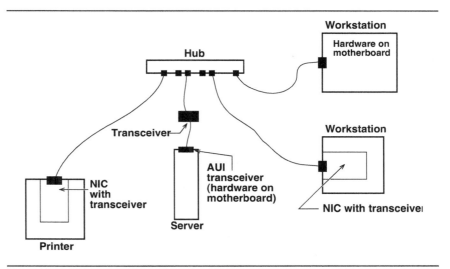

Figure A-12:   Constructing a 10BASE-T network using a hub

An alternative to a desktop hub—often used in multifloor office buildings— is a *wiring closet,* a locked cabinet that contains the wiring for the bus. All devices are connected to the bus inside the closet using a *patch panel.* The wiring closet also typically contains hardware that connects the bus on a single floor with other networks in the building. (Today's "wiring closets" are often server rooms that contain servers, switches, and routers.)

Note: Wiring closets are locked for security purposes. Anyone with access to the bus itself can easily tap into the network by simply plugging in a computer.

B

TCP and UDP Ports

Well-Known Ports

Software ports are used by TCP/IP to associate segments with application programs running on a host that receives a message. The *well-known ports* are used primarily by communications processes and other privileged applications, and have numbers between 0 and 1023.

> *Note: Application developers can register ports for their programs with IANA. Registered ports are in the range of 1024 through 49151. Ports between 49152 and 65536 are dynamic and/or private.*

Table B-1 contains a selection of well-known ports that you may want your firewall to block. In almost all cases, both TCP and UDP have the same port number assignments.

309

Table B-1 Well-Known TCP and UDP Ports

Port	Protocol or Application
1	TCP Port Service Multiplier (TCPMUX)
5	Remote Job Entry (RJE)
7	ECHO
17	Quote of the Day
18	Message Send Protocol (MSP)
20	FTP (default data port)
21	FTP (control port)
22	SSH Remote Login Protocol
23	Telnet
24	Any private mail system
25	SMTP
29	MSG ICP
35	Any private print server
37	Time
38	Remote Access Protocol
39	Remote Location Protocol
41	Graphics
42	Host Name Server
43	WhoIs
44	Message Processing Module (MPM) Flags Protocol
49	Login Host Protocol (Login)
53	DNS
57	Any private terminal access
58	XNS Mail
59	Any private file service

Table B-1 Well-Known TCP and UDP Ports

Port	Protocol or Application
65	Terminal Access Control Access Control System (TACACS) Database Service
66	Oracle SQL*NET
67, 68	Bootstrap Protocol Server
69	Trivial File Transfer Protocol
70	Gopher
71, 72, 73, 74	Remote Job Service
75	Any private dial out service
77	Any private RJE service
79	Finger
80	HTTP
80	Nimda[a]
84	Common Trace Facility
85	MIT ML Device
86	Micro Focus COBOL
87	Any private terminal link
88	Kerberos
92	Network Printing Protocol
93	Device Control Protocol
103	X,400 Standard
107	Remote Telnet Service
109	Post Office Protocol (POP2)
110	Post Office Protocol (POP3)
115	Simple File Transfer Protocol
117	UUCP Path Service
118	SQL Services

Table B-1 Well-Known TCP and UDP Ports

Port	Protocol or Application
119	Network News Transfer Protocol (NNTP)
123	Network Time Protocol
129	Password Generator Protocol
137	NETBIOS Name Service
138	NETBIOS Datagram Service
139	NETBIOS Session Service
143	Internet Message Access Protocol (IMAP4)
150	SQL*NET
152	Background File Transfer Protocol
153	SGMP
156	SQL Server
158	PCMail Server
161	SNMP
162	SNMP TRAP
197	Directory Location Service (DLS)
201–208	AppleTalk
209	Quick Mail Transfer Protocol
213	IPX
389	Lightweight Directory Access Protocol (LDAP)
395	Novell Netware over IP
402	Genie Protocol
407	Timbuktu
443	HTTPS
444	Simple Network Paging Protocol
445	Microsoft-DS
445	Sasser[b]

Table B-1 Well-Known TCP and UDP Ports

Port	Protocol or Application
458	Apple QuickTime
512	biff
513	login (remote login using telnet)
514	who
515	shell
546	DHCP Client
547	DHCP Server
563	SNEWS
569	MSN
591	FileMaker 6.0 Web Sharing
592	Eudora
666	Doom
729–731	IBM NetView
749, 750	Kerberos
989, 990	FTP data over TLS/SSL
991	Netnews Administration Services
992	telnet over TLS/SSL
993	imap4 over TLS/SSL
994	irc over TLS/SSL
995	pop3 over TLS/SSL

a. This worm uses the same port as HTTP, which is, of course, an unauthorized use of the port.

b. Another piece of malware using a port without authorization.

Registered Ports

Table B-2 contains a selection of widely used or important registered ports. Note those that represent malware are not registered but are nonetheless using ports in the registered ports range. Also notice that the heaviest port users are network games!

Table B-2: Selected Registered TCP Ports

Port	Name
1027	ICQ
1080	SOCKS
1214	Kazaa
1337	WASTE (Encrypted file sharing program)
1524	Trinoo (TCP)
2555	RTSP Streaming Media Proxy
3001	Remote Control Service
3128	HTTP (Used by web caches)
3150	DeepThroat
3306	MySQL
3380	SOCKS Proxy Server
3381	Telnet Proxy Server
3382	WWW Proxy Server
3383	FTP Proxy Server
3384	POP3 Proxy Server
3385	SMTP Server
3521	Netrek
5000	Universal Plug and Play
5190–5194	AOL and AOL Instant Messenger
5432	Postgres
5800	VNC (Remote desktop protocol for use over HTTP)

Table B-2: Selected Registered TCP Ports *(Continued)*

5900	VNC (Remote desktop protocol)
5999	EverQuest (UDP)
6000	X11
6667	IRC
7000	EverQuest (TCP)
8000	iRDMI
8080	HTTP (Alternative port often used when a second Web server is running on the same machine as a Web server using port 80.)
8998	Sobig.F
26000	Quake
27444	Trinoo (UDP)
27500	Quake World
27665	Trinoo (TCP)
27910	Quake II
27960	Quake III
31335	Trinoo (UDP)
31337	Back Orifice
34555	Trinoo (UDP)
35555	Trinoo (UDP)

Port List References

You can find complete lists of port assignments in several places:

- ◆ Complete list of assigned ports:
  http://www.iana.org/assignments/port-numbers

- ◆ Ports used by Trojan horses:
  http://www.simovits.com/trojans/trojans.html
- ◆ Searchable database of assigned ports:
  http://ports.tantalo.net/

Products and Vendors

The body of this book mentions many specific products as examples of Ethernet concepts. This appendix contains contact information for the manufacturers of those products. Web addresses were correct at the time this book was written.

A mention of a product in this book does not constitute an endorsement of that product. It is up to you to evaluate products yourself to determine which best meet your particular needs.

Allied Telesyn
Transceivers, switches, hubs
19015 North Creek Parkway, #200
Bothell, WA 98011
Voice: (800) 424-4284
Fax: (425) 489-9191
Web site: http://www.alliedtelesyn.com

Apple Computer
AppleTalk, AppleShare, Macintosh OS
1 Infinite Loop
Cupertino, CA 95014
Voice: (408) 996-1010
Web site: http://www.apple.com

Belden Wire & Cable Company
Network cabling
2200 U.S. Highway 27 South
P.O. Box 1980
Richmond, IN 47374
Voice: (765) 983-5200
Fax: (765) 983-5294
Web site: http://www.belden.com

Belkin Components
Network cabling
501 West Walnut Street
Compton, CA 90220
Voice: (800) 2-BELKIN
Fax: (310) 898-1111
Web site: http://www.belkin.com

Caldera, Inc.
Network-ready operating system (Linux)
240 West Center Street
Orem, Utah 84057
Voice: (801) 765-4999
Fax: (801) 765-1313
Web site: http://www.calderasystems.com

Cisco Systems, Inc.
**Interconnection hardware (routers, switches, gateways, firewalls,
    and so on)**
170 West Tasman Dr.
San Jose, CA 95134
Voice: (408) 526-4000
Web site: http://www.cisco.com

Citrix Systems
MetaFrame
6400 Northwest 6th Way
Ft. Lauderdale, FL 33309
Voice: (954) 267-3000
Fax: (954) 267-9319
Web site: http://www.citrix.com

ConceptDraw (CS Odessa LLC)
Project management and network diagramming software
1798 Technology Dr. Ste. 244
San Jose, CA 95110-1399
Voice: (408) 441-1150
Fax: (408) 441-1138
Web site: http://www.conceptdraw.com

Farallon Communications, Inc.
**Daisy-chainable Ethernet adapters (EtherWave), PCMCIA
        network adapters**
3089 Teagarden Street
San Leandro, CA 94577
Voice: (510) 814-5000
Fax: (510) 814-5015
Web site: http://www.farallon.com

Hewlett-Packard
**Hubs, switches, hub and switch management software
        (NetCenter), hardware print servers**
3000 Hanover Street
Palo Alto, CA 94304
Voice: (650) 857-1501
Fax: (650) 857-5518
Web site: http://www.hp.com

IBM
Network operating system (OS/2 Lan Server)
1133 Westchester Avenue
White Plains, NY 10604
Voice: (800) IBM 4YOU
Fax: (770) 863-3030
Web site: http://www.ibm.com

Linksys
Interconnection hardware (hubs, switches, and routers)
121 Theory Drive
Irvine, CA 92617
Voice: (949) 823-3000
Fax: (949) 823-1100
Web site: http://www.linkss.com

Microsoft Corporation
Network operating systems (Microsoft Windows LAN Manager,
        Windows NT, Windows 2000, Microsoft Vista), Windows OS
One Microsoft Way
Redmond, WA 98052
Voice: (425) 882-8090
Web site: http://www.microsoft.com

Neon Software
Network mapping software (LANsurveyor), multiprotocol
        network analyzer (TrafficWatch, now integrated into
        NetMinder Ethernet)
3685 Mt. Diablo Boulevard
Suite 253
Lafayette, CA 94549
Voice: (800) 334-NEON
Fax: (925) 283-6507
Web site: http://www.neon.com

NetCracker Technology Company
**Network design and simulation software (NetCracker Designer,
NetCracker Professional)**
1159 Main Street
Waltham, MA 02154
Voice: (800) 477-5785
Fax: (781) 736-1735
Web site: http://www.netcracker.com

Netopia, Inc.
**Multiplatform network integration software (Timbuktu Pro),
routers**
2470 Mariner Square Loop
Alameda, CA 94501
Voice: (510) 814-5000
Fax: (510) 814-5025
Web site: http://www.netopia.com

Novell Corporation
Network operating system (Novell NetWare)
2211 North First Street
San Jose, CA 95131
Voice: (408) 968-5000
Web site: http://www.novell.com

Red Hat Software, Inc.
Network-ready operating system (Linux)
P.O. Box 13588
Research Triangle Park, NC 27709
Voice: (800) 454-5502
Fax: (919) 547-0024
Web site: http://www.redhat.com

The Siemon Company
Network cabling
Siemon Business Park
76 Westbury Park Road
Watertown, CT 06795
Voice: (860)274-2523
Fax: (860) 945-4225
Web site: http://www.siemon.com

3Com Corporation
NICs, hubs, and switches
5400 Bayfront Plaza
Santa Clara, CA 95052
Voice: (800) NET-3COM
Fax: (408) 326-5001
Web site: http://www.3com.com

Triticom
Network monitoring software (LANdecoder)
9971 Valley View Road
Eden Prairie, MN 55344
Voice: (612) 937-0772
Web site: http://www.triticom.com

Glossary

AAUI (Apple Attachment Unit Interface): A generic port on an Apple Macintosh or Macintosh-compatible network device to which a specific Ethernet transceiver is connected.

Acknowledged connectionless exchange: A data communications exchange in which each packet is routed by the most efficient pathway. The receiver lets the sender know when each packet has been received.

AppleTalk: A set of protocols designed primarily for use by Macintosh computers. However, AppleTalk protocols are also available for Windows 95, Windows NT, and Linux.

Application server: A file server that contains applications for network users to run.

Attenuation: Loss of signal strength due to friction on the surface of the wire.

AUI (Attachment unit interface): A generic port on a network device to which a specific Ethernet transceiver is connected.

Auto-negotiation: A process during which a hub and a NIC exchange information about the highest speed each can handle to determine the speed at which transmission will take place.

Backbone: A network to which only other networks are connected.

Bandwidth: The number of bits that can travel together at the same time on a single transmission medium.

Baseband: A transmission medium that can carry only one signal at a time.

BNC (barrel) connector: The type of connector used to attached devices to a thinnet network.

Broadband: A transmission medium that can carry multiple signals at one time.

Bus topology: The fundamental topology of an Ethernet network segment, in which all devices are connected to a single transmission medium with unconnected ends.

Carrier: A signal on an Ethernet transmission medium indicating that a frame/packet is currently on the network and that another frame cannot be transmitted at that time.

Category 3, 4, 5, 5e, and 6: Grades of UTP cabling. The higher the grade, the more often the wire is twisted.

Coaxial cable: Network cabling made of a central copper wire, layers of shielding, and a copper mesh.

Collision: The event that occurs when two devices on a network attempt to transmit frames at exactly the same time.

Collision domain: A section of a network, comprising a single Ethernet bus, to which devices attached to that bus compete for access; a more precise term for an Ethernet network segment.

Connection-oriented exchange: A data communications conversation that assumes that there is a virtual circuit between a sender and a receiver and that every packet that is part of a single message travels through the circuit.

CRC (cyclical redundancy check): The last field of an Ethernet packet, used for error checking.

Crossover cable: A cable in which the input and output wires are reversed at one end.

Crossover port: A port on a hub for use in daisy chaining with another hub. The input and output wires are reversed so that the two hubs do not send and receive on the same wires.

Crosstalk: The bleeding of signals from one pair of wires in a cable to another.

CSMA/CA (Carrier Sense Multiple Access with Collision Avoidance): The MAC protocol used by many wireless transmission devices. Unlike CSMA/CD, this protocol does not detect collisions.

CSMA/CD (Carrier Sense Multiple Access with Collision Detection): The MAC protocol used by Ethernet. Devices detect the presence of a frame on the network by listening for a carrier signal. If none is present, a frame can be transmitted. Devices also detect collisions and repeat colliding transmissions after a random wait interval.

Data field: The portion of an Ethernet packet containing meaningful data.

Database server: A file server that runs a database management system and provides data management capabilities to a user.

Datagram: The TCP/IP term for a network packet.

DBMS (database management system): Software that interacts with stored data to store and retrieve data based on commands issued by a user or application program.

Destination address: The physical address of a network device that is to receive an Ethernet packet.

Drop cable: A single, unbroken stretch of thick coaxial cable into which transceivers tab by cutting through the cable shielding to make physical contact with the copper mesh layer and central copper wire.

DTE (data terminal equipment): Any device that will be connected to a network.

E-mail server: A computer dedicated to the sending and receiving of e-mail.

Ethernet: A standard describing the way in which computers on a network gain access to the network media.

Fast Ethernet: Ethernet that transfers data at a maximum of 100 megabits per second.

Fax server: A computer connected to a modem that dials out to send faxes and answers incoming fax calls.

FCS (frame check sequence): The last field of an Ethernet packet, used for error checking.

File server: A repository for files that are to be shared over a network.

Frame: A package of data and control information that travels as a unit across the network; also known as a *packet*.

Frozen yellow garden hose: The nickname given to thick coaxial cable, based on its yellow outer coating and inability to bend easily.

FTP (file transfer protocol): The TCP/IP protocol that supports file transfer over a network.

Full-duplex: Transmissions in two directions at the same time.

Gigabit Ethernet: Ethernet that transfers data at a maximum of 1000 megabits (1 gigabit) per second.

Half-duplex: Transmission in only one direction at a time.

HTTP (hypertext transfer protocol): The TCP/IP protocol that supports the transfer of hypertext documents.

Hub: A network device that contains the wiring for a bus.

IEEE (Institute of Electrical and Electronic Engineers): The organization whose LAN standards committee prepares Ethernet standards for adoption and potential adoption.

Internet: When written in all lowercase letters (*internet*), a WAN that connects multiple LANs into a larger network. When written with a leading uppercase letter (*Internet*), the global network that supports the World Wide Web.

Intranet: A LAN that includes a World Wide Web server.

IP (internet protocol): The TCP/IP protocol that provides connectionless service along with logical network addressing, packet switching, and dynamic routing.

IPX (internet packet exchange): The IPX/SPX protocol that performs translations between physical addressing from layers below to logical addressing for layers above and connectionless routing functions.

IPX/SPX: Protocols developed for Novell NetWare, a network operating system, based on work by Xerox at its PARC (Palo Alto Research Center) facility.

ISO (International Standards Organization): The international body that approves technology standards.

LAN (local area network): A network confined to a small geographic area— such as a floor, a single building, or a group of buildings in close physical proximity (for example, a college campus or an office park)— that is almost always owned by a single organization.

Length field: In an Ethernet data packet, the number of meaningful types of data; in an Ethernet management packet, the type of management information present in the frame.

Linux: An open-source, free implementation of UNIX used extensively for hosting Web sites.

LocalTalk: Apple Computer's proprietary cabling that can be used with the AppleTalk network protocols.

MAC (media access control) address: A unique address assigned to a piece of hardware on a network. MAC addresses must be unique throughout the entire network.

MAC (media access control): A method for managing the access of multiple devices to a single, shared network medium.

MAN (metropolitan area network): An outdated term describing a network that covers an entire city. Today, the concept of a MAN has largely been replaced by the WAN.

Managed hubs: Hubs that can capture statistics about network traffic and accept control commands from a workstation on the network.

MAU (medium attachment unit): The hardware used to connect a network device to a hub, switch, bridge, router, or gateway in a star topology.

MDI (medium-dependent interface): The cable that connects a Fast Ethernet transceiver to the network medium.

MII (medium-independent interface): A device used with Fast Ethernet between an external transceiver and a NIC.

Mirror: A copy of a web server to which traffic can be routed to balance the load on the primary web server.

Multicast address: An address recognized by a group of devices on a network.

Multimode cabling: Fiber optic cabling that reflects light at more than one angle.

Multispeed hub: A hub that can handle more than one transmission speed, typically 10 Mbs and 100 Mbs.

NetBEUI (network BIOS extended user interface): Protocols used by Windows 95, Windows 98, and Windows NT.

NetPC: A stand-alone PC with a hard drive but no floppy or CD-ROM drives.

Network: A combination of hardware and software that allows computers and other peripherals (for example, printers and modems) to communicate with one another through some form of telecommunications media (for example, telephone lines).

Network discovery: The process of using software to determine the devices on a network and the layout of that network.

Network management: In terms of software, software that can monitor network traffic and report on network performance; in the fullest sense, a group of tasks that includes the maintenance and upgrading of a functioning network.

Network segment: A section of network transmission medium to which devices attached to that medium compete for access.

NFS (network file system): The TCP/IP protocol that supports file sharing between networks.

NIC (network interface card): An expansion board that contains the hardware necessary for a piece of hardware to communicate with a network. NIC hardware may also be built onto a motherboard.

Node: Each distinct piece of hardware on a network.

Noise: Any unwanted signal on network transmission media.

NOS (network operating system): Software that manages the transfer of data throughout the network.

Novell NetWare: A network operating system.

100BASE-FX: The Gigabit Ethernet standard for 1000 Mbps transmission over fiber optic cable.

100BASE-TX: The Fast Ethernet standard that supports 100 Mbps transmission over Category 5 UTP wiring.

1000BASE-T: The Ethernet standard that supports 1000 Mbps transmission over Category 5 UTP wiring.

OSI (Open System interconnect) Reference Model: A worldwide standard protocol that provides the underlying theory for protocol implementations.

Packet: A package of data and control information that travels as a unit across the network; also known as a *frame*.

Passive hub: A hub that accepts an incoming signal, amplifies it, and broadcasts it to all devices on the network.

Patch cable: A relatively short cable that connects a network device to a wall outlet or directly to a hub or wiring closet.

PHY (Physical layer device): A Fast Ethernet transceiver.

Physical layer: The bottom layer of a protocol stack that refers to the network hardware.

Plenum cabling: Cabling that has a plastic coating that is less toxic when burned than standard cabling. Plenum cabling is required for installation in spaces through which breathable air passes.

Port: A connector on a network device used to connect the device to the network.

POTS (plain old telephone service): Standard voice-grade telephone service.

Preamble: The first portion of an Ethernet packet that is used to synchronize the transmission.

Print queue: A list of jobs waiting to be printed.

Print server: Hardware, software, or a combination of both that manage a shared network printer.

Propagation delay: The time it takes for a signal to be broadcast and read by all devices on a network.

Protocol: A specification of how a computer will format and transfer data.

Protocol stack: A group of layered protocols that work together to effect network data transfers.

Remote control: Controlling the action of another computer over a network.

Repeater: A piece of hardware that amplifies and retransmits a network signal. Repeater functionality is built into hubs, switches, bridges, and routers.

RJ-11: The connector used with UTP wiring for standard telephone connections.

RJ-45: The connector used with UTP wiring for Ethernet.

Router: A device for connecting network segments that can optimize the path along which packets travel.

Server farm: A group of file servers all on the same network file segment, usually connected by fiber optic cabling.

Single mode cabling: Fiber optic cabling that reflects light at only one angle.

SMTP (simple mail transfer protocol): The TCP/IP protocol that supports the transfer of e-mail.

SNMP (simple network management protocol): The TCP/IP protocol that provides basic functions for managing network devices.

Source address: The hardware address of the network device sending an Ethernet packet.

Spanning-tree algorithm: Software within a switch that ensures there is only one path in a network from one switch to another, avoiding looping problems.

Spooling: Saving print jobs on a disk where they will wait until a printer is free to print them.

SPX (sequenced packet exchange): The IPX/SPX protocol that provides connection-oriented service between the addresses identified by IPX.

Stackable hubs: Hubs that can be connected so that they appear to be a single, large hub to the network.

Standard Ethernet: Ethernet that transfers data at a maximum of 10 megabits per second.

Star topology: A network topology in which all devices are connected to a single central device.

Start frame delimiter: The last eight bits of the Ethernet packet preamble that mark the preamble and the start of the information-bearing parts of the frame.

Structured cabling system: The design of the wiring of commercial buildings for data and telecommunications.

Switch: A device used to connect multiple network segments or devices. Switches can perform routing to the correct network segment rather than broadcasting transmissions to the entire network as hubs do.

TCP (Transmission Control Protocol): A TCP/IP protocol that provides connection-oriented service, including error correction and flow control.

TCP/IP (Transmission Control Protocol/Internet Protocol): The protocols used by the Internet.

Telnet: The TCP/IP protocol that supports remote terminal sessions.

Terminator: A connector at each end of a thinnet network that prevents the unwanted reflection of signals from the ends of the bus back down the network medium.

10BASE5: The Ethernet standard that supports 100 Mbps transmission over thick coaxial cabling.

10BASE-T: The Ethernet standard that supports 10 Mbps transmission over UTP cabling.

10BASE2: The Ethernet standard that supports 10 Mbps transmission over thin coaxial cabling.

Thicknet: An Ethernet network using thick coaxial cabling (10BASE5).

Thin client: A network device that has a CPU and therefore may be able to process data locally. It may or may not have a hard drive, and does not have a floppy or CD-ROM drive. A thin client loads all its software over the network from a file server and processes the data locally (10BASE2).

Thinnet: An Ethernet network using thin coaxial cabling.

Throughput: The number of bits that arrive at a destination per unit time.

Topology: The physical layout of network devices and the transmission media that connect them.

Transceiver: A piece of hardware that sits between a network device and the network medium, ensuring that the device receives the correct type of signal, regardless of the medium in use. Today, transceiver hardware is often built into NICs or on motherboards.

Transceiver cable: A cable that connects a transceiver to a NIC.

UDP (user datagram protocol): A TCP/IP protocol that provides connectionless service.

Unacknowledged connectional exchange: A data communications exchange in which each packet is routed by the most efficient pathway. The receiver does not let the sender know when each packet has been received.

UNIX: An operating system that includes network operating system capabilities.

Unmanaged hub: A hub that accepts an incoming signal, amplifies it, and broadcasts it to all devices on the network.

UTP (unshielded twisted pair wiring): Network cable containing one or more pairs of copper wires that are twisted in a spiral manner.

Vampire clamp: A 10BASE5 (thicknet) transceiver that cuts through the coaxial cable to make physical contact with the copper mesh and wiring inside.

Virtual circuit: A single identified transmission path between a sender and a receiver, made up of a collection of transmission media and hardware that connects network segments. A virtual circuit remains in place for the duration of a single conversation.

Virtual server: A file server that appears as a single hard drive to users but is made up of a portion of the hard drives of more than one computer.

WAN (wide area network): A network that covers a large geographic area, such as a city, a state, or one or more countries.

Web server: A file server that is hosting a World Wide Web site.

Windows-based terminal: A device with no local processing power. It is designed to access Windows programs stored and executed on a server through the Windows Terminal Server program.

Wiring closet: A locked cabinet that contains the wiring for an Ethernet bus.

Index